"*The God Who Is Here* is a needed book.

—TIM KELLER, Senior Pastor, Redeemer
Presbyterian Church and author of
The Reason for God and *The Prodigal God*

"It is obvious to me that *The God Who Is Here* comes from Peter Haas's deep love and commitment to the Christian contemplative journey. This book presents many issues facing Christianity today—not to discourage the reader, but to offer a wake-up call to the beauty and depth that the contemplative Christian dimension gives to those seeking a deeper relationship with God."

—GAIL FITZPATRICK-HOPLER,
President, Contemplative Outreach, Ltd.

"Peter Haas presents us with a compelling vision of the God who is here, and teaches us how that presence is available to us and can change us—and the world."

—GREG GARRETT, Baylor University Professor and author, *Stories from the Edge, The Gospel According to Hollywood*, and *We Get to Carry Each Other: The Gospel According to U2*

"*The God Who Is Here* is a powerful presentation of the almost forgotten mystical side of Christianity—an alternative path to the Divine presence free of the ghastly inhumanity of Fundamentalism or the spiritual vapidity of liberal theology. It draws on traditional concepts and new learning to create a revolutionary theological map into contemplative territory. Haas weaves together a rich contemplative tapestry gently inviting the reader into a deeper place in the soul, a more expansive place in the universe, and into a more 'fully human' spirituality. A fresh new contemplative voice, Haas beautifully illuminates the divine/human mystery that Christ embodied, and we are invited to continue."

—DAN MCGOWEN, Consultant, McGowen Publishing

"In the 1960s, Francis Schaeffer's book *The God Who is There* opened a door in my mind to the wonders of Christian Truth. At the dawn of a new decade in a new century, Peter Haas has given us the gift of *The God Who Is Here*. This is a book for our times and our churches. As the technological age squeezes our relationships and seduces us with a plethora of options that keep us burning the candle at both ends, Haas opens a door for attending to the 'mystery' of Christ in us the hope of glory. With a contemplative heart, Haas guides us into deep and expansive places of God that form us into fully human icons of his love in the world."

—ADELE CALHOUN, Co-pastor, Redeemer Community Church, and author, *The Spiritual Disciplines Handbook*

THE GOD WHO IS HERE

*A Contemplative Guide to Transforming Your Relationship
with God and the Church*

———◦———

PETER TRABEN HAAS

Matt,

Every Blessing   3/12/14

Peter

LANTERN BOOKS • NEW YORK • A DIVISION OF BOOKLIGHT INC.

Lantern Books
128 Second Place
Brooklyn, NY 11231

Excerpt from *Prayer: The Spirituality of the Christian East*, Vol. 2. Copyright © 2005 by Cistercian Publications. Published by Liturgical Press, Collegeville, Minn. Reprinted with permission.
Excerpt from the *A Monk in the World*. Copyright © 2002 by Wayne Teasdale. Reprinted with permission of New World Library, Novato, Calif. www.newworldlibrary.com.
Excerpt from *Christophany*. Copyright © 2004 by Raimon Panikkar.
Reprinted with permission of Orbis, Maryknoll, N.Y.
Excerpt from *The Mark* and "Mission Statement." Copyright © 2010 by The Church of Conscious Harmony. Reprinted with permission.
Excerpt from *A Different Christianity*. Copyright © 2003 by Robin Amis. Reprinted with permission.

Library of Congress Cataloging-in-Publication Data

Haas, Peter Traben.
The God who is here : a contemplative guide to transforming your relationship with God and the church / Peter Traben Haas.
p. cm.
Includes bibliographical references (p.   ).
ISBN-13: 978–1-59056–239–0 (alk. paper)
ISBN-10: 1–59056–239–9 (alk. paper)
1. Spiritual life—Christianity. 2. Contemplation. I. Title.
BV4501.3.H32 2011
248.2—dc22

2010036308

Printed in the United States of America

To:

The early morning hours in Crowell Hall—where I began to pray in the silence and to Deneen—who helped me come into fuller being

green
press
INITIATIVE

Lantern Books has elected to print this title on Rolland Enviro, a 100% post-consumer recycled paper, processed chlorine-free. As a result, we have saved the following resources:

10 Trees (40' tall and 6-8" diameter)
4,786 Gallons of Wastewater
3 million BTU's of Total Energy
291 Pounds of Solid Waste
994 Pounds of Greenhouse Gases

As part of Lantern Books' commitment to the environment we have joined the Green Press Initiative, a nonprofit organization supporting publishers in using fiber that is not sourced from ancient or endangered forests. We hope that you, the reader, will support Lantern and the Green Press Initiative in our endeavor to preserve the ancient forests and the natural systems on which all life depends. One way is to buy books that cost a little more but make a positive commitment to the environment not only in their words, but in the paper that they were published on. For more information, visit www.greenpressinitiative.org

Environmental impact estimates were made using the Environmental Defense Paper Calculator. For more information visit: www.papercalculator.org.

MIX
Paper from
responsible sources
FSC® C013483

Yes! With us is God—not up above the azure vault,
Not out beyond the edge of countless worlds,
Not in evil fire and not in stormy breath,
And not in the drowsy memory of ages.
He is here, now—among the causal bustle.
In the turbid flood of life's alarm.
You rule with an all-joyful mystery;
Evil is impotent; we—eternal; God—with us.

—*Immanuel* by VLADIMIR SOLOVYOV

CONTENTS

[The angels] said, Men of Galilee, why do you stand looking up toward heaven . . . ?

—ACTS 1.11a

For in fact, the Kingdom of God is within you.[1]

—LUKE 17.21I

*O Lord, my heart is not lifted up, my eyes are not raised too high . . .
but I have calmed and quieted my soul.*

——PSALM 131.1a, 2a

PREFACE

———◄○►———

Jesus Christ, the same yesterday, today and tomorrow.

—Hebrews 13.8

I am in labor pains until Christ is formed in you.

—Galatians 4.19

T HE GOD WHO IS HERE aims to show how the biblical story of God's presence culminates with our transformation into Christ by the power of the Holy Spirit (Galatians 4.19). The book also aims to convey that awakening to and participating in this process are crucial for the ongoing development of human community and the future well-being of our planet. I trust it is a book for people who want to experience and participate in God's presence; a book for people who long for a vibrant Christian spirituality and intuit that such a spirituality is integral for the future of humankind. As such, the book seeks to address many of the needs and concerns of Christian spirituality in the postmodern era.

The renewal of contemplative Christianity in our time is a graceful occurrence. Our participation in Divine presence as individuals and communities is at the heart of the contemplative Christian experience. Increasingly, the wider Christian community is being invited to mine the depth of its own mystical, contemplative, Trinitarian tradition. And to that end, my wish is that these ideas bless and inspire deeper exploration, and contribute to the further articulation and embodiment of contemplative Christianity in the third millennium of Christian faith.

The motivation to write *The God Who Is Here* began in 1995. I was fresh out of college and on my way to seminary, taking a year off to work as a pastoral intern at Elmbrook Church in Brookfield, Wisconsin. During my internship, I began to recognize my own spiritual immaturity and started to search for a deeper experience of God's presence.[1] As I read the scriptures, I began to see the experience of Divine presence as an important thread running throughout the entire biblical story line, and I felt drawn to find out where it led. This book is one result of my journey.

I completed the manuscript during the winter of 1996. I wrote at night and on Saturdays in a cozy lakeside room in Delafield, Wisconsin. After seminary, I completely rewrote the manuscript, and revised it again in 2007. While the book's basic structure has remained the same, much of the content evolved as I grew in knowledge and life experience. While much could probably be improved herein, I see it as the resource I often wish I'd had to give to others. I believe it conveys an important message for the Christian community, and contributes to the ongoing rediscovery of the contemplative Christian path. I close this personal preface with two wishes for the reader and this book:

I hope that what's conveyed in this book resonates at deep levels in your being, bringing about an increased awareness of the vast, immediate, personal love of God in, for, to, and with you and all of the creation; and that through this awareness, the incarnation of Christ continues in and through you for the sake of further human flourishing.

I also wish that this increased awareness leads you to experiences that personally verify what this book can only imperfectly point to.

MANY DESERVE THANKS for joining me on my journey and for offering me blessings, counsel, and friendship. They have all, in some measure, contributed to my spiritual formation and the development of this book. I thank Dr. Joseph Stowell, former President of Moody Bible Institute and current President of Cornerstone University, for modeling spiritual leadership and personal discipline to me at such a formative time in my life; and I thank Dr. Stuart Briscoe and Dr. David Seemuth for giving me the opportunity to explore my sense of calling to the pastorate during my residency at Elmbrook Church (August, 1995–August, 1996).

Recalling my years at Princeton Theological Seminary, I give thanks for the profound teaching and friendship of Dr. Peter Ian Cass, and the luminous teaching of the late Dr. James Loder, from whom I first began to understand the mystery of the Trinity for personal transformation.

During my first pastorate at the First Presbyterian Church of Flint, Michigan, I was blessed by the congregation's nurture and love for me as I grew as a pastor and a person. I'm particularly in awe of the friendship, wisdom, and love given to me by Gene and Beth Dolby, who'll always be my "Michigan parents." Gene's vast wisdom and wit are rivaled by his joy for life and learning. Words cannot convey the love I feel for you, Gene, nor the meaningfulness of your "fatherly" mentoring. Joe and Alice Coyner also remain dear friends who continue to encourage me to live into my mission. At First Presbyterian Flint, I was mentored by two men of faith and joy: thank you Dr. Larry Kent and Dr. John Musgrave for modeling pastoral excellence and spiritual leadership.

I thank Deneen Elizabeth, my spiritual midwife, who helped me see my true and false selves more clearly, and revealed the love and presence of Christ to me at a spiritual retreat in the Teton Mountains during my spiritual crisis.

Similarly, I'm also deeply grateful for my community of contemplative friends and teachers in Austin, Texas—*especially* Rev. Tim Cook, and certainly Rev. Barbara Cook, Mary Anne Best, Mimi Conroy, Donald Genung, Pamela and Michael Begeman, and Vivek Bakshi. While so much could be said in gratitude, I shall let the silence speak for itself.

I give thanks for the congregation at Westlake Hills Presbyterian Church, where I have the privilege to serve as associate pastor under the thoughtful leadership of Dr. Peter Barnes. I'm inspired by our mission to nurture our relationships with God and one another, and I trust you find this resource useful in living into our relational vision. I'm especially grateful for the kind encouragement and friendship at WHPC from Phil Haag and Janis Claflin, whose contemplative Christianity Sunday school class has been a source of deep joy to me. I also give thanks to Sam Cangelosi whose steady counsel and friendship have helped me more than I can say.

I've been blessed by the kindness and professional expertise of my editor, Dan McGowen, whose personal encouragement came at just the right moment, conveying the affirmation and giving the continued certitude that my manuscript needed to become a book. Thank you for helping me do so with such skillfulness. Similarly, without the support and timely guidance of Father Carl Arico of Contemplative Outreach the book would never have made the beautiful connection with Gene Gollogly and the exceptional team at Lantern Books, with whom I am honored to collaborate in releasing this work into the world beyond my laptop—if such a place exists.

Finally, to beloved Christina: bearing your name rightfully, you embody the love and presence of Christ to me. Thank you for following the Word and doing the Work together. Your loving imprint endures on every page of this book and in every day of our life together with the God who is here.

Christmas, 2010
Austin, Texas
Peter Traben Haas
www.ContemplativeChristians.com

NOTE TO READER

———◇———

AS A TREE BEARS FRUIT in multiple seasons during the course of its life, and as a mother may bear several children during her fertile years, this book represents only a first-birthing that now, upon its fruition in the world, seems incapable of conveying the mystery of what I first hoped to share.

The reader should bear in mind that virtually everything herein was written from what's known in the developmental literature as the mental/egoic level of human development. As such, the content should be viewed, in part, as a theological autobiography of one person's longing for God. It's only a snapshot of one segment of the ever-unfolding journey to God. I send the book into the world, and now to you dear reader, with the suspicion that these ideas may be helpful to others on their journey toward a deeper participation in God's presence and life in Christ.

Because this book was written from the vantage point of one side of the river, gazing across to contemplative territory, the majority of its content doesn't describe the contemplative life experientially, only theoretically. For those who wish to read someone who does write from the actual state of unitive wisdom, and who can teach a more complete Christian understanding of the spiritual journey, please first read the writings of Thomas Keating or Bernadette Roberts, especially Keating's *Invitation to Love* or Roberts's, *What Is Self?*

THE GOD WHO IS HERE

A CONTEMPLATIVE BRIDGE

———◁◯▷———

*May that which is above be as that which is below, and may that
which is below be as that which is above.*

—ANCIENT PROVERB

*I have come to find the term "presence" a more central and more useful category for
grasping the unifying note in the varieties of Christian mysticism. Thus we can say
that the mystical element in Christianity is that part of its belief and practices that
concerns the preparation for, the consciousness of, and the reaction to what can be
described as the immediate or direct presence of God.*

—BERNARD McGINN[1]

I N MOMENTS OF SILENT WONDER we often intuit God's presence. We
feel swept up in sheer joy or grounded in an unexplainable peace. In these
moments, worship rises spontaneously and scripture reading seems profound.
We are easily touched by nature and beauty, and more open to love. We cherish
such seasons of enchantment. We feel free. Awake. Alive. While we may not have
the words to convey what we experience, memories of these peak moments linger
in our minds and feed our hearts during seasons of sorrow or pain.

When such painful "dark nights" occur we grope to know that we are not
alone; that our life has a purpose. We long for relief from depression, provision
of income, and healing from sickness or disease. We groan with grief and ache
for sleep, laughter, or love. Worship seems empty and scripture-reading dull.

Often, beauty, hope, and love are as strangers passing by unnoticed. While in the shadow of suffering we ask, "Where is God?" The question haunts us like a minor chord echoing in the waiting room of life. Our encounters with suffering seem to contradict such Divine presence the most. We assume God is distant, "up there," and so we conclude it impossible that God could be *here* with us.

Yet such a conclusion is not exclusive to the suffering. It permeates our global mediums of thought, entertainment, politics, and opinion. For many, the depleting power of cultural conditioning with its materialistic mindset casts a foggy pallor over life, veiling the presence of God with the rote habits of being *merely* human, eclipsing our destiny as "participants in the divine nature" (2 Peter 1.4) and "co-heirs with Christ" (Romans 8.17).

This book explores an alternative, one that can't be fully understood but that can be experienced: God is here, there, and everywhere by the relational presence of the Spirit.[2] This may seem unbelievable, and in a sense it is. Still, insights are available to help our understanding, inviting a profound paradigm shift. For example, in the wake of the discoveries of quantum physics, developmental psychology, evolutionary theory, and the emergence of postmodernity, many of our ancient and Newtonian conceptions of God are finally being replaced by a more relational perspective.[3]

By "relational" I mean the living dynamic of personal love pulsing within the heart of the Trinity. Relationality is the personal force of love pouring from the Divine Source holding the universe together and imbuing it with meaning. Relationality is the vibration of light, life, and love that still lingers in every cell of the creation and in which we continue to "live and move and have our being" (Acts 17.28). Relationality is how God is God and what we are more fully to become. Relationality is the heart of the human experience. Reality is relational. We exist relationally. I and Thou. You, Me, and Us. Reality exists as an economy of interactions: light from light, life from life, love from love. If the manifestation of relationality has a name, we might call it *logos* or Spirit. In a sense, they are similar ways of speaking of the deepest mystery underneath the living field of all existence.

In the Christian tradition, the personal experience of Divine presence became more available after the Spirit was released to humankind at Pentecost. Remember, Jesus said that he must go away so that the Spirit could come; that the Spirit would lead us into deeper truth. So why did God start with Abraham? Why didn't God just start with Jesus and the Spirit? It would have saved a lot of trouble and time! In part, it seems that time allowed for our species' growth and development, and along the way God accommodated to our human level of understanding.

For example, first God was the revealer, calling certain individuals through angels and prophets, a whirlwind or a burning bush. Then, God was with us in the person of Jesus, playing out on the stage of history the mystery of Divine love for humankind. After the ascension, the Divine was released in a new way universally (i.e., "to the ends of the Earth," Acts 1.8) by the Spirit who brought and brings God relationally close so that we might experience the non-separative, relational life right here and now in our normal, day-to-day life. So what might the Divine be doing now?

Like all living things, the Divine relationship with humankind is a developing relationship. From one degree of glory to the next, God revealed more and more of the Divine intention for humankind, which took a significant leap forward with the release of the Holy Spirit for the transformation of all humanity into Christ. According to the prophets, the consummation of this process will be the occurrence of the "kingdom of God" and the "new heavens and new Earth." We can't think ourselves into God's presence or the transformation God desires for us or the creation. Ultimately, we consent to it. We participate in it. God's presence and action are hidden in the profound eloquence of silence and sacrament, an interior space accessed through "deeper" or "higher" levels of knowing and being that supersede, yet include, our familiar rational level of knowing. Our journey through the levels of spiritual faith is voluntary and open-ended. No one compels us to move beyond our current level of being. We're free to remain where we are. However, the Spirit of God woos us, deepening our knowledge and filling out our being. Such a move invites us to expand how we conceive of God, ourselves, others, and the world. This shift in perception is an ongoing, personal process each of us can experience throughout our lives.[4] Because the Holy Spirit initiates us into the presence of God, the invitation of contemplative Christianity is to be with God and others, and simply *be* with the One who's with us, even when we cannot see, feel, or understand. There's more beyond this union, but it's beyond what I can say.[5]

WHAT IS CONTEMPLATIVE CHRISTIANITY?

The ideas of this book are set against the background of an ongoing cultural conversation.[6] While some have recently suggested the problems we face as a civilization should be solved by ridding ourselves of religious faith, I believe that what humanity needs is not the end of religious faith altogether, but the rediscovery of the contemplative way within the religious traditions.[7]

The contemplative path can provide a passport for spiritual pilgrims looking for a way forward in faith, rather than an end to it. In my experience, the church needs a third way to help us move beyond the mutual checkmates of Liberals and Conservatives, Evangelicals and Emergents. The contemplative bridge is such a way.

The contemplative Christian bridge is not new.[8] It's part of the ancient infrastructure raised at the dawn of the church. Over the centuries, the bridge has often been forgotten or neglected in favor of more external forms of Christian expression.[9] With the rise of religious pluralism and global interconnectivity, religious boundaries that have physically demarcated the world are blurring. What we are slowly learning from our human interconnectivity is that we are one human community, and that we've run out of room (and maybe even time) on planet Earth to remain divided.

In light of such challenges, one of the most compelling qualities of the contemplative path is that it celebrates the common human spiritual quest for God. Beyond all doctrines, creeds, and faith statements is the unyielding human heart awakened by grace to the experience of and longing for Divine love. Through the contemplative path, humankind is being drawn by grace into the mystery of Divine presence and love.[10] Gregory the Great described contemplation as the knowledge of God infused with love. Indeed, the very word "contemplative" conveys the experiential knowledge of God that is saturated with love, which is the key to our future on planet Earth. This leads us to a definition of contemplative Christianity. While no one definition will convey all the dimensions of such a vast subject, I summarize it as an ever-deepening awareness and experience that one's life "is hidden with God in Christ" (Colossians 3.3). This requires grace, and grace returns us to the heart of Divine love.[11]

Philosophically, some have spoken of this state as *non-dual* or *integral*.[12] St. Paul puts it this way: "In Christ nothing can separate you from the love of God" (Romans 8.28). Recent scholarship has described the developmental levels of the human spiritual experience and the characteristics of contemplative Christianity.[13] While this subject is vitally important, we won't delve into these characteristics here, but will instead articulate a biblical theology for contemplative Christianity, thus reconfirming the soundness of the bridge and its usefulness for moving beyond more "adolescent" levels of faith, such as religious fundamentalism and its twin brother, biblical idolatry.[14]

Theologically, the contemplative Christian path can be identified by several core concepts, many of which we will discuss further throughout the book:

- The recovery of the *logos* as the vehicle for our participation in the Divine presence.
- Salvation as a journey of increasing union with God through Christ by the Spirit.
- A rediscovery of silence, meditative prayer, and the spiritual practices, and a renewed openness to reading scripture with the heart as means of grace.
- A renewed understanding of our relationship with the Earth and cosmos; an integral view of the human person.[15]

THE GOD OF CONTEMPLATIVES IS RELATIONAL AND CLOSE

The church fathers first discerned that God's personal presence in Jesus meant that God was a relational being, whom they designated as Trinity, a term summarizing the biblical relationship of the Father, Son, and Holy Spirit. Today, we might say Be–Being–Becoming; or, echoing St. Augustine, Love–Loved–Loving.[16]

Contrary to the concept of God as a patriarch or monad so often conveyed over the centuries by both the church and its critics, the God of Jesus and the early church fathers is a vibrant, interrelating, loving communion of personal relationality, one for the other, pouring out love and communication.[17] The recovery of relational Trinitarian insights is moving traditional monotheism into a deeper understanding of God as a being-in-relationship, present with humankind in the mystery of love. The relationality of God means that humanity cannot be separated from God's love; the two have been wed in Christ—the heart of the incarnation and the grace of the Trinity, uniting Divine love with the human condition once and for all, even on our worst days and at our lowest levels of consciousness. In Christ, God loves us totally. (You can read more about the relationality of God from a theological perspective in Appendix A.)

The word "Trinity" inherently means God's participation in a dance of light, life, and love. From the farthest reaches of our expanding universe to the deepest dimensions of micro-cellular structures, reality is in relationship with the ultimate generative source—what and whom we call "God," and whom Jesus called *Abba*. Throughout history, humans have pictured God the Father as a "Sky God"—distant, rational, masculine, ruling, and exercising judgment over humankind. This being was often referred to as "king" and "lord." Vestiges of this "up-there" conception are still common: "Don't mess with the big guy," or "Ask the man upstairs."

Michelangelo's Sistine Chapel illustrates this concept perfectly. The transcendent God is above the Earth reaching down to humanity. Why? Michelangelo didn't invent this "up-there" God. This worldview is conveyed quite clearly in the scriptures by the Psalmist who announces, "God looks down from heaven on humankind to see if there are any who are wise, who seek after God" (Psalm 53.2). It's only natural that the Bible reflects the ethos of the culture in which its stories and characters were conveyed. It was written during a time in human development when it was normal to view things from a patriarchal, as well as ethnocentric and Earth-centered, cultural mindset, all of which inevitably influenced Christian ideas about God, ideas that were harmonious with the Ptolemaic and Newtonian worldviews. Although these concepts have dominated for centuries, in light of new scientific models many people are moving beyond them and making way for new perspectives.[18]

A further reason our theological conceptions are shifting is because we've seen images of our galaxy and beyond. New perspectives often bring new insights, and new insights have the potential to increase our level of faith and consciousness. Images of billowing galaxies beamed back from the Hubble Space Telescope have enabled us to conceive of our place in the universe in new and different ways.[19] We grope to comprehend the grandeur of the universe and are humbled by our seemingly small place in it. Surely, the answer to the question, "Where is God?" is affected when we look at a photo of Earth and compare it to the Milky Way, where our own solar system gets lost among the billions of other solar systems, and our galaxy is just one of billions of others! Such knowledge will continue to shift our cosmology, and inevitably our spirituality, and shape how we answer the question, "Where is God?"

Admittedly, such a change of perspective can be frightening. This fear is normal, but fear suppresses the experience of love, and love is what's propelling and attracting our further development into the maximum realization of our God-intended destiny.[20] As our concepts of the universe and reality expand, so too do our ideas of God. God is no longer seen primarily as an up-there "Sky God" (Psalm 113.4), but a relational presence within the cosmos. This concept is emerging slowly, but its impact will be undeniable and profound. And it isn't pantheism; everything is not God. It's Trinitarian relationality experienced personally—meaning that, in Christ, nothing can be separated from God's presence. To repeat: God is not in everything. But, through Christ (i.e., the *logos*), everything is in God, and Christ is, "all in all" (Colossians 3.11).[21]

PERCEIVING PRESENCE

In the past, the Christian establishment was afraid of such shifts in perception—for example, when Copernicus proposed that the Sun doesn't rotate around Earth, or when Galileo concluded that Earth wasn't the center of our solar system. Instead of fearing such shifts or retreating into the past and ignoring new information, we can remember and reclaim the truth that God's presence has no center or circumference. Creation is simply with God, and for this reason we can say God is simply here with us.

In Christ, God infuses and relates with all reality so that the hereness of humanity, the Earth, and the universe are all continuing manifestations of God's generative presence. In the Christian system, we believe that God was with us in Jesus, called Emmanuel, meaning, "God is with us" (Matthew 1.23). The presence of God didn't cease with Jesus' incarnation or ascension. In this era, we're discovering that the expanding, relational universe is teaching us a similar story as Jesus' incarnation—just as the Psalmist said, "The heavens are telling the glory of God" (Psalm 19.1)[22]—and the glory of God is God's presence among us (John 1.14).

How we conceive and perceive God, ourselves, each other, and the world are very tricky processes because, as Flannery O'Connor put it, "The roots of the eyes are in the heart."[23] What we see is filtered by who we are. We see through the lens of our identity, or more accurately, through the lens of our thinking-machine.[24] If we're ever going to experience a change in our perspective that will enable us to perceive more fully the presence of God here and now, we'll first need to experience the "renewal of our minds" (Romans 12.1). Such a paradigm shift will help us remember that we're beings of light, life, and love, created in love, by love, for love, to love and manifest the continuing presence of God. This is what Jesus came to teach us, and more importantly demonstrated for us and our salvation.

In a spirit of awe and gratitude for the affirmation that "nothing can separate us from the love of God in Christ Jesus our Lord" (Romans 8.39), I present myself here as a pilgrim-muse, drawing connections for those called and compelled to carry forth God's relational presence with humanity. At every hinge-point of human history is a heightened sense of fear and anticipation toward what is emerging. At present, there's widespread interest in spiritual transformation and awakening. In light of this, how can the Christian tradition adapt with both integrity and openness to the relational story the creation is telling?

The universe is telling us new stories and providing new experiential information, revealing more of the truth Jesus conveyed long ago: that we too can participate in the life of God (John 14.17). We catch glimpses of the vastness of the story when we gaze into the heavens. Perhaps you, too, have stood beneath the canopy of the Milky Way in wonder, humbled and awestruck, in a manner like T. E. Lawrence in the Arabian Desert: "In the naked desert night we were stained by dew and shamed into pettiness by the innumerable silences of stars."[25]

It's good for us to feel small under the grandeur of the heavens. It's good for us to come to the end of our rope. When we do, we can let go and return to an awareness of Divine presence.

Yet in the midst of the mystery of God and the machinations of being human, many don't know what to do with their holy longing for Divine presence. For many, this longing is met by other means than the relational God.[26] Some leave Christianity altogether. Others just stop gazing at the stars in wonder and longing. Some just think that their doctrines or spiritual programs explain all we need to know. Some get caught in the pettiness of life's webs, including potent and confounding situations where light, life, and love seem to be smothered out completely, leaving only a burning ember of pain. Some get encrusted in the external forms of faith, forgetting the inner life of spiritual experience that's given to undergird and sustain our more external forms of faith. Meanwhile, the contemplative path of Christian tradition is neglected and feared. In the present generation, it calls to all spiritual pilgrims to surrender in the silence of simple faith, listening for the voice of love, the voice that will instruct on the one necessary way of being.

TWO WAYS OF BEING CHRISTIAN

Traditionally, there are two ways of being Christian and doing ministry, both of which Jesus conveyed in his visit detailed in Luke 10.38–42, where Martha and Mary served Jesus appropriately, yet in a different manner. Commentators and spiritual writers have identified Martha with the active, *kataphatic* way of mission and action in the world through service. Mary represents the contemplative, *apophatic* way of silence, solitude, and interior transformation through spiritual practices. Remember, Jesus says that Mary chose the better part—simply listening to the Master as the one necessary thing.

The contemplative way offers wisdom gained during two centuries of communal prayer, solitude, simplicity, and service under both blessed and hostile circumstances. In the last twenty-five years, it has gained exposure through the work and writings of Thomas Merton, Richard Foster, Dallas Willard, Eugene Peterson, Dorothy Butler Bass, Brian McLaren, Richard Rohr, Bernadette Roberts,

Robin Amis, and especially Thomas Keating—a Roman Catholic monk, writer, cofounder of Contemplative Outreach, and principal teacher of the meditative prayer practice referred to as Centering Prayer. They have reintroduced the contemplative dimension of Christianity to an ever-growing audience within the Christian community. It is in the spirit of Mary that I offer this book.

The contemplative path is both personal and communal. It's a unique contribution to the human conversation regarding the way forward for religious faith and spiritual community. *It is the way of Spirit, whereby ordinary human beings become the continuing incarnation of Christ in the world.* If this is a compelling idea, read on and discover how God is here by the Spirit, in you and me, and through us as spiritual communities gathered in love for the future flourishing of humankind.[27]

AN OVERVIEW

The God Who Is Here begins with theology and moves toward embodied experience. Chapters One through Four progressively unfold a biblical spirituality of God's continuing presence by the Spirit, in individuals and through community. Chapters Five through Seven present various examples of the contemplative Christian experience and show how contemplative Christianity is a hopeful way forward for humanity and the Christian church. The Appendices are offered as a further conversation on particular aspects related to contemplative Christianity that I've found useful in responding to the questions that naturally arise out of the book's ideas.

This book aims to contribute to the further unfolding of the contemplative path and to remind the church that for every chasm we see, there's always a providential bridge we don't, and that this contemplative bridge can span the space between head and heart, drawing us into our birthright-state of being here with God.

PART ONE

Contemplative Christianity

ONE

HERE WITH GOD

—◇—

Where can I go from your Spirit? Or where can I flee from your presence?
If I ascend to heaven, you are there; if I make my bed in Sheol, you are there. . . .

—PSALM 139.7–8

What is here is there. What is not here is nowhere.

—VISHVASARA TANTRA[1]

The kingdom of God has come near.

—MARK 1.15

CONTRARY TO ALL DOUBTS, fears, longings, and suffering, God is with
us. God is here with you and you are with God. The only thing separating
us from this knowledge and experience is the veil of self, smothering the
experience of God's presence with the myriad diversions and dualities of life.[2]

If you have a hard time believing this, you're not the only one. For most of
my life, including several years as a pastor, I struggled with a profound sense of
separation from God. This manifested itself as deep longings, and I wasn't aware
of how these longings were actually masking my deeper yearning for God's love
and presence in my life.

During my teens and twenties, my longing for romantic love propelled me
through a series of intimate relationships, a marriage that ended in divorce two
years later, and an engagement two years after the divorce, which I subsequently

broke off. After this series of painful events, I broke down emotionally and spiritually. I was thirty-three years old. Yet from the depths of my breakdown I was lifted into the loving presence of God, in an awakening encounter with the love I'd longed for. It was an experience that initiated me on a journey of discovery, leading me into the contemplative life. I share more of this story of personal awakening in Chapter Five.

For now, it's sufficient to know that in the living and doing of life, I'd forgotten what it was like to *feel* God's love. I'd become a professional at *talking* about God's love. I was adept at theorizing about God's love. But *feeling* God's loving presence in my life had disappeared. We're built to feel God's love, and when we don't we atrophy, turn blue, and gasp for air. While many of us seek other ways to satisfy our full-chested hunger for God's life-giving breath, we soon discover that all the alternatives leave us panting.

I used romance to appease and cover my sense of separation from God, but there are many other ways—seeking power, control, wealth, health, sex, beauty, or a career, to name just a few. No matter our preferred substitute, the result is predictably the same: a sense of separation from God, self, others, and from life itself. This sense of separation can feel like a thick fog blanketing our human condition, smothering our capacities to know God's loving presence and action in our lives, and altogether blurring our purpose for living. In this foggy-minded, disconnected state, we tend to blame others for our problems and believe if only something would change in our external situation *then* we'd begin to feel better. So we keep longing for the ideal partner or job or situation. We keep chasing the money regardless of the toll it takes on us or those we love. We keep running what Thomas Keating calls our own "programs for happiness,"[3] until we've suffered enough to cease our useless striving and surrender to the unveiling.

THE UNVEILING

Although we come under the fog of separation very early in life, the good news is that, as with all fogs, the blazing rays of sunlight can unveil our true situation. This isn't *just* poetry. Throughout the Bible and many other religious texts, the word "light" is often used to describe consciousness. Such light actually exists:

it's the "light of the glory of God in the face of Christ" (2 Corinthians 4.6). In this One who is the "light of the world" (John 8.12) our human condition finds its remedy. The light of Christ can illuminate our mind, lifting our whole being up, through, and above the fog and revealing "separation" to be a primal, yet ephemeral smokescreen.

When this happens, it's transforming. In the invigorating words of Emily Dickinson, the unveiling becomes a "route of evanescence,"[4] where we "bubble up" through the darkness into the light of conscious awareness. Asleep no longer, we awaken to the full glory of being human, and the fullness of God's presence within us as the continuing incarnation of Christ. Then the journey begins; deeper in and higher up, unfolding step by step, the heart of reality calls us to our God-intended destiny.

During our route of evanescence (which theologians might call "sanctification" or *theosis*),[5] the light of Christ transforms us and we begin to grow and change on the inside. This is the essence of what it means to be "born again" and the purpose of all spiritual practices. When this unveiling occurs, we may experience it in our feelings (heart), thoughts (mind), and sometimes even our body. It can personally verify the truth that nothing can separate us from the love of God in Christ (Romans 8.38–39). Everything looks and feels different. Spiritual transformation can provide many moments of unveiling on our journey into evanescence. It's a journey of transformation and healing, the return to God mapped out for us in Jesus' life, death, resurrection, and ascension. It's our journey into love, and the purpose of our spiritual birth, whose destiny is the unveiling in, to, and through all things—Christ![6]

In all honesty, we don't always feel God's presence. There are times of absence and darkness that mark the contemplative way. Such shadows and clouds possess untold gifts for spiritual pilgrims, yet are usually experienced as gifts only after the darkness passes. In the darkness, life seems unbearable and God feels broodingly distant. The "dark night" of the soul and senses is a purgative time. Through it, our senses are cleansed of their gunk, such as negative emotions, painful memories, addictions, and other unconscious behaviors.[7]

An ancient parable illustrates the gift of the unveiling. It begins with ten Japanese warriors who go out on a mission.[8] Returning home, they come to a fast-flowing river and decide to cross it by linking arms to form a human chain. When they reach the other side, the leader counts the warriors and soon despairs because he counts only nine. Sadly and slowly, the nine conclude that the tenth warrior has been swept downstream and has drowned. Grieving, they return to their village. On arriving, the leader counts the party again, and is overjoyed to discover ten warriors, not nine. He'd forgotten about himself in the first count because he'd been focusing outwardly on others. He and his men had despaired for no reason, and they now rejoice in their wholeness, which had been their true condition all along.

We're like the warriors' leader—all along possessing what we think we've lost. The presence of God is always infinitely and perfectly with us, if we just surrender our hearts to the cleansing of the Spirit of God. This cleansing transforms our patterns of perception, freeing us to see more clearly and correctly, enabling us to experience God's life-giving presence.

PRESENCE

Today, the notion of "presence" is stimulating significant cultural and academic conversation. From Bernard McGinn's use of the term to define the contemplative and mystical experience,[9] to Peter Senge's and C. Otto Scharmer's groundbreaking research on its role in personal and communal transformation, "presence" has become a useful concept with which to discuss spiritual experience.[10]

Biblically, presence is a longstanding idea related to the human perception of the Divine. Its history in the Hebrew scriptures begins with the understanding that God and the world are in a beautiful relationship. God is the Source of all life, and God's presence with humanity is conveyed in various ways, such as "dwelling in Zion" (Psalm 9.11) and dwelling with the people in the house or tent of the Lord (Psalm 23.6, 61.4). On a personal level, the people confess to God in prayer that "you are with me" (Psalm 23.4, 46.7). The scriptures tell a story of God's graceful presence. In grace, God initiates relationality with humanity. Motivated by love, the One whose "greatness is beyond understanding" (Psalm 145.7) and whose being "surpasses the heavens" (1 Kings 8.27), is also the one who draws near in presence.[11] Yet as the scriptures unfold, God's relationship with humanity appears to shift slowly from a pure presence to a representative one. The movement begins in the Garden of Eden and proceeds outward with God apparently withdrawing and instead revealing God's self through angel, prophet, tabernacle, ark, and temple.[12]

The story of God's presence doesn't end there though. It continues in the story of the Christian scriptures, where God's presence manifests itself through the life of Jesus and the sending of the Spirit. The story is beautifully summarized by St. John's first letter: "By this we know that we abide in him and he in us, because he has given us of his Spirit" (1 John 4.13).

It's to this dimension of God's presence that we now turn, to understand more fully how God is here by the Spirit.

TWO

HERE BY THE SPIRIT

———◄◇►———

These things God has revealed to us through the Spirit; for the Spirit
searches everything, even the depths of God.

—St. Paul[1]

Nevertheless the paradox remains; the Spirit becomes a thing in the midst of other things;
what is intangible and impossible, unknown and unobservable, becomes concrete and
possible, known and observable. Such is the paradox of the Spirit.

—Karl Barth[2]

It is inherent in the nature of the Spirit . . . to be relational. . . .

—James Loder[3]

God is difficult to understand, for God is first One, then Three, and then Seven. . . .

—Ancient saying[4]

THE WORD BECAME FLESH and dwelt among us. So begins the Gospel of John, and with it the Christian message.[5] This famous sentence forms Christianity's theological bedrock. It conveys transformational ideas, without which Christian history and theology would likely have developed very differently.[6] But what does the *Word* have to do with God being *here by the Spirit?* To answer this question, we need to delve briefly into some rich, if challenging theological insights.

THE UNFOLDING, UNSEEN RELATIONSHIP

What we may call "Christian spirituality" occurs when individuals and communities remember, receive, and relate to the presence and power of the Spirit of Christ, whom we refer to as the Holy Spirit. In phrasing the experience this way, we're faced with something that's primarily secret and hidden—a life of faith and relationship with the Spirit and the interior world of consciousness. St. Ignatius articulates this inner life in his majestic *Spiritual Exercises*, written in the sixteenth century. Christian spirituality, says Ignatius, is manifested by those who "practice seeking the presence of our Lord in everything: their dealing with other people, their walking, seeing, tasting, hearing, understanding, and all [their] activities. For his Divine Majesty is truly in everything by his presence, power and essence."[7] In sum, the Spirit is God's personal presence to us, experienced beyond the mind, but through our body and breath, as the eternal Source of light, life, and love. The Spirit is our Source of true self (Ephesians 4.16–24).

By understanding God's continuing presence as the Holy Spirit, or Spirit of Christ, we shift into the realm of unseen reality. By "unseen reality," I mean our relationship with God through our interior union with Christ by the Holy Spirit. John Calvin spoke of the Spirit's work to and with us as "the secret working of the Spirit," through whom "we come to enjoy Christ and all his benefits."[8] One of the best benefits of Christ is the awareness of and participation in the presence of God.

This is not new. It's rooted in the earliest Christian confessions of faith, sung in our hymns, and written about by our theologians, contemplatives, and mystics, both Eastern Orthodox and Roman Catholic. But for many Christians the Holy Spirit is a nebulous idea that has very little to do with daily living, much less with continuing the presence and power of God to and through us! It is to the spiritual secrets of the universe we now turn.

RELATIONALITY

The recent paradigm shifts in science have revealed what we might call "the relationality of our reality."[9] Physicists and biologists are returning from their realms of inquiry astounded at the complexity, mystery, unfathomable beauty, and apparent anthropic orientation of the universe, billions of light years "above" and billions of times smaller "underneath" us.[10] In fact, the more science has inquired in both directions—above and below—their research seems to be revealing a quirky communication among all that is; an interrelatedness giving the vibration that maybe, just maybe, God is not somewhere "out there," but has always been here among us. When we use the worn and weary word G-O-D, laden with all our ancient conceptions and all-too-human projections of a being "up there," we're actually speaking of a presence and reality that cannot be separated from our own experience within the living universe through the energetic exchange of love.[11]

With this in mind, I propose that when we speak of God, maybe what we're speaking of is relationality. What if God is the Source and dynamic of relationality among and within all that is? Even our tradition of the Trinity hints at such an interconnected relationality by reminding us that humanity was brought to life—a being in relationship—when the Source of Life "breathed the breath of life" into us (Genesis 2.7). Thus, if God is the Source and dynamic of relationality throughout all that is, then Jesus the Christ is the embodied demonstration of this relationality in human form enacted among us, and accommodated to a particular culture and context.

This would explain why Jesus said such revolutionary things such as, "the father and I are one" (John 10.30). *If Jesus the Christ is the embodied demonstration of Divine relationality enacted among us in human form, then the Spirit is the non-embodied continuation of Christ's relationality to and within us for the purpose of reawakening us to our role in embodying the reality of the Divine relationality.* And if that is the case, then the church is the gathered, exponential enactment of beings-in-relationship who have been awakened into the miracle that once and for all the old conceptions of a separate, distant God above us are no longer necessary.

As a community embodying the relationality of the Spirit, we are members of the household of God. Since God is the Source and dynamic of the relationality of all that is, then through Jesus' demonstration of love, and our union with Christ by the Spirit, we too can participate with the Divine loving presence and experience the state of no separation (i.e., union). In this way, God through Christ by the Spirit is all in all.

SPIRITUAL SHIFTS

Long before the Hubble Space Telescope revealed the transcendence (i.e. height) of life, or the Human Genome Project revealed the immanence (i.e. depth) of cellular and organic life, the early Christian tradition intuited a significant spiritual shift. While it was a radical claim to confess the fullness of the Divine presence in a Jewish male named Jesus from Nazareth, even more radical was the re/evolutionary early Christian confession that Jesus' followers experienced the person, power, and presence of the Holy Spirit at work through them (Acts 2).

Although it appeared that Jesus had left his disciples, Christ by the Spirit continued his ministry—transforming, healing, and filling both Jews and Gentiles with the power of the Spirit of Christ. This new reality was so revolutionary that the scriptural tradition employed the ancient imagery of Yahweh's habitation with Israel to confess that now, in union with Christ by the power of the Holy Spirit, mere humans could become majestic "temples of God" (1 Corinthians 3.16, 2 Corinthians 6.16), and even more beautifully, "heirs with God and co-heirs with Christ" (Romans 8.17).

I believe that many of our ancient conceptions of God need to be released, and that we're awakening to a deeper realm of relational reality that verifies our most intimate personal and communal experiences of Divine presence. It's important to remember that the Christian tradition, carried along in the scriptures and self-experience, isn't the only Divine gift that is God-breathed. The word of God is living and active, inspired and God-infused, not just in Jesus the Christ or the scriptures, but in humanity and all of creation. For God spoke and the heavens came to be—God breathed, and humanity came to life.

We are just beginning to understand that the ancient sense of separation is just that: a sensory perception. We can move beyond it, as one moves from sickness to life, by reaching to a deeper awareness that encompasses and transcends the senses. It's a consciousness accessed by faith that the tradition calls the "new birth" (John 3.3), or "new creation" (2 Corinthians 5.17), which, at its core, is a way of relating within our ultimate Source of life. Thus, the classic biblical definition of faith is actually a matter of shifting perception: "Faith is the assurance of things hoped for, the conviction of things not seen" (Hebrews 11.1).

Beyond the observable, and underneath the thoughts of the mind, is the realm of relationality, which is the realm of the heart. We're learning there's no further reason to live separated from the Source of life. This is the message of Jesus the Christ, and that of the universe: God is with us, hidden in, underneath, beyond, and through the surface of our senses, a reality that only heightens our awareness of the exquisite beauty, wonderment, and power of life. It's truly a sensuous knowing by faith, and a relational journey that sustains and opens us more and more to the presence of Divine light, life, and love.

Surely, this is something of what Jesus meant when he said, "I am the way, the truth, and life, no one comes to the Father except through me."[12] The "through" Jesus speaks of is a relationship and state of being—a virtual fourth-dimension, an interior realm of memories, experiences, hopes, confessions, perceptions, fears, desires, and the extended range of all human expressions. This *through* opens us to a process of transformation, which we'll call "spiritual formation."

SPIRITUAL FORMATION

Spiritual formation is the formation of Christ in us by the Spirit. How does the Spirit do this?

How do we, in the words of the Christ-centered evolutionary paleontologist and theologian Pierre Teilhard de Chardin, "come little by little to feel that the individual shapes of all we have laid hold on are melting away in our hands, until finally we are at grips with the single essence of all subsistencies and all unions?"[13] We do it by surrendering ourselves as living resources to the Spirit of God in our physical form. In the words of Thomas Keating, we *consent*.[14]

How do we consent? One of the primary ways we surrender to the Spirit is by cultivating a spiritual practice or discipline, what many refer to as "spiritual formation," which is the shaping of Christ in us. Spiritual formation occurs when we put off the old, false self, and put on the new self in Christ (Colossians 3.5–11). Another term for spiritual formation is "sanctification," the process whereby we're transformed further into the new self in Christ.[15] The goal of spiritual formation is to be more fully shaped by the Spirit into the image of Christ through the release of our old self (Ephesians 4.22), so that Christ is increasingly all there is. Formation is activated by the Holy Spirit in a process that we consent to, which means we participate in it, but don't control.

The primary practice whereby this formation can begin is prayer, especially meditative prayer, or what is called today Centering Prayer. I explore Centering Prayer in depth in Appendix C, so for now, we'll limit our discussion to the key points for unfolding this chapter. As the Spirit is our source of life and our life circulates in us through breath (John 20.22), so Centering Prayer draws practitioners into the depth of Christ, beyond the doubts and thoughts of the mind. Christian masters such as John of the Cross, Teresa of Avila, and Thomas Keating have all detailed the importance of meditative prayer for our spiritual development. Closely related to Centering Prayer is the practice of spiritual reading, or *Lectio Divina*, which helps focus the mind upon the written word of God.

Such spiritual practices—Centering Prayer and *Lectio Divina*—are means of grace that form in us a deepening sense of freedom and love, which propels us outward to serve others. It is to this outward movement we now turn. We're reaching an important synthesis: the merging of spiritual formation with the outward mission of incarnational love embodied in this world through us.

SYNTHESIS: FROM INWARD FORMATION TO OUTWARD MISSION

The Spirit of God takes our inward, personal transformation and begins to move outward into the world through our relationships. Life in relationship with the Spirit is a shared journey. When we're united to Christ, we receive the gift of the Spirit's presence and action in our lives. The Spirit then enables us to move outward into our relationships as a transformed and transforming person. It helps us during our lifelong spiritual journey when we encounter the shadows of suffering, fatigue, hardness of heart, or spiritual melancholy.

As we move from inward transformation to outward mission, our spiritual life begins to shape our social ethics, giving courage to speak to the various dynamics occurring in our globalized life, such as:

- The distortion of human nature through the neglect and materialistic rejection of Spirit. This distortion manifests itself in a vast constellation of psychosomatic, social, familial, and personal dysfunctions and diseases.
- The corruption of the political, social, and religious structures. This corruption occurs through the rejection of servant-leadership and love.
- The mutation of economic structures. This mutation occurs through systems that promote domination for the few and limitation for the many.
- The pollution and destruction of ecological resources. This occurs through self-absorbed, shortsighted, non-sustainable, and overly consumptive lifestyles.

As our inner transformation impacts our external relationships and guides our ethics, we participate more and more in God's mission of reconciliation and liberation: reconciliation as we return home to the presence of God; liberation as we're released from the lower levels of human consciousness into the awareness of our interconnectedness to and with God, each other, and the Earth. This process summarizes the ancient Christian claim that, in Christ, God reconciled and liberated the world by the Spirit. An example from the gospels that illustrates the reconciling presence of God in Jesus is the theme of the kingdom of God.

THE KINGDOM OF GOD

The "kingdom of God" demonstrates the claim that, in Jesus, God was *here* among us by the power of the Spirit. This demonstration occurs with signs of the kingdom. For example, Jesus manifests the *rule* of the kingdom through his power over sickness, sin, death, and the evil one—all dynamics of the "kingdom of this world." It's intentional that the first encounter Jesus has after his baptism (where we're informed that Jesus is God's "beloved son"—Matthew 3.17) is with the evil one, the ruler of the "kingdom of this world," who tempts Jesus with security, affection, and power. Jesus overturns each temptation by drawing deeply upon the truth of his identity as the Son of God, and replies to each temptation with scripture (Luke 3–4).

Many of Jesus' most famous miracles also demonstrate signs of his right to rule in his reordered kingdom: he heals the leper, restores sight to the blind, raises the dead, and heals other kinds of physical sickness, even from afar. Jesus manifested the presence and power of God among us, reordering what had been distorted by other powers at work in contradiction to the kingdom of God. He even began overturning social injustices, with special attention to the poor, the disenfranchised, and the most vulnerable.

For Christians, Jesus demonstrated the presence of God's power among humanity. But the message is even more wonderful when we see that God's power and presence as Christ can be continued and embodied through us by the ongoing presence of the Spirit who unites Christ with us. The first Christians understood this. In the wake of Jesus' ascension they waited in anticipation for the gift he promised. The gift was given as Christ returned to them personally and communally in the manifestation of the Spirit, thus shifting the means of incarnation from the historical person of Jesus to the entire family of Christ, now heirs to Christ's ministry and benefits by the indwelling Spirit (Romans 8.17, John 1.12).

With those first Christians, we too, through our union with Christ by the Spirit, partake in the spiritual authority that Jesus demonstrated. We become the way by which God continues to manifest this spiritual reality among our relationships and with creation, which is the theological foundation for loving one another and, of equal importance, our stewardship of the Earth.

JESUS IS A WHO, CHRIST IS A WHAT

We began this chapter with the bedrock Christian statement that in the beginning the Word became flesh. Wrapped up in the phrase "the Word became flesh" (John 1.14) is the notion that "in Christ the fullness of God was pleased to dwell" (Colossians 1.19). This is extraordinary enough, but there's more: "In

Christ God was reconciling the world" (2 Corinthians 5.16–21).[16] Scriptures such as these have enabled the Christian community to claim that Jesus embodied the fullness of God for the purpose of healing the fullness of human nature. To put it more simply, Jesus was the historical person in whom human nature and Divine nature were united. In our abiding participation in the vine of Christ, we too are transformed more and more into the vice, which is Christ![17]

How can this be? First, Jesus is the "flesh" that the Word (i.e. *logos*) became. Second, Christ is what occurred when the *logos* united itself to human nature in the person Jesus. Christ is the union of the human nature and the Divine nature. As contemplative author Bernadette Roberts says, "Christ is a What, not a Who."[18] Jesus is the "Who." Christ is the "What." Third, in the incarnation the two are combined and we see for the first time in history Jesus the Christ. Jesus is the location where the Christ (i.e. Messiah) is occurring, in the words of the Nicene Creed, "for us and our salvation." While Jesus models God's loving plan of salvation on the stage of human history, after Jesus' death, resurrection and ascension, the Spirit is released to humankind at Pentecost to be the activating power and presence that initiates our union with the Divine nature of Christ (2 Peter 1.4) so that Christ might be "all in all" (Colossians 3.11). The all in all involves us!

Another way of saying this is that without the *Word* part, Jesus was just another ordinary first century Jewish man. But, because the Word became flesh in him, he was the *Christ*. The earliest Christians began to experience, recognize, and understand this fact, especially in light of Jesus' life, ministry, teaching, death, resurrection, and ascension—and the experience transformed their lives as they began to realize that Christ also invited them to follow him as the way, meaning that they too were to become transformed into Christ by the power of the Spirit through word and sacrament on the spiritual journey of dying to self, and being raised to life in God through Christ.

What this means for humankind is that God's loving plan continues without the main actor Jesus remaining with us in person. In his place, the Spirit of Christ was released at Jesus' ascension so that our life might now be "hidden with Christ in God" (Colossians 3.3) by the power of God who is here by the Spirit.

The miracle of the incarnation is that in Jesus the human and the Divine natures were united and are now inseparable. Thus, our human nature is hidden with God in Christ. At Pentecost, the Holy Spirit began the miracle of distribution. What was distributed? Christ. The fire of Christ. The Spirit of Christ. Now not just for Jesus, Christ was released with the abandon of Divine love for humanity conveying the healed human nature obtained on our behalf through Christ in the person of Jesus.

SPIRIT AND THE SPIRITUALITY OF OTHER FAITHS

Christ reconciles two truths: the *logos* "was in the beginning with God" (John 1.1) and Jesus was born "in the time of King Herod" (Matthew 2.1). Christ is the union of the *logos* and human nature. In a similar way, the Spirit reconciles the opposites: East and West, male and female, Jew or Gentile. The Spirit is what unites us back to God through Christ's union with us.

How might this inform how we relate with other faith traditions? Consider the following four axioms to guide us in our relationships with other faiths while remaining faithful to the Spirit of God among us all:

- Humility and love in the midst of the reality of diversity and plurality.
- Solidarity in breath with all living beings, including the Earth, in the certitude that Christ is all in all.
- Clarity of ideas in the midst of difference so to illuminate points of resonance.
- Charity and compassion in the midst of suffering.

I believe that in Christ a way opened for humanity to return home to the presence of God (Ephesians 3.19). Our way has been made clear by Jesus the Christ who demonstrated what the fullness of our human relationship with God was intended to look like. Now, because of Christ's continuing presence through the Spirit, we are co-heirs with Christ and "participants in the divine nature" (2 Peter 1.4). Christ, by the Spirit, invites us to remember, receive, and return to

God, and sends us into the world as individuals and a community to be the missional manifestation of Divine light, life, and love to one another!

WHO IS THE HOLY SPIRIT?

But just who is the Holy Spirit and what does the Holy Spirit do? Theologian J. I. Packer defines the Spirit as "conscious personhood in action and reaction."[19] Similarly, the *Theological Dictionary of New Testament Theology* conveys that "spirit denotes that power which [humans] experience as relating to the spiritual realm, the realm of reality which lies beyond ordinary observation and human control."[20] The New Testament includes over 250 references to the Holy Spirit, while the Old Testament speaks nearly a hundred times of "the Spirit of God." Based upon these references, the Christian tradition describes the personal action of God in relationship with human beings and the world as the work of the Holy Spirit.[21]

Yet, beyond all theological learning and speculation, the Holy Spirit is someone we cannot contain by definitions or categories. In the scriptures, the Spirit of God is described in diverse metaphors as fire, wind, and breath. Such words communicate only a part of the nature of the Spirit. It's appropriate for us to think of the Spirit in such terms as force, power, influence, energy, and movement, but to do so grounded in relationship to other beings and the very cosmos itself.[22] Bear in mind that the Spirit is beyond our normal human consciousness, yet interacts with us in deeply personal and communal ways.

Although, as we'll soon see, the Spirit is more than an impersonal force of nature or energy, the Spirit is indeed a dimension and manifestation of God, beyond our language apprehension and metaphorical images. Certainly, humility and vulnerability before the mystery and power of the Spirit of God are appropriate, for it was the very breath of God that gave life to the first humans, and it was the "Spirit" of God who hovered over the formless void of the cosmos moving chaos into order and nothingness into life-filled being.

In order to see a more complete picture of who the Spirit is and what the Spirit does, we'll explore three impressions of the Spirit of God in scripture: power, person, and presence.[23]

Power

The Spirit is the power of God personally interrelating with human beings and sustaining the cosmos.[24] While Christ is the "source of our life" (1 Corinthians 1.30), we experience this life by the Spirit (Romans 8.11). Thus, life and power are from God through Christ by the Spirit. Spiritual power is creative and trans-formative, finding ultimate expression in servanthood and suffering rather than dominance and victory: it's, therefore, counterintuitive to current cultural power-structures.[25] When we think of power, we tend to think of powerful people like kings, presidents, and billionaires. Yet one can have great power with little authority. The Holy Spirit's power is related to authority. Indeed, the Spirit, as part of the Trinity, *is* the authority.

Thus, when the Holy Spirit anoints us, we're given an inner authority to bring about change and transformation. That authority manifests itself through forgiveness, mercy, hope, and many other psycho-spiritual behaviors. Spiritual power occurs through a self-emptying in love for others in recognition that through the Spirit the one whom we think is other, is actually one with us.[26] Through this union and love, the power of the Spirit is life-generating; counter-ing the forces of evil, hatred, and death; a force to be reckoned with because it's behind, beyond, and within the whole structure of the cosmos.

Another way to say this is that *the power of God is manifested by the Spirit who is the relationship between everything and everyone. This power was demonstrated most supremely in the person of Jesus the Christ who lived a powerfully weak life through love—overturning the powers of sin, suffering, and death, absorbing violence and injustice in his being and releasing it all with tears, transforming reality through resurrection, the ultimate counterpoint to the powers that be.*[27] Yet as fully as this power was manifest in the life and love of Jesus the Christ, it's also possible for it to manifest in our lives too. Without the Spirit, our lives would be devoid of the spiritual power of God, and our union with Christ elu-sive. Just after Jesus' resurrection, Jesus confirmed that this spiritual power was to be ours as well. Jesus clearly draws the connection for the disciples between spiritual power and the gift of the Holy Spirit when he says:

"Peace be with you. As the Father has sent me, so I send you." When he had said this, he breathed on them and said to them, "Receive the Holy Spirit. If you forgive the sins of any, they are forgiven them; if you retain the sins of any, they are retained." (John 20.21–22)

Thus, spiritual power is based upon the gift of the Holy Spirit. The continuation of Jesus' spiritual power was lavished upon the disciples and continues through the church. This underscores the encouragement Jesus gave during his ministry that the disciples would do miracles much greater than the ones they saw him doing (John 14.12). In sum, spiritual power bears spiritual fruits, chief of which is love, and love fosters freedom and joy, especially in relationship with others in community.

Person

The word "person" has a tempestuous theological history. As such, it's important to be very clear: the word "person" in relationship to God doesn't mean three separate "people" (tritheism). Nor does it mean one person who wears different masks or takes on different personas, as a cosmic schizophrenic (modalism). Rather, "person" means the idea of the personal as opposed to the impersonal.

The Spirit relates to people in personal, organic ways. The Spirit isn't a mere force, energy, or power, such as electricity or gravity. Such dynamic dimensions cannot be related to in personal ways. The Spirit is the personal dimension of God. Indeed, we might say that the Spirit of God is the very emergence of intelligence, love. and relationship that proceeds from within the being of God's inner relationship to God as Father, Son, and Spirit. If an analogy is necessary, this relationality is much like breathing: a living, life-giving interchange and interaction.

It's also important to caution that the Spirit isn't a person as a human is a person. Yet the Spirit, as person, is also like us: the Spirit communicates, emotes, and expresses fellowship.[28] The paradox of the Spirit is that the Spirit is like us as a person, and yet also not like us as a supernatural power, energy, and force. The paradox of the Spirit is a mysterious manifestation from the depths of God's loving, relational essence and I cannot speak beyond that. The Spirit relates to us in personal ways, which is what makes the Spirit so beautiful. The Spirit is the power of God with us as God's agency of person and presence, yet so magnificently beyond our understanding, experience, and powers of observation. We only know the Spirit in relationship with the Spirit.

The knowing is a state of being, a matter of the heart, a way of life. Indeed, the Spirit must be much more than a creedal assent; so much more than a white-winged dove descending upon Jesus in an oil painting hung in the church foyer. The Spirit is God's personal closeness to us, Christ with us—transforming, re-creating, empowering, synchronizing, comforting, blessing, showing up and moving in mysterious ways.[29]

Presence

The Spirit now dwells within or among us as individuals and communities. This reality is the fulfillment of God's promise to Israel when God said that "I will dwell among them and they shall be my people" (Ezekiel 36.26). The Christian interpretation, at least according to St. Paul, was that this has been fulfilled in the coming of the Holy Spirit to the community of believers (2 Corinthians 6.16). Such a view opens immense implications for the individual and community, including:

> **The indwelling of the individual:** "but you are not in the flesh; you are in the Spirit, since the Spirit of God dwells in you" (Romans 8.9).
> **The indwelling of the community:** "In him the whole structure is joined together and grows into a holy temple in the Lord; in whom you are also built together to be a dwelling place for God" (Ephesians 2.21–22).

The relationship between the individual and the community is a spiritual synthesis. It emerges in various ways through the spiritual life of the Christian in community. There are five predominant manifestations of the Spirit's presence through and in us. Let's review each one briefly:

> *As spiritual gifts.* The gifts of the Spirit are given for the inspiration of abundant community life.[30] The fruits of the Spirit are manifestations of Christ in our life. Spiritual qualities produced by the Spirit in our lives include: love, peace, kindness, faithfulness, self-control, humility, joy, patience, generosity, gentleness, compassion, and meekness.[31]

As miracles. Miracles are occurrences of extraordinary grace conveying the presence of God. The Spirit brings the power of God to bear in unexpected ways over sickness, suffering, and need through healing, comfort, and provision (Acts 2.43, James 5.13–18).

As prayer. As individuals and as communities, we interact with the Spirit before God, interceding together for the sake of the world. Prayer is a primary way whereby God is made present by the Spirit. We pray in, through, and by the Spirit, and this is the most radical action humans can engage in. Rooted in the Spirit/prayer logic of Romans 8.26–27, the community moves with the Spirit through all things. Even in the depths of suffering and the heights of bliss, in prayer the Spirit intercedes on our behalf with wordless words from the everlasting springs of God.

As creative inspiration. God created creators. Inspired by the Spirit, the Christian community seeks to create the most beautiful and highest quality of artwork, music, architecture, design, and literature. The Spirit leads us into deep beauty, first in our hearts and minds, and then outward through our creativity into the physical world. We must also be creators in a generation of ecological crisis. Rather than merely consumers, we're led by the generative Spirit of God to foster healing and re-creation for that which we have wounded, depleted, and abused. The church community has a theological basis for engaging in proactive renewal and creativity in our confession of faith that the creator God is, by the Spirit, with us, bearing the fruit of life not death, fecundity not barrenness, beauty not banality, order not chaos.

As worship. The community of Christ can be a place of worship that is relevant, excellent, and engaging. Rooted in the ancient traditions, we must converge with the best of aesthetics to engage the human: heart and mind, body and soul. If we believe that we become temples of God wherein God dwells by the Spirit, we should seek to honor this reality with beauty and excellence in worship.

These are five areas whereby the Spirit, who is God's power, person, and presence, is made visible in and through our lives. Teilhard de Chardin summarized this incarnational reality in his majestic prayer *Hymn of the Universe*, where he lyrically embraces the human experience as the temple of the Spirit: "So my God, I prostrate myself before your presence in the universe which has now become living flame: beneath the lineaments of all that I shall encounter this day, all that happens to me, all that I achieve, it is you I desire, you I await."[32]

May the flame of the Spirit transform us into living flames of God's loving presence as individuals and as spiritual communities in relationship to the vast, infinite presence of Divine love, which while unseen, is deeply real, continuing through and with us. To this end, we now explore the promises Jesus made regarding the Holy Spirit, and their subsequent fulfillment.[33]

PROMISE

According to the earliest Christian confessions and creeds, we live in the time between Jesus' ascension and Jesus' physical return. *During this time, we don't have the privilege of experiencing God's incarnational presence in the person of Jesus. What we do have is the continuing personal presence of Christ by means of the Holy Spirit.*

We know this because Jesus promised that he wouldn't leave his disciples alone. Prior to his death, Jesus explained to his followers that he'd be physically leaving them.[34] After three years together, his tangible presence to his disciples would no longer be physical. It would now be inwardly personal. Jesus demonstrates his care and concern for his disciples by promising a continuing presence through the gift of the Holy Spirit. Consider a few of Jesus' most poignant statements from his farewell speech in the Gospel of John regarding this promise:

- "I will not leave you orphaned: I am coming to you. In a little while the world will no longer see me, but you will see me, because I live, you also will live" (John 14.18–19).
- "Do not let your hearts be troubled and do not let them be afraid. You heard

me say to you, 'I'm going away and I am coming to you.' If you loved me you would rejoice that I am going to the Father" (John 14.27b–28).

Not only does Jesus say he's leaving, but that he's doing so for a reason—so that we can be in him and he in us:

"The glory that you have given me I have given them, so that they may be one, as we are one, I in them and you in me, that they may become completely one. . . ." (John 17.22–23)

This mystical union is the heart of Christian spirituality, and the message of God's continuing presence to us through Christ by the Spirit.[35] The message not only gives us hope and comfort in our present life, but provides a deeper understanding of how Jesus understands the way in which God will continue to be here with us even after the apparent physical absence of the person of Jesus the Christ. Most importantly, through the power and presence of the Holy Spirit we can participate with others in continuing the presence of God through our personal union with Christ.[36] With that in mind, listen carefully to Jesus' last words before his departure. He speaks of a new reality of continued Divine presence:

- "Nevertheless I tell you the truth: it is to your advantage that I go away, for if I do not go away, the Advocate will not come to you. But if I go I will send him to you." (John 16.7)
- "I have said these things to you while I am still with you. But the Advocate, the Holy Spirit, whom the Father will send in my name, will teach you everything, and remind you of all that I have said to you." (John 14.25–26)

Those first Christians' hope after Jesus' departure was that the Spirit of Christ would come to the community of faith in a new way. The Spirit of Christ is the Spirit of God, and the Spirit brings new life for the individual and community. In this new way—*the Spirit way*—the Christian and the church can seek to live and learn. This Spirit-way of life unites us to God the Father through Christ the Son, whose Divine light, life, and love continued to radiate in and through the apostles to others, including you and me. But first, the promise needed to be fulfilled.

FULFILLMENT

The story of the fulfillment of Jesus' promise to his disciples is detailed in the book of Acts, which immediately follows the last scene in the Gospel of John. In the hours after Jesus' ascension, the first Christians return to Jerusalem. They proceed to the upper room and devote themselves to prayer. On the day of Pentecost, as they're all gathered in one place, the Spirit of God fills the room. The promised Spirit has come to the community. We're also told that the Spirit came to each individual—for suddenly, as a sign of God's presence, tongues of fire appear upon each of them, symbolizing that "all of them were filled with the Holy Spirit" (Acts 2.4).

The literary structure of promise (Acts 1) and fulfillment (Acts 2) is very clear. The Spirit Jesus promised has come. From here on, the storyteller can begin the account of the Acts of the Apostles, or more accurately: *the continuing acts of Christ through his disciples by the power of the Holy Spirit.*[37] Indeed, the promise continues to be fulfilled, again and again. Jesus' disciples are now empowered by the Holy Spirit to continue the presence of Christ in an expanding, life-giving way. Thus, Jesus continues his ministry of teaching (Acts 2.14–36), healing (Acts 3.1–6), and miracles (Acts 5.12) through his disciples. This ministry manifested the kingdom of God among them, confirming the authenticity of their message. *This means for us that whereas Jesus was born the Christ, now Christians are reborn into Christ, anointed by the Spirit as the continuing presence and power of Christ who is now not just present in Jesus, but in all who spiritually abide in Christ.*

If the disciples were to become apostles fulfilling Jesus' charge to "go into all the world as his witnesses" (Acts 1.9), they needed the empowering presence of the Holy Spirit. Indeed, to be Christians, they needed the Spirit of Christ. Without the presence and power of the Holy Spirit, the entire Christian life is impossible. The Christian community was given the "communion of the Spirit," and from this relationship came illumination of the scriptures, growth in holiness, spiritual gifts, and most of all, personal transformation into the image of Christ. Such empowerment enabled the disciples to endure suffering and persecution.

It's the same for you and me. We need the Spirit of God to be Christians: to teach, to heal, to proclaim the gospel, to participate in the sacramental action of the church, and manifest the kingdom of God among us in love, truth, and healing power. Because the Spirit has been given, the incarnational ministry of Jesus the Christ has leapt forward in a momentous developmental, distributive move expanding the relationality of God's life and love.

God's presence now continues, embodied through all who have been awakened and returned to the Divine sonship and daughtership that Jesus the Christ demonstrated and made possible. It's this family, often called the church, or the communion of saints, who by the power of the Spirit continues the presence of God and mission of Jesus in the world.

THE HINGE OF SCRIPTURE

The Pentecost narrative in Acts is the hinge of scripture. It's a visible stage of spiritual development in human history, demonstrating a new plane of spiritual reality potentially available to all people. It shows Jesus continuing and establishing his community by his Spirit.[38] The flow of biblical history is now seen at the magnificent moment of fulfillment! However, we mustn't stop there. We must continue to the consummation of God's promise that's now being fulfilled because "he has sent the Spirit . . . into our hearts" (Galatians 4.8).

The coming of the Spirit transformed history and is now transforming our lives. One day, we'll experience the final transformation of our bodies as demonstrated by the resurrection and ascension of Jesus. We mustn't take Pentecost lightly. Not only is it meaningful in a literary sense, it's necessary theologically, psychologically, spiritually, and communally.

For therein the Spirit comes in a new, permanent, and personal way as fulfillment to God's promise to Israel, then to the disciples, and out from their witness and mission to the entire body of Christ, which is the church, and from the church into the world as the unfolding, missional light, life, and love of God.

We now know the universe is expanding; why not also the presence of God by the Spirit in our lives?

IN THE NOW, NEVERTHELESS

The church and the Christian live in a time and space characterized by the apparent physical absence of Jesus Christ. Amidst terror, war, fear, and suffering, one is confronted with penetrating questions: Where is God? What difference does the Christian message make in a world in need of the presence of God? Is Christianity just another fabled journey to the great Wizard of Oz? In the end, will we find it was just old men playing at the levers, inventing the majesty of the gods for their own purpose and power?

The unique power of the gospel story is it announces that "the Word became flesh and lived among us . . ." (John 1.14), that Jesus was to be called Emmanuel, meaning, "God with us" (Matthew 1.23), and that, as Jesus once said, "to know the Son is to see the Father" (John 14.7). As compelling as these narratives and theological assertions are, we need to be honest: Jesus is no longer physically with us. This apparent absence creates a credibility problem for a reality-minded generation. The story teaches that after a period following Jesus' resurrection, his disciples gathered on a hill overlooking Jerusalem and Jesus departed from their midst, taken out of their sight. Jesus' disciples watched their Lord transition from being the God who was with us (Emmanuel), to the ascended one.

While the Apostle's Creed says that Jesus "ascended to the right hand of God the Father almighty," we now know that there is too little oxygen above twenty-thousand feet to survive very long, much less in space where there is no atmosphere at all! So during the ascension event the body of Jesus must have been transported to a different dimension or dissolved back into the *logos*. Bear in mind that one biblical account of the event simply says that he was "lifted up, and a cloud took him out of their sight" (Acts 1.9), and that after the ascension there are no biblical accounts of Jesus' reappearing physically as there are after the resurrection. It might also be helpful to reflect on the nature of Jesus' resurrection body, but that is beyond my reach. Interestingly, contemplative Bernadette Roberts says that when she died and ascended to heaven she did not see

Jesus in the Trinity, but she did "see" Christ, and that the Trinity was "literally unbelievable."[39] We do know that at St. Paul's conversion, he did not see Jesus. He only heard his voice and was blinded by a light (Acts 9.3–4).

So it is important to realize that the man Jesus is not sitting on a physical throne in a palace somewhere in the sky. That was fine to believe in the First Century when they thought there were seven heavens and that the vault of the sky had various physical doors leading to "mansions." Today, in the light of the images from the Hubble Space Telescope we now know that "heaven" is much more incomprehensible than that. We do not know how or if Jesus continues to exist physically (i.e., in the flesh), but we do know that he promised he would remain with his disciples "to the end of the age" (Matthew 28.20) and that he would be among us "whenever two or three are gathered in his name . . ." (Matthew 18.20). Yet the question remains *how*?

What I am suggesting is that the Spirit conveys Christ to us, and in this way the sense of what Jesus promised is fulfilled through us! Such a view could open the possibility of interpreting the "second coming" as the occurrence of individuals consenting to Christ's formation in them by the power of the Holy Spirit. Nevertheless, this is a dimension of the Trinity that is total mystery, and an aspect of how Christ continues in us, which we will consider further in the next chapter.

The crucial point here is this: At the ascension of Jesus Christ, salvation history shifted into the *now*—the present era of Christian faith, worship, and mission marked by the physical absence of Jesus but the spiritual presence of his Spirit. Thus, the church has the unique responsibility of believing and proclaiming at once what was, and also what will be. The church lives in the tension between the physical presence of Jesus among us and his anticipated return as the Lord who's overcome death, who'll make all things new in the eternal city of God (Psalm 46.4, Revelation 21). Yet in this era of anticipation, God remains with us. This is the claim we must explore to understand the full implications of Jesus' ministry and purpose, his presence and absence. Let me explain.

In the hours preceding his death and departure, Jesus promised something extraordinary. He promised we wouldn't be alone, that "he would not leave us orphaned" (John 14.18). He pledged that the Father would give to us someone—the Spirit, the Advocate—who'd be with us and abide with us. Even more revolutionary, Jesus said he would, by this Spirit, be in us (John 14.16–20). Thus, the ultimate mystery of the incarnation is that Jesus came to us so he could give us the Spirit who's the continuing presence of Jesus Christ himself. It's the personal being of the Holy Spirit who, through word and sacrament, inspires our confession of faith:

> We are not alone.
> God is with us.
> God is still here by the Spirit.
> God is personally relating to us as God's personal closeness.[40]

These confessions of faith are grounded in the shift of history that occurred at ascension and Pentecost, the deep theological and spiritual transition-point in time and space that provides the primary basis for understanding what it means to be and live as Christians in the post-ascension *now*.

Here are several specific examples of this idea located in the story before Christ's crucifixion. Notice that Jesus speaks of *someone else* who would come after him: "And I will ask the Father, and he will give you another Advocate, to be with you forever . . ." (John 14.16). After his resurrection, Jesus again promises his disciples the presence of *Another* who'll come in his absence: "But you will receive power when the Holy Spirit comes upon you; and you will be my witness . . ." (Acts 1.8).

In promising the Holy Spirit, Jesus was promising the presence of God, and was revealing the new spiritual reality made available through his life, death, resurrection, and ascension. This new reality was and continues to be the means by which we become the people of God, bound to the Father through Christ the Son in fellowship with the Holy Spirit. Jesus is hinting at the promise of a community that will be his continuing presence and "body" in the world, a people who represent the first fruits of the kingdom of God who are comforted, led, and drawn by the Spirit to participate in Jesus' continuing mission to the world: our transformation into love.

The apparent physical absence of Jesus is one of the inner tensions built into Christian faith. The one we follow is no longer physically present with us. So we live in the *now* by faith, believing there is indeed a reality to our relationship with God through Christ. Yet this reality is still unseen and not yet in full bloom. It's a spiritual and relational reality still emerging. It is Spirit shaping Christ in us. Therefore, we live between promise and fulfillment, presence and absence. We anticipate in faith the world to come, living in the *now* with an unseen reality in worship and prayer, mission and mercy, sacrament and silence.

We live in relationship with an invisible reality where we are brought into communion with God the Father through Christ the Son by the fellowship and power of the Holy Spirit.[41] This relationship is experienced by faith. It's here, in this confession of Trinitarian faith lived out in worship and community, that we can begin to understand what a Trinitarian, contemplative Christian spirituality looks like and how we are to live as Christians after the ascension of Jesus.

THE INCLUSIVE NATURE OF THE SPIRIT

The expansion of the presence of the Holy Spirit also demonstrates the inclusive nature of the gospel. Spirit-empowered inclusivity is a dominant theme in the book of Acts. The inclusive message of the gospel is seen most clearly when covenantal life is made available to Gentiles. The shock that the Spirit had *also* come to the Gentiles proved transformative for the early Christian community, including its apostolic leaders.[42]

How? Profoundly, the message of the gospel by the Spirit breaks through cultural fragmentation with the bond of love and fellowship. Thus, the Spirit, bringing reconciliation, is the essence of community and the means by which true communion in relationship can occur. Consider two separate passages in light of each other:

> So if anyone is in Christ, there is a new creation: everything old has passed away; see, everything has become new! All this is from God, who reconciled us to himself through Christ, and has given us the ministry of reconciliation; that is in Christ God was reconciling the world to himself. . . . (2 Corinthians 5.17–21)

And:

> As many of you as were baptized into Christ have clothed yourselves with
> Christ. There is no longer Jew or Greek, there is no longer slave or free, there
> is no longer male nor female; for all of you are one in Christ Jesus. And if
> you belong to Christ, then you are Abraham's offspring, heirs according to the
> promise. (Galatians 3.28)

As beautiful as this inclusivity is, it hasn't been the consistent mark of Christian history or culture. Regrettably, the church hasn't consistently embodied the justice, freedom, and beauty that exude from the Spirit of God. We've often been caught up in separation, spending energy declaring our own "rightness" and another's "wrongness." This is one reason the postmodern generation is so uninterested in the church. To them, the church defines itself by what it is not versus attracting by what we are: vessels of Divine love and presence.

So we struggle and grope along, awaiting the final fulfillment of the beautiful kingdom of God's relationality, where peace and love unify through the bond of the Spirit. In the meantime, through our union with Christ we are enabled to serve humanity, and in so doing become the continuing presence of God by the power of the Holy Spirit (Acts 17.28). Indeed, in Christ this sense of separation is subsumed by Divine love, enabling not just deeper spiritual understanding, but also spiritual union. Union with Christ and with one another is a state of being that helps dissolve our demands for airtight answers to the intellectual and emotional conundrums and conflicts we confront in life and our perplexing experiences of existential pain.

This incongruity between our longings and reality was the situation Jesus entered into in his incarnation. When we say that "Jesus became sin" for the salvation of the world, we mean that Jesus experienced the full terror of being separate from his *Abba*—the Aramaic term for "daddy." Jesus couldn't have imagined this state, since his whole life was defined as being one with the Father. Thus, when he was asked to give up his oneness with the Father and become sin—that is, the state of conscious separation from the Father—it's no wonder he cried out in agony alone in prayer ("If there be any other way") and from the cross ("My God, my God, why have you forsaken me?"). Jesus understood the core of what it meant to be human—to feel separate from God—because he experienced it. However, this experience is no longer the sole destiny for the human condition. A connector exists to mediate the mystery: the Spirit who awakens us in Christ to the essential interconnectedness that is our birthright way of being with God, our self, one another, and creation.

A HOPEFUL WAY FORWARD

God is here by the Spirit! It's a developmental move made long ago in the heart of God, for us and our salvation (Joel 2.28–29). And not just ours, but potentially for everything and everyone. Consenting to the Spirit is a hopeful way of being human and Christian that may correct past mistakes and reconnect with visions cast long ago, but forgotten in the mist of time and progress, wars and suffering, empires and power. Consider: Why did God become so terrible and distant? Why did we become so certain? So judgmental? So hesitant to love? Could it be that it had more to do with our human projections and psychological needs? It's time we came to our senses and returned to the Source of all good gifts. In this return we'll learn again the joy of being in paradise together—a relationship of being to Being and spirit to Spirit, available right here and now.

The Christian miracle is that Jesus demonstrated who we're meant to be: beings united with Christ—Christophanies,[43] the continuing incarnation and mission of Christ. For this reason, we are to receive Christ, believe in Christ, trust in Christ, be united with Christ. For this miracle we need the Holy Spirit. In Christ the ancient enmity between Spirit and flesh was appeased. In Jesus, and also in us, "flesh" was and is the vehicle to God. Why? Because God loves us this much. A crazy, in-loveness that wants to take us all—body, soul, and mind. It turns out that through Christ, the spiritual is actually quite physical!

We now turn from the mystery of God's presence by the Spirit into the vast territory of our personal union with Christ. In our union with Christ, we receive many of the benefits that Jesus demonstrated, especially our participation in the Divine nature.

THREE

HERE IN YOU

◄─◦─►

*Spirituality is not easy to define, but its presence or absence can easily be discerned. . . .
It is the power to change the atmosphere by one's presence, the unconscious influence
that makes Christ and spiritual things real [present] to others.*

—J. Oswald Sanders[1]

*As you, Father, are in me and I am in you, may they also be in us, so that
the world may believe that you have sent me.*

—The Gospel of John[2]

*Enter eagerly into the treasure house that is within you, and so you will see the things that
are in heaven—for there is but one single entry to them both. The ladder that leads to
the Kingdom is hidden within your soul. Flee from sin, dive into yourself, and in your
soul you will discover the stairs by which to ascend.*

—St. Isaac the Syrian[3]

THE INCARNATION CAN CONTINUE. Not the incarnation of Jesus the
Christ that began in Bethlehem long ago, but the incarnation of Christ in us
right here, right now by the Spirit. This is the radical claim at the heart of
Christian orthodoxy;[4] to experience this truth is akin to remembering that hidden
treasure is available to us right now.[5] So how can we remember and claim the treasure? Remembering begins by understanding Christ's union with us and therefore
our union with God. Christ's union with our human nature is a spiritual mystery.
It's difficult to describe, but Jesus gave us an analogy when he said:

"Abide in me as I abide in you. Just as the branch cannot bear fruit by itself unless it abides in the vine, neither can you unless you abide in me. I am the vine, you are the branches." (John 15.4–5)

Abiding is an image for union with Christ, and in our union with Christ, we're conformed more and more into the image of Christ by the power of the Holy Spirit. For example, a branch of an apple tree is conformed increasingly to the trunk through which the branch receives its life. The more the branch "abides," the more it'll bear its proper and abundant fruit, becoming a further expression of the tree.

Another analogy for discussing the spiritual mystery of our union with Christ is the story of Mary, the mother of Jesus. Mary believes the unbelievable. Her rational perceptions are transformed by an interior faith. Listen to Mary's reply to the Divine encounter: "Here am I, the servant of the Lord; let it be in me according to your word" (Luke 1.38). This is the nature of surrender. It is active and passive. She chooses (active) to surrender (passive). Mary consents to receive the transforming presence of the Holy Spirit who brings to life (in and through her body) Jesus the Christ. Mary surrenders to the Spirit by trusting the Word of the Lord, and the Spirit forms Christ in her.

Whereas in Mary the Spirit literally formed Jesus the Christ, in each of us the Spirit unites us by faith with Christ and begins to transform our human nature further into the image of Christ. Another word for image is *nature*.[6] In our union with Christ, our human nature begins to be transformed and healed. Its exclusive power over us begins to be replaced by the power of Christ's nature in us. In this way, we begin to experience new freedom and gifts through our new nature, as the Divine nature of Christ at work within us (2 Peter 1.4).

The role of the Holy Spirit in this union is to "birth" or "form" Christ within us. As Christ is formed in us, we become "participants of the divine nature" (2 Peter 1.4), and in this way icons of God's presence in the world. The inner transformation of our nature is at the heart of what it means to be "united" to Christ in faith.[7] Thus, the essence of Christian spirituality is one's surrender to the Spirit's formation of Christ within so to manifest Divine presence.

CHRIST IN YOU BY THE SPIRIT

But there is a "catch." Jesus died, resurrected, and in the last scene of the story physically left the human stage in the ascension (Acts 1). It's a catch, because if the foundational Christian claim is that God was fully present with humanity *as the person of Jesus*, then any further discussion about the continuing presence of God needs to address the reality of Jesus' physical absence from humanity after his ascension. While we are sympathetic with the personal piety conveyed by such song lyrics as "Jesus walks with me and he talks with me" or sentiments such as "Jesus never leaves my side," if we're honest, we'll acknowledge that for most of us the physical Jesus is *not* here with us.

However, that doesn't mean we're alone. God has made provision to be present even though Jesus is no longer with us physically. How can this be?[8] The short answer is: *Jesus remains present by the Holy Spirit who unites us with Christ so that we become participants of the Divine nature.* After Jesus, the Holy Spirit is the next act of God in human history. The Spirit is the continuing sequel to the great events of Jesus' life and ministry—for the personal distribution and continuation of Christ. We could put it this way: the Word became flesh to make each of us a sentence in the Book of Life.

Whereas John's gospel begins with the famous lines of the Word becoming flesh (John 1.1, 14), Acts teaches us that at the time of Jesus' physical parting, the Spirit was released to continue Christ's presence through individuals surrendered in faith (Acts 2). This is theologically possible because the Spirit of Christ is transferable to us through the spiritual grace of what St. Paul calls becoming "heirs with Christ" (Galatians 4.1–7) or experiencing "union" with Christ (Ephesians 3.17), and what Jesus referred to as "being born from above" (John 3.1–21).[9] These are synonyms for the effect of the Holy Spirit in our lives bringing Christ to us, and symbolized and experienced in the sacraments of baptism and Eucharist. When human beings surrender in faith to Christ, they're "filled with the Spirit" (Acts 2.38), and become "participants of the divine nature" (2 Peter 1.4) "filled with the fullness of God" (Ephesians 3.19).

The way we participate in this Divine nature is through our union with Christ by the Holy Spirit, which *is and was and will always be* the Divine nature of Jesus. Theologian Raimon Panikkar summarizes this situation well: "Jesus is Christ but Christ cannot be identified completely with Jesus."[10] By completely, I take Panikkar to mean *exclusively*, because Christ is given by grace through the Spirit to others so that "Christ might be the firstborn of a large family" (Romans 8.29). Please bear in mind that this is not a program to create "superhuman" individuals, avatars who ascend to Christ-consciousness in this life on their own terms and in their own power. Not at all. The Master, our Lord Jesus Christ, is inviting us to simply be foot washers, not superhuman spiritual gurus.[11]

The reason Jesus could say things like "the Father and I are one" (John 10.30) is because there was a miraculous union of natures in his being, human and Divine. Here is how it plays out: whereas Jesus could say "the Father and I are one," Christians can say, "Christ and I are one by the Spirit." Whereas Jesus was born the Son of God by nature through the Spirit, we are reborn as children of God the Father by grace through faith in the Son by power of the Spirit.[12] Grace anoints us and transforms us through the "second birth." Then, the Spirit initiates us into union with Christ and the life of love Jesus modeled: humble service to our fellow human family. Yes, there is a profound transformation that occurs, but it is not our own doing. We are not promoting our own name or power. We live by the sacramental words: I am not worthy, yet only say the word and I shall be healed.

In the person of Jesus, an unbreakable union occurred uniting our human nature and the Divine nature, or *logos*. Theologians call this the hypostatic union, through which human nature was healed.[13] The divinity or *logos* in the person Jesus was like sunshine soaking up the water of our disordered human nature, drawing that which was broken back to God and bringing the order and wholeness of his Divine nature back to humanity. As our representative, human nature was healed in Jesus from the inside out in what John Calvin called, "the wonderful exchange." St. Irenaeus summed up the whole Divine program this way: "Christ became what we are so that we could become what he is." This is the sole purpose of the incarnation and brings deep insight to the most famous verse in the Bible: John 3.16. It was not an easy process. It occurred through Jesus' obedience to the Father, and came often at great personal cost (Philippians 2.1–11): such as his agony on the cross (Matthew 27.46), his grief in the Garden of Gethsemane (Matthew 26.42), and his temptations in the wilderness (Matthew 4.1–17).[14]

The limitlessness of Christ does not diminish the uniqueness and particularity of Christ's incarnation in Jesus, nor the power of Jesus' name to which every knee shall bow (Philippians 2.10).[15] We bend low as new creations because Jesus was the firstborn among a large family, the forerunner for what we are becoming.[16]

"JUST JESUS" IS JUST NOT CHRISTIANITY

One of the most beautiful truths of Christianity is that it isn't a system of knowledge alone, but a means to experience and participate with the Divine presence. This happens by the Spirit who mystically conveys an inner healing through our union with Christ. Just as Jesus had a hypostatic union, we too can experience our own hypostatic union with Christ (i.e., the Word or *logos*) by the Spirit. In Christ, each of us is one person with two natures: the human and the Divine, or in St. Paul's terminology, flesh and Spirit (Romans 7.13–25). By the secret working of the Holy Spirit we become the body of Christ to such an extent that, as St. Paul put it, "it is no longer I who live, but it is Christ who lives in me. And the life I now live in the flesh I live by faith in the Son of God, who loved me and gave himself for me" (Galatians 2.20–21).

Notice that the text does *not* say, "Jesus lives in me." At first, this may not seem important, since the New Testament rarely uses Jesus' first name, but more frequently refers to him as either "Lord Jesus" or "Christ Jesus" or simply as "Christ."[17] However, there's another deeper, theological truth as to why it's "Christ" who lives in us and *not* Jesus. "Christ" is the Jewish messianic title given to Jesus. The Greek word *christos* was chosen to translate the Hebrew word *messiah*, which meant "anointed one."

It's important to see that the title "Christ" (i.e. Messiah) became the way of referring to Jesus' divinity within the Jewish theological context and historical hope for an heir in the line of King David (2 Samuel 7). Still, "Christ" wasn't the only way of conveying the Divine aspect of Jesus' nature. The Greek way, which emerged years after Jesus' departure, was conveyed by John's gospel (John 1.1, 14). Thus, at a theological level the Divine nature of Jesus can either be called the *logos* or the *Christ* aspect. They are, in essence, *synonymous titles that refer to the Divine nature of Jesus.*

The upshot of all this terminology is that the Divine or "Christ" nature of Jesus is *not* exclusively limited to Jesus. It's transferable to human beings through a spiritual union consented to by faith to such an extent that it's not the human, historical, physical Jesus who dwells within us, but the Divine nature spoken of as the Christ or as *logos* (2 Peter 1.4). Jesus is somewhere else. As we mentioned in the previous chapter, the nature of Jesus' location is a holy mystery that the Apostles' Creed attempts to convey in its culturally bound way saying, he is "at the right hand of God the father almighty."

Unlike the mystery of Jesus, Christ as the *logos* was at the beginning of creation, is now present with all of the creation drawing humankind into relationship with the Father by the "connecting" third person of the Trinity, whom we call Spirit (from the Greek *pneuma* and Hebrew *ruah*).[18]

Lest you think this line of logic is misguided, you're invited to dig deeper into this rich vein of theological truth by contemplating two important passages, one from John Calvin and the other from scripture. They're well worth reading in their entirety.

From Calvin:

> Therefore . . . that indwelling of Christ in our hearts—in short, that mystical union—accorded by us the highest degree of importance, so that Christ, having been made ours, makes us sharers with him in the gifts with which he has been endowed. We do not, therefore, contemplate him outside ourselves from afar . . . but because we put on Christ and are engrafted into his body—in short, because he deigns to make us one with him. For this reason, we glory that we have fellowship of righteousness with him.[19]

And from scripture:

> He [Christ] is the image of the invisible God, the firstborn of all creation; for in him all things in heaven and on Earth were created, things visible and invisible, whether thrones or dominions or rulers or powers—all things have been created

through him and for him. He himself is before all things, and in him all things hold together. He is the head of the body, the church; he is the beginning, the firstborn from the dead, so that he might come to have first place in everything. For in him all the fullness of God was pleased to dwell, and through him God was pleased to reconcile to himself all things, whether on Earth or in heaven, by making peace through the blood of his cross. And you who were once estranged and hostile in mind, doing evil deeds, he has now reconciled in his fleshly body through death, so as to present you holy and blameless and irreproachable before him—provided that you continue securely established and steadfast in the faith, without shifting from the hope promised by the gospel that you heard, which has been proclaimed to every creature under heaven. I, Paul, became a servant of this gospel. I am now rejoicing in my sufferings for your sake, and in my flesh I am completing what is lacking in Christ's afflictions for the sake of his body, that is, the church. I became its servant according to God's commission that was given to me for you, to make the word of God fully known, the mystery that has been hidden throughout the ages and generations but has now been revealed to his saints. To them God chose to make known how great among the Gentiles are the riches of the glory of this mystery, which is Christ in you, the hope of glory. It is he whom we proclaim, warning everyone and teaching everyone in all wisdom, so that we may present everyone mature in Christ. For this I toil and struggle with all the energy that he powerfully inspires within me. (Colossians 1.1–29).

Through such passages as this, the church fathers intuited the importance of the hypostatic union for us and our human transformation. Other passages add further insight, such as: "If anyone is in Christ, there is a new creation . . ." (2 Corinthians 5.17) and this classic declaration from St. Paul's Letter to the Romans:

But you are not in the flesh; you are in the Spirit, since the Spirit of God dwells in you. Anyone who does not have the Spirit of Christ does not belong to him. But if Christ is in you, though the body is dead because of sin, the Spirit is life because of righteousness. If the Spirit of him who raised Jesus from the dead dwells in you, he who raised Christ from the dead will give life to your mortal bodies also through his Spirit that dwells in you." (Romans 8.9–11)

There is much depth of meaning in these passages, and one immediate impression is that Jesus' work didn't end with the cross. It continued to Pentecost where a new reality of relating to God opened up for humanity, *the Spirit way.* Notice that it's the "Spirit of Christ" that dwells within us, and it's this Spirit that brings life, the same life that raised Jesus from the dead. The same life that was in the beginning with God, is God, and is the essence and Source of all life. Thus, through this spiritual union with Christ by the Spirit we can partake in eternal and abundant life (John 10.10), which is, in part, living now in the presence of God.[20]

What these passages and theological ideas reveal is that whereas Jesus is located "at the right hand of God," Christ is located non-spatially, and has been released to the human community by the Spirit of God through Pentecost so to be united with human individuals relationally, interpenetrating with all reality and the cosmos. Christ is simultaneously infinite yet personal. When we personally experience Christ as the *logos*, by the Spirit and through nature and the Eucharist, we begin to move beyond the demands to know more information about Jesus, into the freedom of becoming the love of God as physical vessels of Christ.

We now explore this relationship further through three connected themes: our encounter with Christ; our imitation of Jesus; and the continuing incarnation of Christ through us by the Spirit.

ENCOUNTER WITH CHRIST

If we are honest, we often have the idea that God is not with us. God feels distant and life seems difficult. Life situations such as accidents, sickness, suffering, death, bankruptcy, and divorce try their best to convince us that God *is not here.* In our minds, such situations don't square with the presence of God. I know that what I'm about to say will be difficult to believe, but it's true:

In all such situations, it only appears that we're separated from God. *The problem is not with God's presence; the problem is our perception.* Our perception needs correction, through remembering and receiving our union with Christ, through which we're invited into the mystery that, in Christ, we can experience *no separation* from God's loving presence (Romans 8.38–39).[21]

Another way of speaking of the transformation of perception is *faith.* This transformation is a mystery, and while we still see through the glass dimly, we *can* see, and often times encounter Christ among us by the power of the Spirit in diverse ways. We may not yet fully know Christ, but we will (1 Corinthians 15.52). In the meantime, Christ remains present to us, to encounter individuals and communities of faith in word and sacrament. In many ways, Christ continues to heal the sick, ease the afflicted, comfort the broken, and guide the lost. That is not to say that all of a sudden faith makes everything better. The *hereness* of God is not a means to instant health and wealth. In fact, at first, it has very little to do with changing our external situation.

In grace, Christ changes our lives even though he doesn't appear to be among us in the same physical form that he once was in Jesus of Nazareth. When Christ does encounter us, we're often deeply transformed on the inside, befitting the Apostle Paul's description that such individuals are as "new creations" (2 Corinthians 5.17–21). This conversion impacts all areas of our human development, altering our perceptions, initiating faith, and uplifting us from spiritual death into spiritual life. After this transformation, it may be that grace begins to bear beautiful fruit in your life in the form of external blessings, but there is not a formula or guarantee. It is all grace.[22]

Where Does the Encounter with Christ Occur?

So how and where does this encounter take place? Because our perception is limited by our level of being, there's more to reality than we can currently ascertain. Many Christians aren't even aware of three important concepts that help explain and locate spiritual encounters.

First, Jesus' last name is not Christ. *Christ* is a title, meaning "anointed one," and designates Jesus as the one in whom the fullness of God's power and presence dwells. As I've indicated, whereas Jesus was born the Christ, we are reborn into the image of Christ. That means that the purpose of our life is to experience transformation of our nature into the nature of Christ, the same one shared by Jesus. We aren't Jesus Christ, but we're united to Christ, and it's no longer just "I" who lives, but "Christ in me" (Galatians 3.21). We begin to experience a different kind of life, one more loving, peaceful, and powerful; one less hateful, resentful, angry, disturbed, anxious, and weak.

Secondly, our capacity to experience the presence of Christ can increase as we rise in consciousness through a deepening surrender to union with Christ. This rising is aided by spiritual practices, and especially meditative prayer. Consider a simple analogy: we're all climbing the same mountain of human existence, but we're at different levels with different equipment and gifts for climbing. Depending upon our location on the mountain we'll perceive and experience diverse views, some taking in less, others revealing more, and some providing *the entire* panorama. In the same way, we encounter Christ through our level of perception, which is our consciousness.

The exciting thing about this is that we're not limited to one level of consciousness. There are several levels above and below what we normally experience as reality.[23] St. Irenaeus intuited this when he wrote, "the glory of God is a human fully alive, but the life of faith is the increasing vision of God."[24] This is why dreams, impressions, intuitions, and visions are valuable, but not required, for our spiritual development. Mystics are those who have fuller, higher, and deeper levels of consciousness, which is why they're so often misunderstood. A popular example of this dynamic was vividly conveyed in the blockbuster movie series *The Matrix*. Neo was able to interact with reality differently because of his level or depth of being, one which both included and transcended the typical human aspects of being. Such extraordinary manifestations are special graces, not to be pursued or desired. More often than not, those who have lived at a higher or deeper level of consciousness have been totally misunderstood or rejected. Think of Jesus, or Gandhi, or Martin Luther King, Jr. While all quite different, they saw new realities and ways of being human and died trying to convey their vision.

Jesus also showed a deepening of his spiritual awareness after his baptism and forty days of fasting in the wilderness. He demonstrated the ability to perceive a different reality and change the "normal" one. He saw wine when others just saw water, and new wine came into being. He saw health and wholeness when others saw a cripple, a leper, or a dead man. He saw through physical form to the interconnectedness of all things and demonstrated this by walking on water (Matthew 14), multiplying physical substances (Mark 6), healing non-invasively (Luke 8), communicating telepathically (John 4), and transporting himself non-linearly (Luke 24.31, John 20). According to Jesus, what we perceive as miracles are actually manifestations of a deeper reality and the way things can be from Christ's perspective.

So what is happening when we're encountered by Christ? In computing terms, we're experiencing a "system reboot." Our human operating system, which is our consciousness, has a virus that prevents us from functioning to our fullest potential. In theological language, we have "fallen." But to be fallen suggests that we were created to live at a higher level. This reboot enables us to return to this intended level of functionality. We experience many such reboots throughout our lifetime, but hopefully we ascend further up (or deeper down) in consciousness each time. To continue the mountain analogy: we increase in elevation, enabling an expanded perception and awareness.

As we develop on the spiritual journey, we gain new knowledge and experience. But we need to be "learner-ready." For example, we don't normally teach a first-grader calculus, but we do a twelfth-grader. Likewise, we won't experience the deeper things of God until we're developmentally ready. We must ascend through each phase, one at a time, with no shortcuts. Spiritual practices can aid us, and spiritual teachers "above" our level can guide us on our journey further into God's loving presence.[25]

Finally, the encounter with Christ also occurs in what Jesus called "your inner room." While this can mean several things, I love the way the church fathers understood this to mean the inner room of the heart. The context of Jesus' teaching was prayer: "Whenever you pray, go into your inner room and shut the door and pray to your Father who is in secret" (Matthew 6.6.). Encounters with Christ are available to us in the secret silence of prayer, which is, in essence, the invitation and gift of the meditative prayer practices, and in particular, Centering Prayer.

Encounter in Word and Sacrament

A further way in which Christ continues to encounter us is through the proclamation of the gospel in word and sacrament. In the gospel, we hear God's story—a story of new life given—where God is presented to us by a bold and pursuing love. God is near us when we remember, proclaim, and interpret the story: Jesus the Christ's birth, life, death, resurrection, and ascension. By embracing and rehearsing these events of the past, in word and sacrament, we're drawn into God's story and life more fully and deeply. In the gospel, God is calling out to the created order to listen and be changed; through the gospel we're called to belong to Christ (Romans 1.6), as well as to be conformed into the image of Christ (Ephesians 5.1).

In the gospel, God encounters and embraces us as God's own people called out from the world to belong and remain by the power of a love so strong it conquered death, so that by this power Christ might be "glorified in you and you in him" (2 Thessalonians 1.11–12). This is one interpretation of the story of the prodigal son (Luke 15), who "comes to his senses" and returns to the father. When we're encountered by the light, life, and love of Christ, we come to our senses and remember who we are and are offered a joyful return home to the presence of God.

God encounters us in Christ, and we encounter Christ through the return to the Father made available by Jesus. We also encounter Christ in worship, especially in the sacrament of Holy Communion. Christ continues to encounter us in word and sacrament and calls us in faith to follow, obey, believe in, and belong to him. It's an invitation to spiritual union made real by the Spirit, as demonstrated by Mary. Christ's call re-orients our identities from self-governed to God-governed, and translates us from spiritual darkness into the light, so that we might be co-heirs of the kingdom of God and participants within the Divine nature. A spiritual encounter occurs as Christ by the Spirit engages our mind and spirit, and awakens faith. We hear first and then believe, and this brings about spiritual illumination.[26] The encounter demands faith, and faith is the transformation of perception, the assurance of things unseen. We cannot see Christ. We perceive Christ. We encounter Christ in the word of truth.

This word of truth is diverse. It includes, but is not limited to, the deep language of scripture, nature, worship, literature, fellowship, prayer, science, service, charity, mission, and most of all, silence. We cannot limit the language God uses to encounter human beings, but no matter the language, it's the one Word of God behind and within all things, and it's ultimately the consent of faith that's awakened by the mystery of God's grace and love.

When we are encountered in our interior self by the Word of God, we realize that we have everything we need, for as Martin Luther said, "When you have Christ you have all; but you also have lost all when you lose Christ. Stay with

Christ, although your eyes do not see him and your reason does not grasp him."[27] This is the miracle of water into wine and walking on water, the grace of the transformation of our perceptions and its blessed outcome: being "transformed by the renewing of our minds" (Romans 12.1).

The presence of Christ calls forth a reaction from those encountered. A dinner party recorded in Luke 7 offers a vivid picture of two opposing responses. A woman comes humbly, contrite of heart and weeping, and begins to wash Jesus' feet with her own tears, using her hair as a rag. Her ointment is an expensive perfume. Jesus encounters her with a startling word of forgiveness and love, both tender and strong: "Daughter, your sins are forgiven" (Luke 7.48). In contrast, the religious leaders can only stand in disbelief, questioning, condemning, doubting. It's a powerful scene in which Jesus as Christ encounters all present, yet only one, an unlikely woman, responds with humility, love, and consent. Jesus himself sums up the situation when he comments to the religious leaders:

> "I entered your house. You gave me no water for my feet, but she has bathed my feet with her tears and dried them with her hair. You gave me no kiss, but from the time I came in she has not stopped kissing my feet. You did not anoint my head with oil, but she has anointed my feet with ointment." (Luke 7.44–46)

Through the gospel, Christ continues to enter the house of our interior being, where we encounter Christ, and Christ by the Spirit encounters us. Maybe it's through a sunset or a major life situation; or maybe Christ encounters us through an unexpected blessing or tragedy. Whatever the means, when Christ by the Spirit enters into our interior home, we stand before Love itself and are given the opportunity to respond. Will we believe? Will we humble our hearts? Will we surrender? Or will we remain cynical, prideful, unbelieving, and resentful?

The invitation to believe and belong is extended to all in the gospel (Ephesians 3.7–9, 2 Timothy 2.3–5). Once we believe, we're sealed with the Spirit, "a pledge of our inheritance as God's own people" (Ephesians 1.14). And the spirit we've received is a spirit of adoption, for, "when we cry 'Abba! Father!' that very Spirit bears witness with our spirit that we are children of God" (Romans 8.16–16).

Our relationship with Christ is not virtual. It must exist in reality. Of course, a certain sense of virtuality exists to all faith, but its essence is rooted in reality: that Christ has met us in word and sacrament, and is now transforming our life. When we're rooted in the reality of relationship with God through Christ by the Spirit, we can confidently expect miracles and dimensions of God's power, person, or presence to manifest through our lives as individuals or as a community! If we desire the presence of God, we must first enter into a reality of relationship by surrendering to Christ with faith and love.

IMITATION OF JESUS

Reality in our relationship with God begins when we consent to Christ. But such consent is sustained by a rhythm of relationship working itself out into all dimensions of our life. The rhythm of relationship nourishes our relationship with God. Often, we're empty because we have no rhythm of relationship. Christian communities have, throughout history, created meaningful ways of living out a balanced relationship, often synchronized with the rhythms of creation and nature, such as the daily office of prayer and the liturgical seasons.

By the grace of God, the goal of the Christian life is to be further transformed into the Divine nature of Christ. This inward, spiritual transformation takes place through the slow and steady growth in Christ through a rhythm of relationship, which begins with grace, but moves toward imitation. This conviction is rooted in the imperative, "Be imitators of God" (Ephesians 5.1). But how do we know what God is like? Jesus' answer is that "it is God the only Son, who is close to the Father's heart, who has made God known" (John 1.18). In the person of Jesus the Christ, humanity gained insight regarding who God was. John the Baptist summarized this process of transformation and formation perfectly when he announced, "He must increase, but I must increase" (John 3.30), or, more to the point: less of self and more of Christ.

Jesus was luminous. As the light of the world, he manifested "glory as of a father's only son, full of grace and truth (John 1.14). In this radiance, we see that Jesus the Christ is the "reflection of God's glory and the exact imprint of God's very being, and [that Christ] sustains all things by his powerful word" (Hebrews 1.3). If you find this somewhat hard to believe, you're not alone. Jesus said, when asked to clarify this point by a confused disciple: "Have I been with you all this time, Philip, and you still do not know me? Whoever has seen me has seen the Father" (John 14.8–9).

To affirm Jesus as the image and essence of God is to believe that in Jesus was God with us. Apart from the Christ-nature, Jesus would have been just a normal Jewish human being. But, joyfully, because of the Christ-nature, Jesus was "one being with the Father" and "fully God and fully human." This confession of faith allows us, as Martin Luther said, to "forget all speculation about God. [And] hold on to the man Jesus Christ, [for] he is the only God we've got."[28] To be an imitator of God is to be an imitator of Jesus the Christ. The unseen God was seen and demonstrated in Jesus, and this manifestation gives us a nature and narrative we can follow and imitate.

Interestingly, Jesus himself said he was simply reflecting what he saw in God, and acknowledged that he was totally dependent upon the Father.[29] His life is the preeminent demonstration of relational obedience, even in the face of suffering. The very human struggle to obey and follow is memorably captured in Jesus' soul-searching Gethsemane prayer uttered on the eve of his own death: "Not my will, but your will be done" (Luke 22.42).

The whole emphasis of the gospel and of the Christian life is one of transformation and maturation through a life of imitation and recapitulation of Jesus' journey. The apostles, the church, and even Christ himself cheer us on as we're more fully formed into the image of the Christ and made more like Jesus so that he might be the first among many brothers and sisters. The very core of what it means to be a Christian is to be one who's becoming like Jesus the Christ, and this becoming involves the growth of Christ in us.

THE GROWTH OF CHRIST IN US

Imitation is rooted in our reality of relationship with God through Christ by the power of the Spirit—an interior relationship that can grow through spiritual practices such as Centering Prayer and worship. In Christ, we're transformed into something and someone different. This process is the reason for our spiritual journey. The experience of being transformed further into Christ is the goal of human life. The key element is the word "formed." To feel the power of this truth, reflect upon the following theological assertion:

> We know that all things work together for good for those who love God, who are called according to his purpose. For those whom he foreknew he also pre-destined to be conformed to the image of his Son, in order that he might be the firstborn within a large family. (Romans 8.28–29)

Our conforming into Christ's image is rooted in the call of God. But notice the call has a specific purpose: that we might be conformed to the image of his Son. This is our potential destiny! And it requires a transformation. The "trans" part of the experience is what lifts us above or beneath our normal level of being. It's what brings the "death to self" and "life toward God" (Romans 5).

Through our spiritual union with Christ, we begin to be transformed more into the image of Christ. It's not a physical transformation. We don't take on the physical characteristics of Jesus, but our personality begins to lessen and essence begins to rise, and we experience healing, or what Thomas Keating calls "Divine therapy." I think of it as a spiritual dialysis: we surrender to the Spirit who takes away that which is fouled in us, and gives to us that which is Divine in Christ. The light of Christ enters further into our depths of unconsciousness and brings healing and transformation, casting the light of love into the deepest recesses of our unconscious human cave.

Such is the grand purpose of each Christian that even in the face of the "all things" of Romans 8, we have the confidence that God will use the "all things" for our good. Why? Because we have a destiny in Christ, and our destiny is to be transformed from death to life, shaped day by day more fully into the image of Christ. It's the "all things" we experience in life that are the very means by which God shapes us more into the image of his Son. *What many call chaos, fate, and tragedy, we call our school for surrender and our teacher unto transformation.*

This doesn't mean we laugh at sorrow and tragedy and pretend pain and suffering don't exist. Rather, in the face of the worst tragedies, even death itself, in the presence of seemingly meaningless pain and suffering, we have the deep assurance that, in the words of Fyodor Dostoevsky, our "hosanna has been through the furnace of doubt." Even when we feel the heat of life burning into our soul, we yet have the assurance that one day we'll emerge with a strong shout of *hosanna*—because through the deepest valleys, God, by the Spirit, is shaping Christ in us using the very things we question, deny, and dismiss in ourselves, others, and our lives, to transform us.

St. Paul had a similar vision for the Christian life. He understood the destiny and difficulty of being shaped into the image of Christ, and the demands it placed upon him as a minister. He once wrote to a church reminding them of their hidden treasure: "My little Children, for whom I am again in the pain of childbirth until Christ is formed in you" (Galatians 4.19–20). Inner transformation is a process of labor not only for those who minister, but for those who are being formed.

Here we're given a glimpse into the vocational role of the minister who lives out this incarnational spirituality: we groan with, we labor alongside, we wait through the process. It doesn't just happen; it emerges after enduring the long and slow process of spiritual formation. To love and care for another is to suffer alongside the process of spiritual birth, interceding with groans too deep to understand rationally, especially when the mysteries of life and death, agony and glory, seem totally confounding. Leadership is love, and love is the will to work for the spiritual well being of others.[30] Love for one another means that we become spiritual midwives, befriending and encouraging others through the journey of life, aiding the growth of the soul and the expansion of love and development of the full psyche into a loving, mature human being.

To be formed comes from the root word "morph," which is where we get words like morphing and morphology. The modern concept of morphing is a good illustration of being made like Christ. We begin in the form of A and over time, by the Spirit and through certain practices, we are no longer only A but also B. We have been morphed into a new form: in the words of St. Paul, "a new creation" (2 Corinthians 5.17–21). And the pinnacle expression of this transformation is St. Paul's personal declaration of his own developmental recognition: "I have been crucified with Christ; and it is no longer I who live, but it is Christ who lives in me" (Galatians 2.19b–20).

Christ's formation in us is not only rooted in calling and labor, but the historic truths of our redemption though Christ: that through Christ's life, death, and resurrection we've been given a new way of life. We have died to sin and have been raised to life. Imitation is our part of morphing. *But we can do nothing unless we are united to and in Christ.* The life of Christ by the Spirit living within us is the beginning point of all our spirituality. It is an incarnational miracle: the Word continues to be enfleshed in and through us!

One further point: the process of morphing into the image of Christ cannot be accomplished unless we, like St. Paul, die to self-centeredness. The way of morphing is a commitment to surrender our life for and to Christ's life, whereby Christ by the Spirit lives in and through us. So we move beyond morphing into the realm of union with Christ. For when we look to Jesus as the one we imitate, we see sacrificial love, obedience even in the face of personal sacrifice, and humility beyond all logic.

This requires effort, for which we've been given the tools of self-observation, non-identification, and self-remembering. We self-observe by noticing thoughts, emotions, and movements in our inner and outer life. Attention alone is transformative because when the light of consciousness shines in our inner world we will never be the same. We non-identify by recognizing that we're more than the thoughts or feelings, ideas, or imaginations we observe occurring in our inner world. Non-identification creates a space within, like opening the window a crack to let the light in. This is the space for grace and the chance for acceptance, the freedom to say *"even this* is not I." This leads to self-remembering, which is ultimately the recognition that our life is hidden with God in Christ and that it's paradoxically "I, not I, Christ in me." We're more than our personalities and preferences, successes and failures, roles or relationships. We're soul-beings created by God for God and destined to be sons and daughters of God.

Jesus demonstrated for us what it would look like to be the Son of God, and then offered to us adoption through faith so that we too might be called sons and daughters of God. In Christ, we're returned to the Father by the power of the Holy Spirit for the sake of love, and the healing of the world. In Christ, we're agents of this healing, invited to continue the incarnational impulse of God in Christ.

CONTINUING THE INCARNATION

The Christian life has a hidden treasure, which is God. The presence of God in and through us is a result of our union with Christ. As we experience this, we become a very different kind of Christian—not just a consumer, but an incarnation. Consider this: Jesus was born the Christ, but we are reborn into the image of Christ! Let's explore this treasure further.

However glorious the life of *imitation* may be, it finds its ultimate expression as it moves from the interior transformation into the external world of relationships and experiences, what I call the continuing *incarnation.* God is made present and visible through the one who is being transformed into Christ. Incarnation flows logically from imitation. Our union with Christ by the Spirit begins an interior transformation that involves our whole being (psychologically, emotionally, sexually, spiritually, cognitively, and behaviorally).

As we consent to the Spirit, the Divine nature of Christ is formed within us. This is a process of many developmental phases toward our full union with God, and one of the most overlooked ways in which the kingdom of God manifests itself in the here and now. The essence of Christian spirituality is the inner transformation of the individual, and the exterior manifestations of this inward transformation into the world. This process affects our thought patterns, habits, emotions, and preferences. Bernadette Roberts, a Roman Catholic contemplative whose books *The Experience of No Self* and *The Path to No Self* are changing the conversation about the nature and extent of the Christian spiritual journey, reports that the essence of the Christian journey is not only the transformation of the self into Christ, but the gradual dissolution of the self altogether.[31] Roberts uses the analogy of a circle whose center is Christ, expanding outward to consume the space until there's nothing but Christ and the self is only a filament of form and function.

The life of incarnation is not a responsibility, but a surrender to Divine grace and love. The image of a river is helpful to visualize this process: flowing from the Source, it carries us inevitably to its destination. This has a liberating effect on our spirituality. We needn't try to control the process; it occurs through our own inner transformation. God is here in us, because God is manifest through us as Christ is formed in us. In her book *The Experience of No-Self*, Roberts acknowledges the difficulty of understanding the presence of Christ in us:

> For me, God-transcendent (the Father beyond creation and self) was never a problem or a mystery, nor was God-imminent (the Holy Spirit in creation and self). The problem was only Christ, and this mystery, more than anything else, is what kept the journey going. Belief and understanding of Christ are only complete once we see, and once we see "what" Christ is, we know "where" Christ is, for these cannot be separated. Once we see how Christ is Everywhere, we realize that without Christ, the very question, "Where is Christ?" could not have arisen. Though we cannot say where God-Transcendent is (because he transcends "where"), we can say, Christ is Everywhere, because there is nowhere he is not.[32]

This "everywhereness" leads us to the mystery of the Spirit in relationship with the material realm, including humankind.

MYSTERY OF SPIRIT IN THE MATERIAL REALM

We exist as a mysterious, indefinable interrelationship of earth and breath, flesh and Spirit. It becomes very personal when we observe the universal human anxiety surrounding the fear of death. Thus, two dimensions interact, the physical and the spiritual, and these two (at least) cannot be separated. In light of this interconnected reality, how are we to live in relationship with the Spirit and the spiritual realm as physical beings?

In our human vulnerability, the Spirit moves inward into our lives as a spiritual grace. The presence and graceful action of the Spirit in our lives propels us outward into the physical world of relationship with a new and transformed spiritual being. Without the presence of the Spirit we'll always remain *on the verge* of life. Spiritual merging involves three principles:

- Be vulnerable to the Spirit's initiation.
- Be submissive to the Spirit through a life of meditative prayer.

- Remember that you can be a continuing incarnation of Christ, bearing Divine love into the lives of others through your actions, words, being, and physical presence.

The spiritual life is an integrated life whereby the Spirit of God brings our entire being (body, mind, spirit) into the sphere of relationship and transformation. This is what I call spiritual merging, what others call transformation, and what St. Paul refers to as changing "from one degree of glory to another" (2 Corinthians 3.18), Divine Spirit to human spirit, bearing us further toward becoming love.

BECOMING LOVE

In our union with Christ, we are given the Spirit, and the Spirit enables us to manifest the presence of God. This presence is what we offer when we do "ministry." Christ's ministry continues through us by the Spirit because, according to Jesus, the Spirit "abides with you, and he will be in you" (John 14.16–17). If the Spirit is the continuing manifestation of Christ, and if the Spirit is now here in us, then the Christian vocation is sharing the presence of God to those in need of waking from the dream of forgetfulness. We aid others in coming to their senses, helping them remember who they truly are and can be.[33]

As we consent to the Spirit, the presence of God will manifest in our life, especially in our capacity to love (1 John 1.4–6). By remaining in Christ, we remain vulnerable to the Spirit, and we're enabled to bring about even greater things than we could ever ask or imagine (Ephesians 3.21). The implication of this spiritual reality is that through a life of vulnerability to the Spirit, we live lives of imitation, and through lives of imitation we continue the incarnation and bear the presence of God to a world that desperately needs and longs for the touch of God's love in the midst of deep pain and doubt.

The progressive renewal of our minds (Romans 12.1), through the developmental process of "putting on the mind of Christ" (Philippians 2.5), is the means by which we can recapitulate the pattern of Jesus' life and ministry: birth, anointing, temptations, teaching, ministry, suffering, death, resurrection, ascension. Our increased illumination and awakening into the light, life, and love of God in and through us is intended to lead us to further humility, obedience, and self-surrender. This is the spirituality of Jesus, and it's now the spirituality of Christ's continuing presence through and in us by the Spirit bearing love.

Regarding the nature of a loving presence, it's vital that we think in terms of the presence of a faithful family member. Now that the divorce rate has surpassed the percentage of "successful" marriages, it's crucial to reassert the language of the Christian family as we seek to be near those whom we care for and love. The bare terms father/mother and brother/sister can be re-imagined to provide a form for our presence. The Christian family is one of brothers and sisters, mothers and fathers tending to each other in love. For those who have damaged images from years of psychological or physical abuse, it's absolutely necessary that we demonstrate a loving selflessness for the sake of healing and reclaiming what should be a beautiful part of what it means to be "children through Jesus Christ, according to the good pleasure of God's will" (Ephesians 1.5), members of the household of God. We now turn to our final component of incarnation: that of *demonstration*.

DEMONSTRATING OUR RELATIONSHIP WITH GOD

Christ is being formed in us through grace by the presence and action of the Holy Spirit. Because we're united to Christ, we bear his light through our life.[34] One of the most important questions for our generation is how someone can experience God personally. It's one thing to say and believe God exists. It's something totally different to say that "God loves me and I experience it, and will show you through my life!"[35]

As Christians, we are to demonstrate our relationship with God.[36] This is precisely what Jesus meant when he taught about being salt and light, and why he told his disciples to go into all the world. The mission of the Christian and the missional movement of the church aren't to spread more information. We are meant to demonstrate personal transformation in our lives, and help others remember and claim their treasure in Christ. Without the internal transformation and healing that occurs through our union with Christ, all we'll have to share is theological information. Evangelism and mission aren't just telling someone to believe something. They mean demonstrating a relationship with God and manifesting the presence of Christ to others.

Demonstrating our relationship with this God in loving and humble ways is the essence of mission. Demonstration also happens to fulfill our human need to honor God and to leave a mark on the world, quenching our human desire to fulfill our purpose and calling. We don't need an office, education, title to be a demonstrator: just be alive and consent to the Spirit.

The concept of spiritual demonstration is meaningfully conveyed by the German theologian and martyr Dietrich Bonhoeffer (1906–1945), who admonished the Christian community that "the religious 'act' is always something partial; faith is something whole, involving the whole of one's life. Jesus calls a person not to a new religion, but to [a new] life."[37] Simply put, the vocation of the Christian is to manifest Christ, and we can do this by consenting to the Spirit's formation of Christ in us through spiritual practices that foster the growth of our inner relationship with Christ. It's our task to demonstrate the interior relationality we experience with Christ by the Spirit so that it may truly be said that "Christ is in our midst."

Yes, the incarnation can continue, in us. Understanding this incredible truth, we can begin to delve into the third way in which God is here with us: God is here *through us*, the communion of saints.

FOUR

HERE THROUGH US

————◆◇◆————

I am the vine; you are the branches. If anyone remains in me and I in you, you
will bear much fruit; apart from me you can do nothing.

—JOHN 15.5

In and through community lies the salvation of the world.

—M. SCOTT PECK[1]

Thus through [the Spirit] we come into communion with God, so that we in a way feel God's
life-giving power toward us. From the Spirit is power, sanctification, truth, grace, and every good
thing that can be conceived, since there is but one Spirit from whom flows every sort of gift.

—JOHN CALVIN[2]

PLANET EARTH is a populous place, and will only grow more so. The United Nations Population Division projects that by 2050 the human family will grow from 6.5 billion to more than nine billion people, with much of the growth occurring in Africa and Asia.[3] The scale of such growth is hard to grasp and will present profound challenges to us as a species. As far as we know, never before has the world faced such a global need to cultivate communities of togetherness versus separation. With populations expanding and habitat and resources shrinking, humankind will inevitably experience intense frictions. Will faith communities, including the Christian church, contribute to the easing of such frictions, or will we follow past patterns and let our doctrines divide us further into unconscious fear, violence, and isolation?

Such sobering challenges await the church of the third millennium, calling us to reappraise our way of being individually and collectively. Thankfully, we have ample spiritual resources to help us face and shape our future. If, as articulated in the previous chapters, the incarnation can continue in and through individuals consenting to the Spirit of God forming Christ in them, so too can the Trinity manifest its communal light, life, and love in and through our gathered communities of worship, prayer, and sacrament. Important conversations about how to be and do church are occurring in many contexts and congregations. Questions abound; theories are abundant; consultants are in demand. The questions require prayerful reflection and discussion. Yet an important, but often marginalized conversational partner in this reflection is the voice and vision of contemplatives.

Contemplative Christianity offers wisdom gained during two centuries of communal prayer, solitude, and simplicity, under both blessed and hostile circumstances, and has many sources for all inclined to listen. The postmodern church can learn a great deal from its own contemplative brothers and sisters, whose shy disposition has kept them in the shadows of their larger, more prominent siblings in the Evangelical, Mainline, and Charismatic American Christian churches. But shy doesn't necessarily mean silent. The contemplative tradition has become more outspoken and attentive to the state of the world and the church.

Even social scientists at the Massachusetts Institute of Technology are tapping into the important role of what we would call contemplative presence. C. Otto` Scharmer, cofounder of the Society for Organizational Learning, sums up the global situation and possibilities with a view to spiritual presence in community:

> What I see rising is a new form of presence and power that starts to grow spontaneously from and through small groups and networks of people. It's a different quality of connection, a different way of being present with one another and with what wants to emerge. . . . When that shift happens, people can connect with a deeper source of creativity and knowing and move beyond the patterns of the past. They step into their real power, the power of their authentic self.[4]

As the human community unfolds further into this emerging shift, I pray we incline our ear to the ancient wisdom of the contemplative traditions to undergird our Christian communities with the ballast of silence, the strength of meditative prayer, and the sustainable rhythms of living all life in an ethos of, and participation in, the presence of God.

In the following pages, we explore what a Christian contemplative community might look like today and how the contemplative dimension of Christianity can help shape positively the future of the Christian church during an era that will bring us challenges and blessings beyond imagination.

EMERGING TRAITS, TRENDING CONTEMPLATIVE

A survey of the Emergent and Missional church movements reveals that these communities share several common traits.[5] Such traits, in my view, portend the future widespread return to contemplative Christian communities. They are: empathy, patience, curiosity, environmental consciousness, integration, and beauty.

Empathy

Christian community must have enough courage to risk its emotions and resources to stand in solidarity and serve in selflessness for the sake of the suffering.[6] The distant, aloof, and preoccupied personality of the church is antithetical to the Spirit. Fortunately, the Spirit helps us to be empathetic. Likewise, we must be willing to be vulnerable and authentic in our ministry. In our weakness, we find strength. Rather than trying to escape our humanity, we must let our humanity teach us more fully, through sharing our own pain and experiences.[7] The Apostle Paul encouraged empathy in the community of Christ. He writes:

> Blessed be the God and Father of our Lord Jesus Christ, the Father of mercies and the God of all consolation, who consoles us in all our affliction, so that we may be able to console those who are in any affliction with the consolation with which we ourselves are consoled by God. For just as the sufferings of Christ are abundant for us, so also our consolation is abundant through Christ.
> (2 Corinthians 1.3–5)

We are members not only of the family of Christian community; we also are members of the human family. We see pain and tragedy in the world just like everyone else does, but we mustn't forget that we have the hope and courage to live in the midst of great suffering by faith in Christ and the reality of the resurrection. But as we live in this world together, enduring its seemingly random tragedies, we don't keep to ourselves. We can be the empathetic community moving outward and interrelating with others because we understand with tender care the pain that sin and suffering create. The Christian message affirms these polarities of existence. Through empathy we cry and draw near to the suffering situations humanity finds itself in, and there seek to be present, manifesting love and tenderness. We may not always have the solution, but we always try to provide a loving presence in the midst of the problems and pain.

Empathy is an imperative for the personality of the community of Christ. Empathy leads to compassion, compassion to conversation, conversation to relationships, and relationships to presence!

Patience

The personality trait of patience tempers the urgency of so much of our program and event-driven lifestyle and ministry. We need to relearn ministry that is relationally driven. The long view of life entails interior stillness before God that allows God to work in our communities. We need to get out of the way. If we were to judge Jesus' ministry by the pragmatic, business model, Jesus' ministry was neither very seeker-sensitive nor highly successful. He was arrested and sentenced to die.

God's methods may seem ineffective to our managerial and success-oriented mind-sets, but God is patient. God doesn't need our ministries, nor our megachurch campuses and global, television ministries. We must never let ministry become our passion; Christ must be our passion. A little hesitancy, humility, and patience would do us well. We don't need to save humanity; God has done and is doing that.

As the Apostle James faced the world and all its suffering, he gave the Christian community some very good advice, which might be appropriate for our Christian communities to reassess. "Be patient, therefore, beloved," he pleaded, "until the coming of the Lord. The farmer waits for the precious crop from the earth, being patient with it until it receives the early and the late rains. You also must be patient" (James 5.7). Like the farmer, the community of Christ must be patient, waiting upon the Lord. This is difficult because waiting requires a surrender of self-interest to a larger one that we're not in control of. It demands the deepest of all human capacities: trust. And trust requires hope.[8] We are participants in God's larger story, and we're being transformed into the Divine image. This is a story line we can settle into and take rest in, surrendering our worry and hurry, and in so doing, learning the lesson of waiting and the spiritual practice of patience.

Curiosity

No one is an expert anymore. Knowledge is expanding at far too fast and vast a rate. Rather, we are lifelong learners, seeking further knowledge on the specific and unique needs and characteristics of the present generation and culture. We should remember the ancient maxim: faith seeking understanding.[9] We can no longer afford to be reactionary and isolationist. If we're going to manifest the presence of God, we must try to understand our moment in time and the people we are in relationship with. Jesus spoke in the language of the people. He used parables and stories from their common experience. This may mean that we need to temper our habit of cultural superiority. We now need the global community of Christ to work together as a community of learners interacting in dialogue with other religions and peoples for the sake of authenticity and sustainability. We are not the essence of cultural sophistication. We can learn from other cultures, and we must do so, or we'll suffer the consequences of irrelevancy in a global community of diversity.

Environmental consciousness

The church needs to be a steward of our ecological resources as we enter into this new millennium. It must raise its voice as an institution uniquely qualified to speak to the subject of the care and love of the Earth. It must take leadership on this issue for the sake of being consistent with our theology of reconciliation. It should demonstrate what it means to be stewards of our resources, particularly the environment. The church could be the lead advocate for creating beautiful gathering spaces in concert with nature.

For one thing, we can all stop trying to become the next mega-church. We can cease competing with each other and start being an interrelated community. How many billions of dollars are spent on church-building projects? How much duplication do we need? Do we really need three brand-new mega-church campuses on the same road in one town? Think of all the identical resources and materials duplicated. This thinking is consumer culture under the guise of doing "excellent" ministry. I'm not advocating diminishment or consolidation. I'm suggesting that we structure our communities in line with the nature of God's presence—which at its core is relational and communal, and not isolated and self-serving. We might also start to think about how the church's building projects might represent us as stewards of creation manifesting God's presence through our worship spaces.

In my vision, the Christian church should build campuses that demonstrate the beauty, order, harmony, and sustainability of paradise. Why do spas, hotels, and Disney World corner the market on beauty and imagination in their buildings and grounds and spaces? These spaces and buildings inspire and foster peace. Couldn't the church lead the way in creating the same? After all, the Christian community has in the past been at the forefront of beauty in architecture. The great sanctuaries and cathedrals of Europe are models of the glory and beauty of God in physical form—spaces that inspire such awe, imagination, and peace that we're still drawn to them. Compare these with the multipurpose, gymnasium-style, or theater-style churches today. Now recall the beauty of nature. Surely our spaces can aid us in our vocation to be icons of God's presence through which the love, power, and healing of God can flow, as light flows through stained glass windows.

Integration

We can seek a spirituality that integrates with the totality of life, including the political, legislative, and judicial. Reactionary politics is fear-based; relational politics is love-based. Relational politics is based on love for our neighbor. And this love creates consensus, and consensus creates creativity.

In our pluralistic culture, the Christian community is one voice out of the many, and in America we're privileged to have a government of the people, by the people, and for the people, so we say. The church can be the conscience of society, not the mirror, engaging in an integrated spiritual politics that practically embodies the love of Christ in very real and tangible ways—such as the power of forgiveness and the necessity of reconciliation in relationships. For this reason alone, the personality of the community of Christ must re-imagine an integrative, spiritual politics.

Beauty

Dostoevsky wrote that beauty will save the world, and for Dostoevsky, this beauty was Christ.[10] Spiritual community is the manifestation of love, and love is beautiful. Love creates, and love can create beautifully. Marko Ivan Rupnik, a Roman Catholic theologian, articulates this vision with depth and luminosity, connecting it to our human privilege of manifesting the continuing presence of God by becoming love:

> The progressive spiritualization of the world and of life leads to the fulfillment of beauty. In a theological sense, beauty is a world transfigured by Love, a world in which many realities exist in harmony. The spiritual esthetic is an index of true spiritual life and of a profound comprehension of the spiritual. This is why spiritual persons can make the world beautiful; their presence indelibly marks the social life, politics, and ecology of the times in which they live. Love is a visible word, just as the spiritual person is visible. Love is eternal, just as the spiritual person is eternal, having passed from death to life because of love for brothers and sisters.[11]

THE FIRST CHRISTIAN COMMUNITY: THE APOSTOLIC CHURCH IN THE BOOK OF ACTS

While such traits give possible glimpses into a more contemplative future, we should also survey our common past. We're given a glimpse of the inner dynamics of the early Christian community in Acts. The Holy Spirit's presence enables and liberates the church to live a relational, contemplative way of life. The apostles possessed a relational spirituality that manifested the presence and power of God in their life together and in their daily common practices: "Day by day, as they spent much time together in the temple, they broke bread at home and ate their food with glad and generous hearts, praising God and having the goodwill of all the people" (Acts 2.44–47a). This life together wasn't complex. It involved three spheres:

- Daily time in the temple together. This would include praying and teaching.
- Eating together. This would include the Lord's Supper as well as daily meals and hospitality to guests.
- Worshiping together. This would include praises, singing, music, and dancing.

Notice that the location of most of this common life was in the early church-members' homes. While the Temple served as a public gathering and discussion forum, relational Christianity began quietly in private homes. Church buildings would emerge in the years to come, but Christianity began in relative simplicity and domesticity.

The experience of the apostolic church was transformative.[12] While we no longer have the physical presence of the apostles, we can still anticipate and share in similar experiences of the Holy Spirit, which is neither limited nor hindered by time. Every Christian community can surrender to this way of life in the Spirit, who's still inviting us to do so for the healing of the world.

Theologically, the contemplative way of life for the community of Christ finds its source in the relational life of the Trinity. When the Spirit was given to the apostolic community, they experienced an inner transformation that propelled them further into the contemplative way of life rooted in God, now revealed not just as the high and holy one, but also as *Abba*, close and caring. It was Jesus who revealed God's personal name as Abba, teaching us that God is a relational being, known through the Son and the Spirit. Abba does not mean that God is a masculine, white-bearded grandfather sitting on a throne. Abba means, *"I love you as a father/mother. I am personally interested in you. You have eternal significance. And I will participate in bringing about your unique growth and destiny."*

Through Jesus, we were given new knowledge. We were educated further about the nature of God. Jesus was teaching us that God is a relational being, not just with humanity, but within God's very selfhood. God is One, yet Three; God is Abba; God is Christ; and God is the Holy Spirit. The One-in-Three waltzes in Divine community, creativity, and communication. This is the Trinity: a relational community of light, life, and love, and we know and ponder this because of Jesus' genius. He revealed the leading edge of knowledge about God and what it looked like to live as one with the Divine, to be caught up with God the Father and the Spirit, and what it was like to be a human Son of God and Son of Man. He showed us on the stage of history that God is a relationship.

The church fathers used the Greek word *perichoresis* to describe this Divine relationship and community. The word means "to move about"—literally, to dance. So we see from the story of Pentecost that it's the Spirit who forms Christian community by drawing us into the Divine relational life so as to "dance" with the Trinity. The Spirit is the extension of the Divine community with us. God, as Trinity, is a *being-in-communion*, and through the Spirit, the church participates in this relational way of being.

If aspects of the apostolic church were to be reclaimed for contemplative Christian community today, what would such a way of life look like? The following envisioning is a creative attempt to connect the two worlds—apostolic and postmodern—with a contemplative bridge. (Those interested in a contemplative interpretation of this apostolic community can read "Contemplative Practices and the Apostolic Church" in Appendix C.)

ENVISIONING CONTEMPLATIVE CHRISTIAN COMMUNITY

Our human role in continuing God's presence can contribute both to a revitalization of Christian spirituality and the healing of the world—a healing Jesus hints at when he teaches us to pray: "Thy kingdom come; thy will be done on Earth as it is in heaven" (Matthew 6.10). This kingdom is a relationship we're charged to foster in community with one another on this exquisite planet we inhabit and share. As a living relationship, it nurtures a web of life held together by God's relational love, which bears the enduring fruit of life.

So what would such a contemplative Christian community look like today? This is an important question as we move from contemplative theory to contemplative embodiment. While the manifestation of Divine presence flows from the particular personality of each community, several general aspects of Christian contemplative community can be considered. These aspects are characteristics and practices that will help communities cultivate their deepening consent to the Spirit's presence.

As a start to what should be an ongoing conversation, I propose the following five aspects for cultivating contemplative, Christian community:

- **Listening for understanding:** the wisdom of scripture, nature, and experience.
- **Consenting in silence:** the grace of Centering Prayer and meditation.
- **Connecting beyond differences:** the experience of oneness in Christ.
- **Becoming love:** the journey toward transformation and union.
- **Living with reverence:** the harmony of all life.

From this initial outline, we will now develop each of these characteristics as a thought-experiment in service of the emergence of contemplative, Christian communities everywhere.

Listening for Understanding

Contemplative community places itself under the authority of the living wisdom carried through the centuries by the ongoing creative conversation between scripture and commentary. Contemplative Brother David Steindl-Rast has noted that the key word in his personal spiritual discipline is "listening," and that "listen" is the very first word of St. Benedict's Rule.[13]

While the Reformation insight of sola scriptura ("by scripture alone") was an important developmental move in the growth of Christianity, it has also created untold damage in the wake of the scientific enlightenment. Today, an ongoing conversation is occurring regarding the role of scripture in the formation and governance of churches, as well as its normative place in faith and practice. The role of scripture is very much in process, and to some this is very troubling.

This situation is not troubling for contemplatives. For contemplatives, the answer to the enduring conundrum regarding the role of scripture differs from the Fundamentalists, Evangelicals, and Emergents. From a contemplative Christian perspective, scripture is only one of the means by which we are given principles that lead to wisdom. While scripture is a means to wisdom and wisdom is a means to a deeper union with God, contemplatives recognize that wisdom is bound up with the living Word of God, but the living Word of God is not limited to the written word of God, or what we refer to as the scriptures.

Moving to this place of perspective requires a journey of spiritual development—one that happens, in many cases, quite naturally. Over time, one's concrete view of scripture begins to open up to multiple dimensions of meaning. Developmental psychologists have mapped this process and refer to it in various terms, such as the fifth stage of "conjunctive faith," described by James Fowler, a pioneer in the developmental psychology of spirituality:

> A way of seeing, of knowing, of committing, [that] moves beyond the dichotomizing logic of Stage 4's "either/or." It sees both (or the many) sides of an issue simultaneously. Conjunctive faith suspects that things are organically related to each other; it attends to the pattern of interrelatedness in things, trying to avoid force fitting to its own prior mind set.[14]

On one level, this is a very good psychological description of the contemplative/mystical way of knowing and experiencing. It's also a very useful way to describe the shift that occurs during one's lifetime as to how one reads and sees the scriptures. Regrettably, many deeply committed Christians and Christian leaders today remain attached to the Reformation era worldview in their use of scripture, yet they are also intuiting that their use of scripture is dissonant and in friction with their own spiritual and psychological human development. Unfortunately, not having a way forward, such leaders often stop growing in order to preserve their sense of control over their faith. In such cases, repression can occur, creating all sorts of distortions, from sexual misbehavior to psychological breakdowns leading them to "leave the ministry." What is most insidious are those spiritual leaders who become Pharisees.

Leaders of great power and position who may know a great deal of doctrine but are not transformed into love or wisdom. While that may sound critical, it's not meant to be a judgment, simply an observation of developmental fact. But it is the propensity of life to grow, and some ideas are meant to be outgrown like an old pair of shoes.

Everyone is free to be at whatever stage of psycho-spiritual development they choose to live at. People are free to walk through life wearing all sorts of different kinds of shoes—some more fashionable, outdated, comfortable, utilitarian than others. Psychological growth is not compulsory in life; neither was going to the moon or climbing Mount Everest. But humanity is further enriched by those achievements. Psychological growth is available and it's an important way out of the box of literal scriptural interpretation, a box made more confining by the Reformation principle sola scriptura in a universe that's certainly not boxed in, but is actually open and expanding. Sola scriptura is a fear- and control-based mentality that can now be superseded by the principles of love, wisdom, and discernment. It was a useful concept in the sixteenth century. In order for it to be of use today in the role of fostering spiritual wholeness and transformation, sola scriptura will require significant re-visioning.

Listening for understanding replaces the Enlightenment tendency of dogmatic interpretation that's still very much with the Christian church. The role of scripture in a contemplative community follows a process of spiritual development that requires listening with an open heart and mind to hear what the Spirit of truth might say, to bring personal understanding, and lead one to further transformation in Christ.[15] This is an ever-emerging process. Wisdom is never cornered, captured, or known completely. Why? Because it's actually a living thing, a being of life whom we call Spirit, who in and through the person Jesus reminded us that this living wisdom was the "way, truth, and life" (John 14.6). Thus wisdom can be experienced with similar intensity in the beauty and power of nature, music, and human art. While these "books" have their own uniqueness, they aren't intended to convey the personal story of Divine love that is, for Christians, particularly embodied in the Jewish and Christian scriptures.

For some, these ideas will be very challenging and raise many concerns. For others, they will be life-giving words of freedom. As Jesus said: "Let anyone with ears, listen" (Matthew 11.15). And what are we listening for? We listen for the personal experience of truth known with interior, relational conviction that transcends yet includes doctrinal categories, leading us to be inhabited by the flame of conscious light and wisdom itself; which was in the beginning with God, before all books, ideas, doctrines, and words ever were, and will endure when these human expressions cease to be.

Consenting in Silence

Contemplative Christian community places itself under the grace of silence. The primary way this occurs is through the spiritual practice of Centering Prayer, which is one form of meditative, silent prayer. The church father Ignatius speculated that silence was God's first word. The reason silence is important is not because it initiates an altered state of consciousness. While fuller understanding and deeper clarity may be obtained through meditative prayer, it isn't the primary reason contemplative community grounds itself in silence. Such outcomes of silence are simply natural by-products of the meditative process, but not its ultimate purpose. The real reason for silence in contemplative community is to surrender to God's grace and initiative. To put it bluntly: human beings need to sit down and shut up. Or to use biblical imagery: we lost our intimacy with God when we were evicted from the Garden and what soon followed was human violence and chaos, symbolized by the stories of Cain and Abel and the Tower of Babel.

Basically, the world is full of noise. Our inner life is spent in thought-chatter, and this drains spiritual force. Furthermore, chatter depletes and distracts us from the ever-present living word of God manifesting as wisdom, available as deeper consciousness, or understanding. Neurology and consciousness studies are discovering the biological basis and benefits of silent meditation. But like all science, it can only go so far in describing how and answering the "what" question. It cannot answer "why."[16] The contemplative Christian tradition teaches us why. We consent to God in silence to return to the Father's peaceful presence that passes all understanding. This return requires a descent from our divided brain, and an entrance into the heart, which follows its own inner logic—the logic of love. The grace of silence is that it can lead us away from being solely "head" people and return us to being "heart" people. The heart is symbolized by the garden, the head by the city, where humankind, generation after generation, builds its towers. It's a noisy, chaotic business. While the life of the thinking brain provides profound gifts of technology, it cannot provide the felt touch of God's loving presence. That requires a grace known and conveyed with the language of love beating in the mind of the heart surrendered in silence.

While it's true that Western Christianity has been dominated by rationalism, this doesn't mean that the contemplative tradition of silence is non-Christian. It's time for the Western church to cease its fearful reaction to the gift of silence. Meditative silence is not the enemy. The enemy is all ideas that keep humanity separate from God. Silence is God's beautiful notion.

What was occurring prior to God's speaking? What could be more Divine and beautiful? What could be a more appropriate posture of humility and adoration than surrendered silence? Just because silence hasn't been on the front burner of the Western Christian tradition, or because it's an important aspect of other religious traditions like Buddhism, doesn't deny its vital importance for Christian spirituality.

Connecting beyond Differences

In fact, all of humanity can connect in the language of silence, beyond words. Everyone understands silence, which connects us beyond all differences. In this way, silence is Christ, reconciling East and West. Contemplative Christian community places itself under the binding power of non-duality, which moves us beyond the charitable statement, "There go I but for the grace of God," into the radical awareness, "There go I," so beautifully portrayed by Jesus' story of the Good Samaritan (Luke 10.25–37).

Sin is the power of separation. Jesus calls the devil *diabolos*, which means "the divider." From the beginning, humanity was tempted to separative thinking: you are not God. The result of this deep separation lingers in us biologically and spiritually. We literally are split-brain beings. Thus, the Christian program of salvation has emphasized the reconciliation of humanity, or a "bringing back together" of the human with God in Christ. In St. Paul's words, we have been "justified," which means brought back together in a balanced relationship (Romans 5).

The very word "religion" comes from the Latin *religare*, which can be translated "to bind back." Sadly, for much of human history religion has not bound us back to God or to one another. It has often done just the opposite, fostering deeper divisions within the human family. Contemplative Christianity, standing in the radical union of human nature with the Divine in Jesus Christ, says, "No more." Once and for all, human beings have been bound back to God and thus to one another. St. Paul puts it this way: "In Christ God was reconciling the world to himself, not counting their trespasses against them, and entrusting the message of reconciliation to us . . ." (2 Corinthians 5.19).

What the contemplative tradition is reminding us is that underneath all our differences is the image of God, and beyond the image of God is the love of God for humankind, now ontologically bound with God through Christ. In this union, a oneness can emerge. All fears and differences are denials of the radical claim of oneness made visible in Jesus Christ. Humanity is embraced in God; creation is embraced in God; the whole is one and the one is also the many. The body of Christ is comprised of different aspects, but it is one body growing in love (1 Corinthians 13).

Thus, where we once saw foreigners and strangers, we now see neighbors to love, who are our brothers and sisters. Indeed, the other is now ourselves—not egocentrically, but in a way that admits that there is not just a "you" and a "me," there is also an "us." Instead, the living Spirit of God manifests itself through all things, bringing an understanding that all of life is at its deepest levels interrelated: a living organism. The problem is that we forget our connectedness and live in fearful isolation. But the truth is that, in Christ, nothing can separate us from God or one another, and this is the binding power of non-dual love.

Becoming Love

Contemplative Christian community places itself under the purposes of love. Such unity as we just discussed can only be possible by the power of love. Contemplative Christianity has become aware through personal experience that the purpose of life, silence, and unity is to become love itself. Each relationship is our best chance to become love. Where we once saw our spouse or child with all their flaws, now we see love itself. Rather than being a relationship that we categorize as "my spouse," or "my boss," or "my family member," contemplative Christianity invites us to simply be in relationship with love itself, for love itself.

From a contemplative perspective, the purpose-driven life is actually a love-driven life, for love is the ultimate purpose of being human. Love is what drove the incarnation; love is what incarnation is for. Our lifetime is given to realize that love. Following Jesus' pattern, this will require the death of self, and a giving up of all that opposes love.

So this naturally begs the question, "What is love?" As profound as the question seems, the answer surpasses it in profundity. Consider St. John's classic answer to this great question:

> Beloved, let us love one another, because love is from God; everyone who loves is born of God and knows God. Whoever does not love does not know God, for God is love. God's love was revealed among us in this way: God sent his only Son into the world so that we might live through him. In this is love, not that we loved God but that he loved us and sent his Son to be the atoning sacrifice for our sins. Beloved, since God loved us so much, we also ought to love one another. No one has ever seen God; if we love one another, God lives in us and his love is perfected in us. (1 John 4.7–12)

The whole existence of humankind and creation is built around God's being love, and love's intention to become us. Love is the juice that drives Divine presence, the glue that holds the essence of life together. Love is everything. It is beyond description: it is felt; it is given. Love is. Worship, music, and prayer and service convey the deepest language of love, and so we pray:

> Divine Love, pour into the vessels of our heart, the presence of love for you and one another. Inspired by your initiative, we choose to become a living gift of love today. Freed from all compulsion to pay for or demand proof of another's worthiness, we simply offer the free gift of love, in word, deed, and countenance. Amen.[17]

Living with Reverence

Contemplative Christian community places itself in humble reverence and relationality to and with all life—human, organic, animal, cosmic, Divine. Contemplative Christians have intuited that love leads to union and reverence. The ecological movement isn't just a modern phenomenon; once, religious traditions lived in deeper harmony with the natural world. While some choose to only see this as paganism, I wish to remind them that God is the God of all life and the creator of all creation! Why would anyone choose to live separate from the creator or the creation? Such thinking comes from one who divides in fear, not one who binds together in love.

Contemplatives understand that reverence is not worship. We don't worship Mother Earth or Gaia, but we do consent in deep reverence to the reality of our interrelatedness. Once again, science can describe the "what" and "how" of this interconnectivity, but our purpose here is to highlight the "why." The contemplative answer to this question is that we live in reverence to all life because all things come from God. Recall that in the beginning God spoke and said let there be light (Genesis 1). The ancient story of Genesis is intended to convey to us the nested hierarchy and interrelatedness of life. What is it that binds all of this life back to God? Yes, love—but beyond love is the Spirit of God infusing the entire cosmos and creation with Christ!

The contemplative dimension of Christianity wishes to order its external life bound to this reverence for life. In this way, we live with humility, lest we think we are the source of our life. While life requires effort against what appear to be the chaotic forces of nature, wisdom leads us further into a harmonious way of being with the creation. It's the contemplative disposition of reverence toward the creation that's of vital importance to reclaim in our Christian communities.

In this third millennium of Christian faith, we're blessed to contemplate the repository of insights gained by those who have preceded us. One such legacy burns more luminously than others—that of Francis of Assisi. St. Francis lived during a time of cultural transition; the "dark ages" were slowly drawing to a close and the Renaissance would emerge within a hundred years of his death. His Canticle of the Sun, sometimes also called the "canticle of creation," conveys a simple understanding of the interrelatedness of all things. This song-prayer beautifully summarizes our whole point of reverence for life:

> O Most High, all-powerful, good Lord God, to you belong praise, glory, honor and all blessing.
>
> Be praised, my Lord, for all your creation and especially for our Brother Sun, who brings us the day and the light; he is strong and shines magnificently. O Lord, we think of you when we look at him.
>
> Be praised, my Lord, for Sister Moon, and for the stars which you have set shining and lovely in the heavens.
>
> Be praised, my Lord, for our Brothers Wind and Air and every kind of weather by which you, Lord, uphold life in all your creatures.
>
> Be praised, my Lord, for Sister Water, who is very useful to us, and humble and precious and pure.
>
> Be praised, my Lord, for Brother Fire, through whom you give us light in the darkness: he is bright and lively and strong.
>
> Be praised, my Lord, for Sister Earth, our Mother, who nourishes us and sustains us, bringing forth fruits and vegetables of many kinds and flowers of many colors.
>
> Be praised, my Lord, for those who forgive for love of you; and for those who bear sickness and weakness in peace and patience—you will grant them a crown.
>
> Be praised, my Lord, for our Sister Death, whom we must all face. I praise and bless you, Lord, and I give thanks to you, and I will serve you in all humility.[18]

The Canticle of the Sun conveys a non-dual, integral awareness of the interconnectivity of all things, as well as the reverent place humanity inhabits: we crown creation not as monarchs, but as surrendered servants who live in reverence for and adoration of the One from whom all things come and are presently moving within, and who will one day return. Reaching this point, we're now ready to go beyond envisioning characteristics of what a contemplative community could be, and into the realm of spiritual evolution, which is in essence a process summarized by our prayerful intention for an increasing correspondence between heaven and Earth.

The means by which this spiritual evolution occurs is a form of grace, drawing us further into God's intentions. It's a graceful movement propelled by the attraction of Divine love to the creation. It's love that draws us into the Divine destiny, and fulfills the mystery of who we shall be. It's Divine love that will make us complete. Scripture summarizes this vision with great beauty:

> May the God of peace . . . make you complete in everything good so that you may do his will, working among us that which is pleasing in his sight, through Jesus Christ, to whom be the glory forever and ever. Amen. (Hebrews 13.21)

In addition to these five aspects for cultivating contemplative Christian community, it's wise for Christian leaders to consider how this internal contemplative dimension might take shape in external, structural ways. For example, how can the church manifest God's relational presence with more integrity and congruency in our buildings? Could our buildings demonstrate our commitment to relationships and community better? Could they manifest a creative and symbiotic relationship with creation that leads the way for ecological and social sustainability and stewardship? I believe the answers to these questions can and *must* be yes! We now explore a few ideas on just how we might envision contemplative community in this very practical way.

THE BEAUTY OF RELATIONAL BUILDINGS

If we are to manifest the presence of God through our community life, we might consider designing campuses that more intentionally manifest the relational presence of God. Such a vision for our churches is rooted in the relational theology of the Trinity, and an implementation of the relational and theological principles of the incarnation. Instead of undertaking building projects that create a "one-stop" destination for spiritual services (worship, education, ministry), why not envision structures that foster community living and ecological stewardship? For example, envision a church redeveloping several downtown blocks.

With that space the church could fashion not just a building, but a functioning community where day by day, home by home, business by business, the relational presence of God could be manifested to the surrounding communities as people lived in tangible community. This is one way in which our function as the relational presence of God in community could take physical expression as a living spiritual ecosystem incarnating the presence of God through life, light, and love, which ultimately *is* beauty itself.[19]

Also, consider this: without the automobile, many suburban churches and most mega-churches would be isolated from their membership. Suburban neighborhoods and subdivisions are connected by a network of roads and highways (many of which don't even have sidewalks) that provide access to schools, parks, churches, grocery stores, and shopping malls. It's not an overstatement to describe this landscape as an isolated grid of homes and consumer outlets highly dependent upon cars and refined oil. What would happen to church attendance or membership if gasoline prices spiked to $5 or $10 a gallon? Can community occur without commuting?

In our culture, face-to-face, personal, and relational presence is important in incarnational spiritual community. The mediated presence through technologies such as sermon broadcasts to multiple "worship sites" is not relational, but commercial. Such church methodologies borrow a page from the book of business-franchising, forgetting the beauty of what can occur in smaller, local settings with the gift of physical presence.

I believe it's necessary to facilitate community and relationships by redesigning church form and structure. Imagine a community surrounded by a circle of homes, apartments, businesses, a school, library, post office, and so on. Such small towns were "normal" until the automobile lengthened our stride and made our communities larger than life. At the center of the circle is a park, near which is the sanctuary where the community gathers to worship. Children could attend community daycare and life-services would also be available. Of course, these ventures would be open to the public, but instead of having a closed building set aside for worship once or twice a week, the community could incarnationally manifest the presence of God through its common life.[20]

The church would become a community where members could live, work, play, and worship. It would be a way of being community with intentional designs impacting physical structures and architecture. It's not a new vision, rather a re-visioning of the parish community that emerged with the development of churches in the center of village life. It's also a vision shared by the monastic communities who desired to demonstrate in tangible forms something of the function, form, and flow of the kingdom of heaven here on Earth.

If this vision is criticized as social engineering or communism, I would argue that it's no different than what many city planners are designing for trendy sites in urban centers and gated communities. City planners have already begun building towns with community and relationships in mind. The oil and ecological crises have added urgency to such developments. But most of all, it's our culture's tacit longing for community and meaningful relationships that is driving such market shifts.[21]

There are critiques to this kind of community design. The first is that we further inculcate a defensive isolation from others not like us. To counter this, I imagine interracial communities that commit themselves to reconciliation and relationship. The second danger is that these communities become Christian subcultures. My response: Each community could also host people of other faiths. What we gain in terms of quality of relationships and communal life far outweighs the perceived risks of spiritual mingling. Such risks forget the understanding of Christ's eternal presence and action before, beyond, and after the historical incarnation as Jesus.

The entire missional church discussion is also in agreement with the church's need to move outward, rather than inward. Such a re-imagination of the form of church buildings supports this outward vision in that the church community actively seeks to live among the world as a people demonstrating the relational presence of God in all our form and flow.[22]

I don't see the "village" or "parish" church model in contradiction to the missional church model. Rather, combined, they balance and strengthen each other. The missional church emphasizes that the church doesn't exist in buildings, but is an outward movement of people in relationship with Christ, participating in Christ's work of love and grace. However, at the core of all our Christian faith is the claim that "the word became flesh" (John 1.14), thus the incarnation gives clear permission to enflesh the light, life, and love of Christ we experience with imagination, intentionality, and beauty in how we design Christian community.

While community is counter-cultural to the American sense of independence, and while many examples exist of the dangerous extremes that can occur in spiritual community (such as the Branch Davidians), the Christian church, at its heart, is a communal experience grounded in relationship—with God and with each other.

Relationships take form; community takes shape. Why not form and shape a village that visibly demonstrates and enacts relationships and community, and that is dedicated to spiritual transformation through worship and spiritual practices? The church building can be more than a mall or a one-stop destination for spiritual services. The church can be a living, enfleshed community, designed and structured with aesthetic beauty, ecological sustainability, and relational reverence, like a spiritual ecosystem.

THE BEAUTY AND FLOW OF THE WEEKLY SABBATH

The seven-day week is central to Christian spirituality. Grounded as we are in the Jewish tradition, it was the Christian shift from a Saturday to a Sunday Sabbath that bears a compelling witness to the resurrection of Jesus. The shift is also more than historical. The Jewish notion of a day of rest is rooted in the creation story where we're presented with God's activity of creation segmented into specific days: but on the seventh day, God rested. The narrative structure of the book of Genesis provides a basis for ordering time in a week, and it's the week that's the essential framework within which we are to establish a rhythm of relationship as well as a Christian spirituality. All of the activities and spiritual practices that nourish our relationship with God such as prayer, reading of scripture, private and public worship are placed within the weekly, seven-day framework.[23]

Sunday is the hinge day between weeks. It's the day of recollection and visioning, the day symbolizing the in-between age we live in now. We go about our rhythm of relationship throughout the entire week, not just one day. Creativity emerges over the whole week, lived daily.

In the Benedictine monastic tradition, each day is a miniature week, broken into seven time periods, some for work, some for prayer, some for rest and fellowship. Each week, like each day, has a beginning and an end, marked by the cycles of light and darkness—as the Sabbath evening approaches, the week is drawing to a close, and as the Sabbath day concludes, a new week is emerging. Therefore, the reality of relationship emerges through the daily disciplines of the entire week, deeply connected to the rhythms of the Earth and its relationship to the sun, moon, and stars; light and darkness; season and cycle.

Yet it's Sunday that consummates the Christian week. Not just because it's the symbolic day of renewal and rest, but because it's the last and first day of each week. It's the day of transition and symbolically bears witness to the resurrection. Similarly, Sunday is very much like the hours between dawn and dusk: the day of remembrance and anticipation. Sunday hinges the week that has passed with the week to come. During this time of reflection and envisioning, we have an opportunity to renew in worship and detect the spiritual relationship with the cycle of the Earth and allow our own beings to be nourished in rest, community, and time in nature.

THE BEAUTY AND CALLING TO
ALL OF LIFE AS WORSHIP

The incarnation affirms the value of being human and doing human things. Our spirituality shouldn't diminish our humanity or lessen the glory of the physical body. Our spirituality attends to our bodies, aware of the interconnection of Spirit to our own energy, breath, and physical well-being.

The rhythm of relationship is one way in which we're transformed as individuals and as a community more into the image of Christ. Through our bodies, the Earth, and our communities, God is working, ministering, and indeed, present. The liberating and joyful message of the incarnation is that we can glorify and manifest God in all we do. All of life can be sacred. The liberating message that God is relational as embodied in Jesus is that the life of Christ returns our humanity to God and brings the kingdom of God to us, here and now.

With such questions in mind, consider M. Scott Peck's suggestion that true community is "a group of individuals who have learned how to communicate honestly with each other; whose relationships go deeper than their masks of composure, and a group of people who have developed some significant ability to rejoice together, mourn together, delight in each other, and make other's conditions their own."[24] This is the essence of Christian community—dwelling together in love and vulnerability for the sake of manifesting the presence of God to one another and the world.

This vision challenges our culture of separation and transience. If we are to nurture and demonstrate meaningful relationships in community, and if we are to demonstrate the presence of God, we as individuals and as the church are invited do at least two things:

1. **Provide a sense of real presence in the midst of diversity, separation, and isolation.** Real presence is essentially attentive, close, and caring relationships committed to intentional covenants and sincere reconciliation enacted in ritual and manifested in love. Another way of saying this is that we live sacramentally, bound by the internal bond of self-giving through faithfulness and forgiveness.

2. **Provide a sense of permanence in the midst of transience and non-commitment.** Permanence is the willingness to remain and endure even at personal sacrifice. The vision is for meaningful communities grounded in the commitment to be a rooted presence in a specific place with specific people, providing emotional, financial, physical, or educational support as it may arise.

THE BEAUTY AND MISSION OF THE CHURCH

The church is a community of persons who are in Christ.[25] The church is neither a building nor a history. The church occurs when those in Christ gather together. As a community of individuals united to Christ, we experience much diversity; yet Christ, by the Spirit, is our common Source of light, life, and love, and the taproot for our corporate function, form, and flow. As Christ shows up among us by the

Spirit, we experience the gift of fellowship or "Christian communion." Joyfully, this mystical communion transcends many human barriers and boundaries.

The contemplative vision of the church invites us to remember who we are and awaken to the participation of God's presence available to us in our union with Christ by the power of the Holy Spirit. The movement of the Spirit flows into the individual, through the community and outward to the world.[26] Thus, the church is relational *and* missional.[27]

Because we've been given the Spirit, we can consent to the Spirit's intention to manifest the presence of God through us. To put it another way: the internal spiritual transformation taking place within the individual is manifested in tangible ways—in our language, actions, relationships, worship, programs, buildings, and so on. It's the outward movement of our spiritual lives that's made visible to the world. This movement explodes exponentially when individuals gather together as the community of Christ and surrender to their calling to manifest the light, life, and love of Christ by the Spirit.

The Spirit intends to fill and form individuals into a combined living organism imbued with Divine life and radiating Divine love. Jesus began this with his disciples and his Spirit continues it today. This living, imbued constellation of life is the church. Gathered together, networked in Spirit, connected in faith, and resonating in the biosphere, the community of Christ is an impression of love upon the soul of this living planet. Beyond buildings and names, this constellation of light, life, and love rises through the centuries as an unfolding and imperfect witness to the One who draws us ever into the life of God. Forever, we're changed by this love, and drawn into the presence of Divine majesty here on Earth, the location of transformation and habitat of holy energies at work in word and sacrament. This heritage of wisdom is guarded by angels and archangels, principalities and powers, seraphim and cherubim.

As this living, radiating constellation, we'll never be separated from the love of God in Christ. Our destination is a reunion with all the saints and brothers and sisters who have fired their hearts in the furnace of the Father to the praise of His glory and honor. Then, kneeling, surrendered, our hallelujah will be our breath and our being. We will be the church: the communion of Spirit and flesh, the bride of Christ, united to our Beloved.

We belong to God. We also belong together, and God, the relational One, pours forth love from the joyful depths of Divine being. This active, faithful love takes the form of will: a strength of intention for us to be participants, to be caught up in Divine overabundance, sharing with one another what we've received in our own hearts. There is much we can yet be. This is the vision of God for you and me when we become *us*, and yours becomes *ours*, and mine, *thine*. When this occurs, the church becomes a non-dual, contemplative community.

THE CHURCH AS NON-DUAL COMMUNITY

The fullness of the Divine intention for humanity can only occur in community with others who possess knowledge for one's continued edification and transformation. This is the school of Christ that every church is meant to be. The community is crucial to the ongoing spiritual formation of each individual. The presence of God reveals itself through individuals, but when individuals gather together by and in the Spirit of God, many manifestations occur to demonstrate our awakened state of sonship and daughtership as a radiating spiritual family, a living organism fulfilling what St. Paul knew long ago—that under such conditions, "Jesus Christ would be the first born of a large family" (Romans 8.29).

When it comes to the mission of manifesting the presence of God as a community, it doesn't really matter what church we "belong" to. What's essential is that we remember we are a child of God as demonstrated by Jesus the Christ, and continue the incarnation through our union with Christ. Regardless of our denominational affiliation or particular expression of "doing church," as a child of God we share in the collaborative experience of continuing the presence of God as the communion of saints, which is the church. Thus, union with Christ is the theological basis for non-dual spiritual community.

THE CHURCH AS METAPHOR

The function (mission) of the Christian community in every generation is to continue the incarnation of Christ. In his classic book *The Cost of Discipleship*, Dietrich Bonhoeffer put it this way: "The church is Christ existing as community."[28] C. S. Lewis once suggested the function of the church is to cultivate "little Christs," where there "is so much of Christ that millions and millions of 'little Christs,' all different, will still be too few to express Christ fully."[29]

The form of this mission is the tangible ways we come into being. Form may even include how we design church buildings, organizational structures, and church governance. The flow of this mission is what occurs when we as a community surrender to the Spirit who bears forth the presence of Christ through us.[30]

To explore the identity of the community of Christ, consider three biblical metaphors: a people, a body, and a building.[31]

People

The community of Christ is the people of God.[32] We are God's people, as individuals and as a community. The concept of "people" invokes ideas of belonging, security, and destiny. Our spiritual transformation comes from our vulnerability to the Spirit of God as the people of God. The Heidelberg Catechism captures this in a unique and comforting way:[33]

> Q: What is your chief comfort in life and in death?
> A: That I belong, body and soul, to my faithful savior Jesus Christ.

In Christ, we have the assurance of belonging despite our lonely outposts; the comfort of security amid uncontrollable events, and the hope of a destiny amid various threats. The seal of the Spirit upon our lives is a balm to our human anxieties, perceptions of lack, and false conclusions of God's absence. We belong to God. We are not alone: God is with us by the Spirit.

Body

The community of Christ is the body of Christ.[34] This means we are the continuing physical form through which Christ manifests to and in the world. Everything we've said up to this point has been leading to this statement: *God is here in our midst through God's people as individuals and as a community.*[35] Bonhoeffer said it this way: "It is necessary to give due weight both to the unity of Christ and his church and to their distinction. The church is one person; it is the body of

Christ, but it is also many, a fellowship of members."[36] Thus the first emphasis of the body concept is that of unity in the midst of diversity.[37]

This unity transcends all differences. It's a spiritual revolution that unites into one community anyone who consents to the Spirit. In a world fragmenting over ethnic and economic inequality, it's imperative for the community of Christ to show unity in very tangible ways. The body of Christ isn't inclusive for ideological purposes; it's inclusive because unity is the essence of reconciliation with God through Christ by the Spirit.

The second emphasis of the body-concept is equality. Consider the Apostle Paul's teaching using different parts of a physical body (1 Corinthians 12). Paul asserts that no one part of the body is in and of itself superior to another. So, for instance, he might say, "What good is an ear without an eye?" A more helpful word would be "interdependent." The body-concept is antithetical to the independent, autonomous person who exists as if there were no need or desire for others. Members of the Christian community are meant to be interdependent upon each other, i.e. neither isolated nor independent. Maybe this is why Paul, at the conclusion of his argument, mentions several very practical issues, such as helping others in their suffering and with their personal needs. He reminds them:

> But God has so arranged the body, giving greater honor to the inferior member, that there may be no dissension within the body, but the members may have the same care for one another. If one member suffers, all suffer together with it; if one member is honored, all rejoice together with it. (1 Corinthians 12.24–26)

The word I use to summarize this beautiful reality is "relationship." As Christ's body, we are in relationship with God and with one another.

The third emphasis of the body of Christ is that the community of Christians becomes the visible Christ to and in our world. Granted, we don't want to overextend the metaphor, but there's legitimacy to the community of individuals surrendering to their union with Christ by the Spirit and visibly manifesting the nature of Christ in word and deed, through our very human forms. This is the incarnational life, and leads us to the metaphor of the church as *building*.

Building

Our union with Christ is both spiritual and physical. Listen to the way Paul explains this crucial experience in terms of the community: "In him the whole structure is joined together and grows into a holy temple in the Lord; in whom you also are built together spiritually into a dwelling place for God" (Ephesians 2.21). The community of Christ is a building in which the Spirit of God lives. Paul adapts Hebrew concepts to the internal fulfillment of the Spirit when he reminds the Corinthian Christians: "Do you not know that you are God's temple and that God's Spirit dwells in you?" (1 Corinthians 3.16). I find this most intriguing and powerful, for it's the culmination of God's presence to the world in those who are now being built into a spiritual building. In order to understand the importance of this metaphor, we must briefly trace the history behind the idea of God's presence in the temple.

Throughout the Hebrew Bible we find the belief that God was present in the midst of the people, particularly as they gathered to worship first in the tabernacle and subsequently in the temple.[38] We've already considered how at Pentecost the Spirit came in a new way, fulfilling Divine promises.[39] Such promises, coupled with Israel's anticipation for a new temple in which God would dwell and rule as their king, begin to find fulfillment and expression in Christian community.

As opposed to a physical building, the Spirit now dwells within individuals who are being "built together spiritually into a dwelling place for God" (Ephesians 2.22). Such a vision incorporates the hope of the ancient Jewish community into the new community of Christ whereby both Jew and Gentile are joined together as members of the same household (Ephesians 2.17–19). Thus, as we gather as a community, we now have the privilege of experiencing the presence and power of God by the Spirit in ways that the Hebrew scriptures only anticipated. We are no longer strangers to the presence of God, we are the very people and means God is using to be present!

Paul also reminds the early Christians how this new reality of being the temple or building of God must affect their lives.[40] The church fulfills Israel's expectations for a new temple and because this is so, we must live our lives as is fitting for a people who are privileged to be members of the "building" God inhabits by the Spirit. We can draw this out further when we realize what our responsibility is as the ones through whom God by the Spirit is present. Our responsibility as the community of Christ is to reflect God to the people of this world. In doing so, God will be here through the community of Christ, which is comprised of individuals gathered together by the Spirit to be a dwelling place for God, exercising their diverse gifts in unity, faith, and love.

Now more than ever, the world needs to experience the presence of God. The community of Christ must be both *visible* and *active*. We are visible in that we manifest Christ's light, life, and love, and active in that we demonstrate and enact in this world the existence and character of God for the sake of love and justice. Such a calling has intensely practical outcomes.

The community of Christ is called to surrender and engage itself to be the visible and active manifestation of God. This is what it means for us to be faithful: to reflect outwardly the beatific vision of the God who is here by the Spirit, in you and through us. We can be faithful by living, as individuals and community, a relational way of life that is ours in Christ by the Spirit. Faithfulness drafts the Divine initiative, ever calling us forward in faith. Such Divine initiatives show up in emerging ecclesial traits and trends, as spiritual communities and leaders lean into where the Spirit may be leading. So what might this be? We turn now to exploring the call to the evolution of the church, congruent with a contemplative vision.

THE EVOLUTION OF THE CHURCH

A line in Bernard McGinn's *The Foundations of Mysticism* is useful for our transition from theory to practice. It summarizes the perennial reality that humankind outgrows ossified forms and ideas, including theological and spiritual ones. Commenting on the impact of Platonism upon Christian mysticism, McGinn suggests that the "apocalypses and the philosophical religious tradition begun by Plato . . . were ways of making God accessible to a world in which the Divine was no longer present in its traditional forms."[41] Plato was a reformer and prophet. He saw how the old forms of Greek mythology were no longer useful or accessible to his generation in a life-giving way, and as a spiritual intellectual and genius of the human condition, he penetrated the depths of mythology to bring forth a renovated and transformed system of thought and being. Platonism would be the foundation upon which subsequent cultures and civilizations, including Christianity, would be built.

It seems to me that, as it was for Plato, so it is for us today. We are experiencing a massive paradigm shift. New forms of thought and ways of being are occurring and unfolding from the significant scientific and technological revelations of the late modern period (such as the human genome and consciousness studies). We are at a crisis point, where many wish to cling to the ways of the past, others are jettisoning them altogether, and fewer still are finding new ways forward. Confusion and tension simmer in our churches and seminaries as we contemplate the social, intellectual, and spiritual conundrum we find ourselves in. They manifest themselves in diverse symptoms, one of which is conflict over the interpretation of scripture and its relationship to science and human sexuality.

We need new thought forms to transcend the presently unworkable theological concepts and presuppositions. Einstein's famous quote aptly sums up our situation: "The same ideas that created the problem will not be able to solve it." For this reason, spiritual elders like Thomas Merton, Thomas Keating, Bernadette Roberts, Ken Wilber, and many others at the leading edge of human consciousness are the present day "Plato" for us.

What if, even now, we're developing from and evolving beyond the deep stream of Christian presuppositions that stretches through the distant bend of Platonism, meandering all the way back to the prophetic headwaters of Judaism? What if, like Plato, we're discovering that the intellectual foundations of Christianity and some of its core presuppositions are no longer widely accepted as given facts? For example, it used to be that Billy Graham and other evangelists throughout church history could show up and speak an inherited spiritual language such as: "Trust in Jesus Christ as your Lord and Savior"; "Confess your sins and trust in his shed blood for the forgiveness of your sins"; "Receive him into your heart by faith." Indeed, as recently as the 1990s, one could be relatively confident that people could understand what these concepts might mean. But we live in a time when the inherited spiritual language of Western culture and Christian theological presuppositions are increasingly no longer accessible or indeed intellectually feasible for large numbers of people.

In *this* context, preaching about the "shed blood of Jesus" is both irresponsible and inappropriate to anyone who doesn't have the inherited presuppositions of the Levitical sacrificial system. To put it another way: disconnected from biblical presuppositions and the gospel narratives, much of the traditional forms of communicating the Christian message of "salvation" and theology are totally irrelevant to people today. If this is so, what are we to do?

Answers are coming from both ends of the Christian spectrum. From the most liberal, Bishop John Shelby Spong has responded with his book *Why Christianity Must Change or Die*—a title that immediately conveys the defrocked bishop's agenda. From Evangelical conservatives comes an equally serious response. Their thoughtful approach to the same dilemmas is best summarized in the writings of Lesslie Newbigin and Darrell Guder's Missional Church movement. In between are the progressive, protestant writings of Brian McLaren and Michael Frost, who attempt to provide language and models for the church to become more accessible at both presuppositional and practical levels, in light of the fact that the tide of postmodernity is now reaching our church shores.

What if all this friction is signaling something? What if Christianity is giving birth, by the Spirit of God, to something new, just as Jesus emerged from the roots of Judaism as something different? Could Christianity also be ripe for a revolution from within, birthing what might be called the third move of God for the third millennium of Christian faith and community? What if all that has gone before us was intended to generate this present growth and evolutionary moment? What if this is the transforming evolutionary moment similar to when earthbound creatures learned to fly?[42]

The love of God is drawing humankind forward in faith. The church is caught up in this Divine romance and we're slowly fulfilling God's intentions. At the core of this destiny is the furnace of the heart, wherein love leads to the personal, contemplative experience, which is "Christ in you, the hope of glory" (Colossians 1.27). Glory is our destiny; where Divine life is taking creation, including humankind. Glory is the presence of God. Whatever crisis we may face in our common human future, we'll do so together—with one another and with the God who is here through us by the Spirit.

As we come to the end of this chapter, and Part One, it's clear the conversation needs to continue beyond these pages. The call is urgent. The invitation is *to remember our primary role as manifesting the presence of God through our relationships, and* *especially in how these relationships take shape in our communities.* Union with Christ actually means that we become locations through which the Spirit of God births love, and such love helps us bear all things for the sake of mutual transformation.

The urgency of the call for incarnational, spiritual community grounded in love is summarized by psychologist David G. Myers, who notices that, "more than ever, we have big houses and broken homes, high incomes and low morale, secured rights and diminished civility. We excel at making a living but often fail at making a life. We celebrate our prosperity but long for connection. In an age of plenty we feel spiritual hunger."[43] Contrast Myers' observation with the invitation we've been given as the community of Christ called to participate in the presence of God in word and deed, with love and justice. It's a beautiful calling. Let us live it out with creativity and intelligence and believe the ancient declaration, shaping our words and deeds accordingly:

> As God's chosen ones, holy and beloved, clothe yourselves with compassion, kindness, humility, meekness, and patience. Bear with one another and, if anyone has a complaint against another, forgive each other; just as the Lord has forgiven you, so you also must forgive. Above all, clothe yourselves with love, which binds everything together in perfect harmony. And let the peace of Christ rule in your hearts, to which indeed you were called in the one body. And be thankful. Let the word of Christ dwell [manifest] in you richly; teach and admonish one another in all wisdom; and with gratitude in your hearts sing psalms, hymns, and spiritual songs to God. And whatever you do, in word or deed, do everything in the name of the Lord Jesus, giving thanks to God the Father through him. (Colossians 3.12–17)

I believe the Christian ecumenical priority in the third millennium must be demonstrating the relational way of life. I believe the ever-spiraling forward circle of truth is more fully completed by the relational (Trinitarian) model. The relational way of life is demonstrated in community, and expressed in liturgy, sacrament, hospitality, prayer, fellowship, mystery, justice, mercy, doxology, mission, community, and ecology (to name a few). To do this, the Christian church and individual Christians are invited to draw upon the rich contemplative heritage common to Catholicism, Protestantism, and Orthodox Christianity.

The Christian church can demonstrate such a spiritual authenticity as individuals and in community. We have a beautiful story and gift to offer the Earth and its peoples: a relational spirituality that addresses the emptiness, despair, and love-longings of our generation, and demonstrates the transforming relationality of the Trinity for all of life—human communities and ecological communities included.

The church can speak and live in such a way that those who long for God, and those enchanted by the endless parade of spiritual options, will experience the power, person, and presence of God through Christ by the Spirit in our worship and living communities, and in our relationship to the Earth itself. The call to spiritual community is primarily a call to wholeness, prayer, and sacramental life. At its core, it means living in joyful, sustainable, communal, worshipful, peaceful, loving, and conscious ways as the communion of saints. Should not those who confess that God was enfleshed as one of us possess the highest view of embodied life in God's creation?

My primary hope for Christianity in the third millennium is that Christian communities reshape their endeavors within a contemplative-relational matrix, reconnecting and completing more fully the circle of truth in worship, community, and praxis, transforming relationships with the past, present, and future, and with ourselves, each other, and all of creation—as continuing incarnations filled with fullness of God through Christ by the Spirit.

God is not only here, God is also there, and indeed, *everywhere*.[44] The *hereness of God* is one way of saying from a contemplative Christian framework what Jesus said two thousand years ago: "the Father and I are one" (John 10.30). He did not stop there. He also wished that humanity might be one and share in his union with Abba (John 17.11).[45] It turns out that the leading edge of non-dual, integrative thought is now just catching up to what our sages have been telling us all along and what Jesus demonstrated on the stage of history. Now, in the light of quantum physics, developmental psychology, and global interconnectivity, we have every reason to embrace our human inheritance of "oneness" in Christ. To this end, we turn from theory toward contemplative Christian experience, and the wish for our further awakening.

PART TWO

Contemplative
Christian Experiences

FIVE

CONTEMPLATIVE AWAKENINGS

—◁◇▷—

*I know that it is not an easy thing to realize that one is hearing new things. We are
so accustomed to the old tunes, and the old motives, that long ago we ceased to hope
and ceased to believe that there might be anything new.*

—P. D. Ouspensky[1]

C HRISTIANS RESTLESS FOR and with God are beginning to realize that
Christianity can change. Christianity is moving into something higher
and fuller, yet interrelated with the ancient foundations of the faith.[2]
The recent uptick in books published for the Christian mainstream about
the ancient, contemplative spiritual practices reveals just how restless Christians are for deeper, fuller experiences with God that bear the fruits of
transformation.[3]

The popularized form of Christianity most know today is in fact the result
of centuries of evolution as the gospel adapted and responded to each unique
cultural context. Even in the development of the written text of the Bible, we
can see this inner process of transformation. It was Jesus the Christ who, from
within the very depths of Judaism, both included and transcended the Jewish
faith of his heritage. Jesus and the gospel tradition stand as luminous developmental moves in the history of God. The teaching of Jesus is rooted within, but

also rises above, its Abrahamic origins.[4] Christianity was and can continue to be a movement of transformation.

We are all created as self-developing organisms. It's never too late to become whom you were meant to be. Even the universe is expanding. So, too, is human understanding. The development of faith is a part of God's unfolding, emerging Spirit. Staying static is not our destiny. Transformation is.

Remember, Jesus promised a *new* way of relating to God *after* his departure. This new way would be the way of the Spirit; a promise both fulfilling the ancient prophecies *and also* transcending them, inaugurating the expanding Divine manifestation and mission at Pentecost to a wider community that surprised all involved. The ensuing apostolic mission indelibly impacted not only the first-century world post-Jesus, but the entire flow of human civilization to date, including you and me.

OUT OF THE DEPTHS

In my case, I was born into a Christian family and nurtured in Christian love and knowledge. At seventeen years old I experienced a God-directed surrender that touched my emotions and psychology in a transformative way. I responded to an "invitation" to "come forward and receive Christ" following a sermon preached at Camp-of-the-Woods, a Christian retreat center in the Adirondack mountains of upstate New York. While I'd spent all my life absorbed in a Christian context and family, this experience was a transforming moment in which I consented to the love and service of God. I felt God drenched me with a waterfall of light and love. I emerged with a hunger for scripture and a longing for more of God, especially in prayer.

As profound and significant as that spiritual experience was, I endured friction and frustration trying to integrate this new level of being with the other experiences and knowledge gained in my young life. Increasingly, I felt fragmented: on one side, Christian faith; on the other, the multiple dimensions of myself and the world that didn't seem to fit with the kind of Christianity I was striving to experience.[5] So several years after my "conversion," I began to question God's existence. I longed to experience God's presence more in every dimension of my life—not just compartmentalized in my worship or "devotional time." I experienced melancholy, doubt, and anxiety. I felt spiritually empty. Because I couldn't integrate my faith with external life and culture, my mind and my heart were strangers, aching for reunion.

In this way, a decade passed during which I studied theology as an undergraduate and received a masters degree at Princeton Theological Seminary. Through these years, I continued to long to know and experience more of God—not just through what I heard or read from others, but personally. I learned that this kind of longing is a hallmark of the contemplative, Christian path, and that St. Augustine famously summarized this mystical longing in the opening lines of his spiritual autobiography, musing that "our heart is restless, until it rests in Thee."[6] I began to see this kind of spiritual, integrated longing all over the place. I read the Bible with new eyes and saw the spiritual depth of such phrases as "abide in me as I abide in you" (John 15.4).

Nature also became vibrantly alive to me as an icon of God's infused presence and I retreated more and more into the solitude and silence of forest, field, and mountain top. I began to understand that Christianity is an invitation into relationality with God, through Christ in prayer and sacrament, bearing us into an experiential spiritual union with God who fills us with the Divine Spirit.

Yet this longing for God's presence was both stimulated and thwarted in college and seminary, where despite the best intentions of professor and student alike, I encountered compelling arguments against Christian doctrines. I wrestled with these ideas and hungered all the more for the relevancy of faith in today's scientific, technological world. I wanted to remain a Christian with intellectual integrity *and* spiritual vitality, without collapsing into either the unexamined life or the brash certainty of religious fundamentalism. When I'd cross the street from the seminary to Princeton University, I'd feel oddly out of place. I felt small compared to what I thought was the "real and rational" learning of the University. Then came the dread of this question: How am I going to make a living in *this real world?*

Surely, I sensed, there was another way—a bridge to span the chasm widening in my heart between faith and unbelief, myth and truth, longing and fulfillment. I lived with this tension well into my first years as a pastor. Like many young ministers I struggled to know what it meant to be a pastor in the first place. But I also wondered what it meant in the context of a confusing world where the Christian story and presuppositions were increasingly considered irrational and irrelevant.

It wasn't until I was thirty-three, and five years into my first pastorate, that I discovered a bridge for my own crossing. The transforming moment in my spiritual development helped reunite my head and heart. I was introduced to the inner dimension of the Christian tradition, broadly termed, "the contemplative way." The contemplative tradition is at the heart of Christianity. But regrettably, for many Protestants the abundant blessings of this tradition have long been forgotten, if not nearly thrown away. Thankfully, however, the treasure remains, and can be experienced through remembering and returning, two dimensions of the spiritual journey modeled for us in the story of the prodigal son.

CONTEMPLATIVE REMEMBERING
AND RETURNING

The story of the prodigal son recorded in Luke 15 helped me understand the essence of the Christian message. At the story's core is a moment of awakening, or what I like to call a remembering and returning to the presence and love of God. This poignant and popular biblical story is, among many things, an analogy of our own spiritual journeys. Let's briefly review it.

A son requests his inheritance from his father. The father graciously gives the son his share of wealth and the young man goes his own way. For a time, he experiences pleasure, parties, friends, and fun. But soon, the wealth runs out and the good life becomes, overnight, one of suffering. Here the story really gets good. The son finds himself working in a very low job, feeding pigs. This, of course, is anathema to the Jewish culture and conveys the depths of misery this man had descended into. Just then, at the end of his tether in suffering and misery, he discovers there's no more rope to hold onto, releases and surrenders.

The breakdown and surrender allows the man to remember who he truly is. Awakening to this truth is of vital importance to all spiritual transformation. Before any of us can return to the presence of the "Father," we too must first remember who we are: children of God. In the story, the man remembers by "coming to his senses"—not his physical senses, but his *relational* ones. He literally begins to think in a different way about who he is and what his purpose in life could be. He remembers not only his identity, but also the benefits that are rightfully available to him. Soon after, the man returns home to his father where he's received with unconditional love and celebration. The Christian tradition desperately needs to restore spiritual practices that help foster this remembering, ways of being that cultivate a return to the awareness of and participation in God's presence.

My remembering occurred when I reached a psychological and emotional breaking point after a divorce and a broken engagement, both within a three-year period. My breakdown revealed just how devoid I was of spiritual life, and how much I had forgotten the truth that St. Paul declared long ago when he wrote that nothing "will be able to separate us from the love of God in Christ Jesus our Lord" (Romans 8.39). Freedom and healing became more available to me when I began to realize that the word *nothing* included my own thoughts, ideas, situations, and emotions.

Importantly, this realization showed me how many of my own ideas and feelings about myself and situation contributed to my sense of separation from God. Yet most of the teaching about "salvation" in Christ never conveyed this deep inner truth or psychological dimension! It was as if most of the gospel teaching I'd heard had been incomplete until I connected what Jesus did for me *and* demonstrated for me to do; namely, remember and reclaim that I'm a beloved child of God, then return home to know and claim God's presence where I'll receive the banquet feast of presence, sharing and celebrating in joy with others. But this required effort. To use a biblical phrase, I realized I had to "work out my salvation" (Philippians 2.12–13). However, work couldn't begin until I'd first longed for freedom from the prison of self and its sense of separation from God and others, and requested a return to the wholeness I intuited in my heart of hearts.

LONGING FOR THE HOLY WHOLE

Many Christians are waking up to their restless longing to experience the presence of God. Christians are also seeking help and healing over addictions, sickness, depression, and other stress-related ailments that are intensified by living in our fast-paced, consumer-driven culture. The answer is not more information.

We need transformation. And transformation requires an effort on our part, a surrendering of will as well as a commitment to be worked on by the presence and action of God's grace.

What we are really after in transformation is a spiritual experience that means something for real life—its joys and sorrows, heights and depths. What we long for is the experience of God's presence that bears the fruit of transformation in our life. The essence of Christian faith is in the interior experience of God's presence, and the healing and transformation that flows from God's presence and action within us. Jesus spoke of such a presence when he prayed for his disciples before his arrest and death. Listen for the inner meaning of God's presence to us in Jesus' prayer: "As you, Father, are in me and I am in you, may they also be in us, so that the world may believe that you have sent me" (John 17.21b–22).

Christianity is meant to be a means for healing and transformation, not just a system of spiritual information or doctrines to believe. Jesus embodied and enacted this healing and transformation for us and our salvation on the stage of history. By salvation, I don't mean "getting into heaven." I mean the healing of our human nature *here and now in us* through our union with Christ by the Spirit. Such a healing brings an increasing wholeness to our humanity, and unites it further with Christ's Divine nature. This is what St. Paul meant when he wrote that in Christ we are new creations, "the old has gone and the new has come" (2 Corinthians 5.17).[7]

So what would this look like at the personal level? I share two personal, real-life stories: the first, from a dear friend; the second, my own. These two stories will help convey the personal dimension of contemplative, christophanic Christianity.

A CONTEMPLATIVE'S STORY:
A SUBURBAN NEW ENGLAND MOM

Through Facebook, I reconnected with someone I hadn't spoken with in nearly twenty years. I call reconnections such as this "Facebook miracles." After a few initial contacts, we discovered we were on the same spiritual path. My friend sent me a profoundly honest email sharing more about her journey into contemplative territory. Her story deeply blessed me and resonated with my own experiences. Sometimes we have images of "contemplatives" or "mystics" as eccentrics walking around with rags on, as "have-nots" who really just don't fit into mainstream society.

From both a religious and a worldly perspective, my friend had a picture-perfect life. She grew up in a good, Christian, loving family and spent her formative years in evangelical churches. She went to an Ivy League school, got a masters degree, married an investment banker, had three children, and was very active in a prominent evangelical church in New England. She had an idyllic suburban life, white picket fence and all.

Yet her story speaks to the deep failure of a certain kind of Christianity. It also speaks to the power of a longing heart. At a critical juncture in her spiritual journey, when her evangelical "answers" lost their relevance, unlike many she didn't lose her faith. She entered more deeply into it and emerged a different kind of Christian. She wrote:

> I had somewhat of a contemplative or mystical experience that has re-oriented my spirituality. In the winter of 2004, I found myself at a point in my life where I allowed myself to go back to square one and become a beginner again in my faith. After over three decades in the church, I came to feel myself as a Seeker of God, whatever I had known of God, I had this sense that there was More.
>
> I don't exactly know what triggered it at that particular moment but I was almost overwhelmed by a raw desire to know God more intimately and directly. It did not really feel like a crisis of faith, but rather a response to something stirring inside—an intermittent sense of malaise mixed with a yearning for "Something More." It was the winter and my husband had been traveling a lot and somehow I managed to block out life to follow this spiritual nudging I was feeling.
>
> I sort of became a little reclusive, let my voicemail and email pile up. I let lots of laundry and bills pile up, let my kids watch a little too many videos, woke up really early in the mornings and sort of indulged myself with a single-minded focus on God and my own soul. How do I know what I know about God? How does anyone know what they know about God beyond second-hand propositional knowing?

Really, how can we as human beings know this Unseen God? Along with this new spiritual curiosity, all sorts of books seemed to come my way that struck an inner chord—Henry Nouwen, *The Cloud of Unknowing*, mystical writings which seemed like diagonal stripes compared to the familiar straight lines of the evangelical language that I was so accustomed to. This venture into this new type of spirituality had been going on in the background for a few years.

I had done some work with the Enneagram which gives a window into your false self and I had this new awareness that my spiritual beliefs were very disconnected from my own humanity. I had "answers," but I did not "know thyself." It was a little unsettling. My spiritual life had stagnated for some time. I had three babies, become a multi-tasking Mother who tried to meet everyone's needs, but never succeeded, and in the process picked up an auto-immunity.

The "evangelical box" had been collecting dust on the shelf of my mind for some time. As I journeyed through adulthood, the airtight "believe-these-things and-be-saved" theology that at one point had given me security slowly became disconnected from my day-to-day existence and to be honest became somewhat boring and routine. How many sermons can one hear?

I knew God more with my head than my heart and I hardly gave any attention at all to my inner life. My religious activities kept me in a comfortable orbit of believing and doing and did little to help me to look inwardly to understand how my ego and fallen psychology created barriers to knowing God. All of my knowing about God and my sense of being "saved" past-tense had become a barrier to knowing God in a more intimate, real way, right now.

I did not discard my beliefs but somewhere along the way, there was a gradual loss of soul, a slow dying on the vine. Unbeknownst to me, life events had been moving the furniture around in my mind and bringing me in closer touch with my own humanity. From a deep and human place within me, something asked "am I missing something?" Maybe I can know God more directly, not just through right answers (which to be honest never totally resonated) which were so wired in from growing up with the idea that if you don't believe this exact thing you are going to hell. All this is the backdrop to my contemplative awakening.

I had this very palpable, felt moment with God where I felt myself as one of my precious babies. I had a sense of being deeply loved the way I love my

little children. I love their uniqueness, their raw little selves, the inner beloved-
ness they each radiate. In this very tender moment with God, I had a sense of
deep rest, of stillness, of having been working a little too much, trying a little
too hard. Coming to the end of my own resources was God waiting for me
with a maternal embrace. Looking back, I can see now that my own experience
of maternal love gave me a blueprint to conceive of the crazy and desirous love
God has for each of us.

After this experience, I had a renewed awareness of myself as a spiritual
being and my vision of God seemed to grow by the moment. Little glimpses
of the Divine seemed to be everywhere—in the trees in my backyard, in patterns in nature and in smells of flowers, and in the profound insights that came
to me as I was running through the woods, connecting with my children or
simply breathing. I felt a new joy in simply being alive and human. Every day
felt like a new adventure of sensing God's presence in my everyday, ordinary
world. God started to seem both more mysterious and cosmic, yet strangely
more intimately close and knowable.

My heart, my humanity, felt more open and receptive. Love. Sweet, peaceful tears. Inner music. Inner enjoyment with simple things. An inner-knowing
of God and my place in God, a sense of my own beingness in God. Seeking
and finding.

Life normalized, yet I emerged from this time with a new lens on Reality, a new sense of self, and a new confidence to trust and go with this inner
knowing of God, and allow this to repackage my faith. I felt a great sense of
release and boldness in letting some of [the] layers of accumulated religious
belief that really never resonated just fall away. In this time of repackaging, I
developed a ravenous appetite for spiritual writing.

Mystics like Julian of Norwich, Thomas Merton, Evelyn Underhill and the
author of *The Cloud of Unknowing* accompanied me on this journey and brought
me into touch with a more ancient, more human Christian spirituality that
sees "salvation" as a journey of falling in love with and becoming whole in
God. I am not one to casually say, "God spoke to me" but through this time
of spiritual awakening, in the deepest place of my soul I heard God say to me,
"You belong to me. Daughter-of-the-Most-High."

What I "know" of God is less, but feels more integrated with my humanity and more like something unfolding rather than something all packaged up.
My life as a mother and as an active person is hardly a monastery. Life always
seems too full. Much of my spirituality right now is finding the "calm within
the storms" of life and seeking to stay present and "in the moment" with Life
and the inner promptings of Love. Christ-in-me the hope of glory.[8]

My friend is one of countless people who've also had similar spiritual breakdowns that have been used by the Spirit of God to further integral transformation.
Such passages often lead to new ways of being human and Christian. While difficult at the time, more often than not, these periods end in a deepening awareness
of God's presence and the discovery of the contemplative Christian dimension that
has been waiting in the silence all along to welcome those who are awakening from
one self to another, who is the living Christ, the way, truth, and life.

AWAKENING: MY JOURNEY
AS A MAN AND AS A PASTOR

My awakening experience further into the life of God occurred on a solo spiritual
retreat.[9] I share this story with holy circumspection and demurral. I experienced
the presence of Christ and was reacquainted with a long forgotten dimension of
myself and the contemplative Christian tradition: the inner dimension, wherein
heart and mind are reunited not out there, or on that side or this side, but right
here in me.[10] I didn't really know what I needed, but I felt that something was
very "off" in my heart. As I mentioned earlier, I'd experienced a divorce and a
broken engagement within a three-year period, both symptoms that masked a
deeper longing for God. Through my misery, and my contribution to another's
suffering, I began to see that I was the common denominator—this thing I
called "myself" needed healing and transformation.

I did what many have done when confronted with a desire to begin again: I
headed West! In the Teton mountains, I walked, prayed, grieved, cried, and sat in
silence for three days.[11] I emerged from my solo retreat and treated myself to a
mountain-sized feast at the Grand Teton Lodge Mural Room restaurant. There,

sitting alone, exhausted, sun-worn, and probably something of a curiosity, I met my new spiritual director: my waitress Deneen.

Deneen's presence was radiant. Her eyes conveyed unconditional love. It wasn't romance; it was holiness. Her beauty was in her innocence and purity, her vulnerability to holy things. She could laugh out loud at herself and swagger like a mama bear. She was gregariously human. She would run in the woods at night. I asked her if she was worried about bears and she told me she trusted in God's love. Deneen was honest to the core, penetrating with clarity and insight in a way that I'd only read about in the scriptures, such as when Jesus says to the Samaritan woman, "No you have five husbands" (Luke 4.17–18). She knew quite quickly, before I shared much, exactly what I needed for further healing and awakening.

We shared little during dinner, yet it was enough for me to recognize this as a Divine appointment. In a moment of courage, I left a note with my number and a request to talk further. Deneen called me the following day and we arranged to meet in Jackson for breakfast. I spent the whole day with her, sharing my story and listening to her wisdom, and grew inspired by her love of our Triune God. Her insights seemed connected and integral in a way I'd never heard before. She taught of "speaking from the open heart" and "standing in truth," and revealed a profound spiritual knowledge and godly wisdom in the most accessible ways. I imagined this is how the disciples felt walking with Jesus on the Emmaus road, as when he explained the scriptures, "their hearts burned within" (Luke 24.32). Everything Deneen said connected spiritually, psychologically, and physically with me.

The ministry she blessed me with was something I'd read about in scripture, but had never personally experienced. For example, during our prayer time, I began to shake uncontrollably. Deneen assured me this was normal. My body was "unloading." I began to cry for reasons I was unaware of. My body was releasing beyond the level of my rationality. This, she said, was a very good thing. As her hands conveyed to me the healing love of Christ, I was reminded of the many times Jesus did the same, and even felt power leave him when once touched by a woman seeking healing (Luke 7.45).[12]

Following the prayer time, I felt deeply warmed, renewed, and energized— like a completely new person, as if I'd shed a skin. I had, in fact, through spiritual healing and tears discarded a layer of my old man—the false-self system attached to my body. Deneen then gave me a worship CD. "I think you'll be needing this," she said. Our parting was tearful. I didn't have words to convey the feelings I was experiencing. She put her hand on my heart and looked into my eyes and said, "I love you." I knew then that this wasn't just Deneen speaking to me, it was Christ. She was conveying the presence of Christ to me.

As I drove north to Yellowstone National Park, I listened to the CD. As the fifth song began to play, the stringed instruments and voice blended in a way that continued the healing process in me. I'll only say this regarding what happened next: I began to weep. I'd never cried that deeply; it was a purging. I pulled the car over near a lake, fell onto the ground, and sobbed while listening to the music. Through the tears, I could see the sunlight streaming through the trees. I could feel the voice of Christ with me—yes, *feel*: "I am with you, beloved one. I am here with you." I cried in this way until all was silent.

I didn't reach my destination. I'd made reservations at a dude ranch in Montana, but I turned the car around and headed back to the Tetons and Deneen. I needed to share this experience with her and I longed for further teaching. I also desired to return to her mysterious and radiant presence.

For two days, Deneen shared her insights and answered my questions. Then I left her and the Tetons with exquisite joy and serenity. I played the song again and cried some more. This time, however, it wasn't purgation, but a celebration of gratitude—tears of joy and love for the holy mystery of what had happened and what was still happening in me. I knew I'd never be the same. Indeed, I haven't. When I returned to my home and church in Flint, Michigan, my first sermon was entitled, "The Open Heart Bearing." I searched for books to help me understand what happened and what lineage of teaching Deneen was drawing from. I deepened my Centering Prayer practice, began eating healthier, and started practicing yoga. The entire experience was important and life-transforming and built the foundation for my present life.

I sold my home in Flint. The same house that had languished on the market for a year was bought after just a month. Deneen had spoken of this when I was in the Tetons. She'd taught me that the past was just that, and the future wouldn't be the same. She helped me understand that "my being draws my life."

She encouraged me to return to Flint with the recognition that "everything you need will be provided." And it was. Not only did the home sell, I received a new call to serve a church in Austin, Texas. Here, I've been blessed beyond what I could have imagined.

Soon after my arrival in Austin I was introduced to Casa de Luz,[13] a macrobiotic, vegan restaurant where I found my first community and was given food for my continued physical healing. For years, I'd suffered from severe acid reflux disease. Within six months of regularly eating at Casa the condition was healed. Then I was introduced to Christina Newton. We recognized in each other the gift of a lifelong love, and married a year later at seven in the morning in the sagebrush fields in front of the Grand Tetons' Cathedral Group mountain range. We were circled by thirty of our family and friends.

Through Deneen's loving, wise, yet severe spiritual counsel, I began to see how, since my Christian conversion, I'd believed that the way to get to God more fully was through my thinking mind. Yet, in the mountains, and in particular, through Deneen's prayerful healing ministry, I experienced psychological and physical healing in the presence of God that both included and transcend my thinking mind. Through this awakening, healing experience in the presence of God, mediated through a human being, I experienced the continuing manifestation of Christ by the power of the Spirit, and began to see for myself how *this* was the essence of the Christian message.

Since my Teton awakening, I've continued to experience the healing of my sense of separation from God, from creation, and others. I've learned that this sense of separation is the essence of sin, and was the source of much of my pain and useless, negative acting-out toward others. I've discovered that it's called duality, and that the contemplative Christian experience in Christ can lead to non-duality.

In the years since those holy summer days in the high mountains of Wyoming, I've observed how I've blamed many external situations, events, and people for my "perceived" pain and misery. In actuality, my misery was of my own making—or to be more precise, my forgetfulness. I'd forgotten the most important truth of all: the immediate adequacy of the relational presence of God. To forget this truth was to believe the lie that something was lacking, and that this lack could or should be met by someone or something else other than the loving presence of God. This is one reason why Jesus invited people to "repent," in order to enter the "presence of God." The word he uses is *metanoia*, which literally means "change your thinking," or as Thomas Keating says, "change the direction you are looking for happiness."

While this sense of separation from God is our inherited human condition, the good news is that this state needn't be our destiny. It's generated and perpetuated in our human minds by our over-identification with negative thinking and emotions, and believing the inner stories spun by the false self that are often grounded deep in the soil of our childhood development. This false self is usually interwoven with our personality, which has been created, layer upon layer, during our formative years. It's this "wrong thinking" that the Christian tradition calls "sin" or "the flesh."

So what do we do? Most of us suffer, and when we've suffered enough we surrender. In this surrender is hidden the liberating discovery that our emotional pain and spiritual angst is the result of our thinking machine working predictably incorrectly. This predictability or mechanicalness is the result of our encrusted personality that has, over time, smothered our essence and its awareness of God, which is our birthright state of bliss and joyful union. Thus, our thinking machines are in need of transformation and healing.

Our failures and pains in life can become our teachers, awakening us to this realization that we are not our life, our feelings, or thoughts. That's just life happening. Our true life is actually "hidden with God in Christ" (Colossians 3.3). This is why we read that we are to put on "the mind of Christ" (1 Corinthians 2.16, Philippians 2). It's the psychological and spiritual truth of St. Paul's Christian mystical teaching that, "nothing . . . will be able to separate you from the love of God in Christ Jesus" (Romans 8.39). Thus, the essence of the word "repentance" means "change of mind."

Through my own experiences of pain and failure, I came to see that my need is not so much answering the question of God's existence *rationally* with my mind, but rather remembering and experiencing the presence of God in my life *relationally*, that is, with my whole being. Because, as Carl Arico of Contemplative Outreach says, "the issues are in our tissues,"[14] the healing presence of God must transcend our rational mind. The mind participates in the healing process but does not dominate. (To be honest, this is easier said than done, and in my experience, doesn't occur without much inner work.)

To guide us on this journey of discovery, many Christian masters throughout Church history have passed on certain practices to help us cultivate the awareness of God's enduring presence and action in our life that can lead us into transformation and healing, and help us begin to live as if nothing really can separate one from God's loving presence and action here and now. Such an experience is a shift in consciousness, moving from the sense of separation that so many of us are shackled by into the awareness of our Divine union with God through Christ.[15]

Cultivating a practice (or spirituality) of God's presence isn't just important for our personal transformation and healing. It's crucial for the well-being of human civilization. Like human beings, human civilization has many spiritual, psychological, social, and environmental stressors, and our human situation as a community only intensifies the need to articulate a contemplative Christian spirituality that helps people remember and experience God's presence.[16] This isn't just a private matter; it's global, and indeed cosmic.[17]

During my spiritual crisis, it seemed that I'd gone as far as my Christian faith and understanding could take me. I'd read and studied the Bible. I'd prayed and practiced spiritual disciplines. I'd worshiped, preached, served, and loved doing it. Yet something was still missing. However, I didn't know what *it* was, much less how to find it! As is so often the case, because I couldn't find it, it found me. But, first, I had to realize how powerless I was to manage my own spiritual and emotional life. And, like the prodigal, in a mess of my own making, I came to my senses, remembered both whose and who I was, and returned to the Father. I didn't return through my thinking mind, but through an embodied experience. Deneen's message to me was clear and simple: "Waking from the dream of forgetfulness, you see my face and remember who you are."

THE FACE OF CHRIST

My story isn't unusual in that, while it's unique, it's also universal. In the face of Christ, we're reconnected with our God-intended self (Galatians 4.19). We see that God loves us and discern what it means to be human. We feel the shock of grace lifting us up from our spiritual death and slumber, reaching down from the great and living ray of creation and awakening us, reminding us who we really are. It is grace that sends the prophets and discloses the scriptures. Grace happens, again and again. Grace connects an empty pastor with a filled-up waitress, who in grace was to me the face of Christ.

The contemplative Christian tradition intuits and teaches that human beings, united to Christ by the Spirit, can awaken, remember, and manifest the face of Christ to one another. By "face of Christ," I mean the "presence of God," because I believe the terms are interchangeable. Such a practice indicates that we're "united to Christ," and in our spiritual union, we become "formed in his image" (Galatians 2.19). Or, to use my favorite phrase from a different apostle, we become "participants of the divine nature" (2 Peter 1.4).[18] This entails a developmental journey from one stage of spiritual maturity to another and "from one degree of glory to the next" (2 Corinthians 3.18). In other words, it's a developmental journey. This is our central purpose in life. Let me say this as clearly as I can: *By the gift of our union with Christ, the Holy Spirit forms Christ in us so that we become participants in and manifestations of God's right-here presence, similar to how Jesus was God with us.*

We move now from these two stories of personal awakenings to a brief mapping of models for contemplative Christian community.

SIX

A MONASTERY WITHOUT WALLS

———— ◀◦▶ ————

A community of faith offers the support of example, correction and mutual concern in the
spiritual journey. Above all, participating in the mystery of Christ through the celebration of the
liturgy, praying the scriptures, and silent prayer binds the community in a common search for
transformation and union with God. The presence of Christ becomes tangible in the community,
especially when it is gathered for worship or engaged in some work of service to those in need.

—THOMAS KEATING[1]

T HE FOUNDING OF the first urban Christian communities by the Apostles began a movement of hope, faith, and love. Inspired by the flame of
Christ's love, the Apostles initiated a trajectory that continues today. These
first Christian communities provided the seedbed for the Holy Spirit to grow
God-lovers. In time, this God-directed life of love drew many Christians away
from the crowded cities and into the solace of solitude and silence.

Often responding to political oppression, or reacting to the rise of Christian
power in the wake of Roman Emperor Constantine's legalization of Christianity, new spiritual communities emerged, first in the Egyptian desert and later
throughout Europe. These communities were populated by individuals who
shared a love for God. Their members weren't running away from culture; they
were running toward God, and a life situation that would, at least in theory,

enable a deeper attention to God's presence. As these early desert and rural spiritual communities grew, they became the basis for what we now know as "monasteries," where work and prayer were integrated into a God-centered life. St. Benedict, considered the founder of the Western monastic tradition, conceived of such monasteries and convents as schools of love. In community, the brothers and sisters loved God, one another, and oftentimes the least among them, such as the sick and dying.[2]

While modern contemplative Christians may love the historic ideal of monastic life and daily spiritual practice, for most of us such a lifestyle is both impractical and impossible. Yet is there a way to participate in contemplative, spiritual community in the world? Are there models where such spiritual community is occurring today? What follows, is an attempt to answer these important questions.

MODELS OF CONTEMPLATIVE CHRISTIAN COMMUNITY

Models of contemplative spiritual community are emerging. While few people are joining monasteries and convents, more of the monastery is entering the church. For example, Christian communities around the world are embracing contemplative spiritual practices such as *Lectio Divina* and Centering Prayer. It's my prayer that in the years to come, the contemplative dimension of Christianity will be more integrated into our church communities, as more and more Christians cross over the bridge into contemplative territory, which is ultimately the non-dual experience of participating in God's loving presence through a deepening consent to the gift of union with Christ by the Spirit. As this integration occurs, we may be able to drop the adjective "contemplative" and simply be Christians. Thankfully, many individuals, organizations, and churches are blazing the trail for all of us.

To learn more about contemplative spiritual community, we'll survey several expressions of the contemplative Christian movement, beginning with churches and organizations engaged in selective contemplative spiritual practices, and ending with a model of Christian community that, from my perspective, seems to fully embody contemplative Christianity. While many monastic communities naturally would fall into this range, we'll limit our study to the non-monastic to affirm the "in-the-world" dimension of the growing contemplative Christian movement.

"Mainline" Contemplative Expressions

Mainline churches are increasingly incorporating contemplative aspects into their worship and community life. For example, St. David's Episcopal Church in Austin, Texas, one of the largest Episcopalian churches in the country, has a downtown congregation with an ongoing liturgical and missional presence dating to 1854. In addition to daily Morning and Evening Prayer, and services for healing, St. David's has created two unique contemplative weekly worship services on Sunday evenings.

At five p.m., a "Celtic communion" service occurs in a newly renovated contemplative worship hall—a soaring, wood-paneled room with central windows open to the southern light and Texas sky. During this service, worshipers engage in a meditative listening to lectionary readings, sing simple Celtic chants and hymns, and after a brief homily, partake in a meditative communion. At nine p.m., a choral Compline of ancient Evening Prayer occurs in what the congregation refers to as their "historic" sanctuary. Compline is the last of the daily offices chanted by monks before retiring for the evening—a short, meditative service chanted by a choir of between eight to eighteen singers. The music consists of Gregorian and Sarum chant melodies, anthems from the Tudor times, and a variety of contemporary hymns. The congregation sits quietly in candlelight, bathed in the aroma and mystery of Somali incense, and participates with the choir in worship through silent prayer and contemplative meditation. In the candlelit sanctuary, surrounded by the ethereal vocal beauty, one feels the simple beauty of worship and emotional awareness beyond the spoken word of the vibrations of Divine love and presence exquisitely conveyed through music.

In addition to these two contemplative worship services, St. David's has also incorporated into an outdoor plaza a contemplative labyrinth—a replica of the one on the floor of the Cathedral at Chartres near Paris. Not only is the labyrinth open for personal prayer walks, but St. David's also hosts a monthly community walk, including a short meditation prior to the walk. The community walk is accompanied by music and candles and is designed to foster a prayerful space in the middle of the busy downtown. A meditative labyrinth walk usually takes about twenty minutes and is a further way to experience contemplative prayer and embodied meditation, just as is kneeling, folding one's hands, or bowing one's head. This simple spiritual practice helps one experience God's presence right there.

A further example of mainline contemplative discovery is occurring at Westlake Hills Presbyterian Church in Austin, Texas (WHPC), where I serve as an associate pastor. Over the years, discovery of some aspects of the contemplative tradition has budded, including a weekly Centering Prayer Sunday school class that both reviews contemplative authors such as Thomas Keating and supports practitioners of Centering Prayer. We've also hosted a monthly "contemplative worship service," using candlelight, Taizé music, and meditative readings to foster a more intimate encounter with the living Christ.

Of particular inspiration to me is WHPC's vision statement, which conveys the personal invitation to Trinitarian, relational Christianity lived out in community and in the world under the authority of the transformative power of the Holy Spirit. It reads:

> Transformed and empowered by the Holy Spirit, WHPC will be a Christ-centered community of faith that intentionally nurtures relationships with God, one another, our neighbors and the world.

Similarly, my denomination, the Presbyterian Church U.S.A., has introduced spiritual practices and formation into its nomenclature and culture, especially through the Spiritual Formation Leadership Network, which provides online resources and training for spiritual direction.[3]

Emergent Contemplative Expressions

The Emergent church movement is exploring the contemplative dimensions of Christianity in its popular expressions. In part, this is a philosophical move driven by a trend toward the "experiential" versus the "doctrinal" notion of faith. Leading institutions such as Rob Bell's Mars Hill Church in Grand Rapids, Michigan, and The Village Church in Dallas, Texas, are seeking ways to convey the love of God in personal and relevant ways, outside the traditional Christian box. Following theorists like Brian McLaren, the Emergent movement has increasingly embraced the contemplative, mystical dimensions of Christianity. For example, in McLaren's *A Generous Orthodoxy* he outlines a manifesto of the kind of Christian he is seeking to be. Among the litany of twenty or so traits are chapters entitled, "Why I am Mystical/Poetic," and "Why I am Charismatic/ Contemplative." With the following description, McLaren offers a trailblazing invitation to a new generation of Christians seeking a way forward in faith:

> There have long been Christian traditions recognizing the profound impor-
> tance of mysticism and poetry, and the corresponding limitations of rational-
> ity and prose, including the *via negativa*—the negative way—and the *hesychastic*
> tradition, which discovers God in silence.[4]

Like McLaren, Rob Bell has also gained international notoriety for his "re-painting" of Christian truths, in books, videos, tours, and at Mars Hill. Together, these theorists and practitioners have helped define what is now referred to as the "Emergent Church." In my view, Bell's work has been more edgy than McLaren's, and while neither McLaren nor Bell explicitly identify themselves as Christian contemplatives, their writings clearly draw upon the contemplative tradition.

It's my contention that the Emergent movement is a stage on the journey into contemplative territory. It's only a matter of time before they fully get there. For example, Bell is aware that the old dualistic categories of theism are no longer working. In his bestselling book *Velvet Jesus*, Bell hints at this contemplative awareness briefly in chapter three, entitled "Everywhere," by which I take it he means God in Christ as the *logos*. Bell writes, surveying the Jewish tradition, that, "God is always present. We're the ones who show up. For the ancient Jew, the world is soaked in the presence of God. . . . For the writers of the Bible, this truth is everywhere. It's here. It's there. It's all over."[5]

"Evangelical" Contemplative Expressions

Similar to the emergent model, Evangelicals are also exploring the contemplative dimensions of Christianity. A leading example is Pete Scazzero, senior pastor of

New Life Fellowship Church in Queens, New York, and author of *The Emotionally Healthy Church* and *Emotionally Healthy Spirituality*, both of which are essentially primers on contemplative spiritual practices, and teach how such practices relate to marriage, life, and church leadership.

Through Scazzero's partnership with the Willow Creek Association, the Evangelical community will certainly receive further exposure to the contemplative Christian tradition. Scazzero's work on emotionally healthy spirituality includes a contemplative dimension that builds in time for God and living a slower-paced life through the cultivation of a daily spiritual practice, called the "daily office," as well as through Sabbath-keeping. Scazzero defines the "daily office" as, "a time to STOP, SLOW DOWN, CENTER, and PAUSE to be with Jesus. Our goal is to create a continual and easy familiarity with God's presence in each day."[6]

Scazzero's work falls in line with Richard Foster's. Foster began introducing the Evangelical world to some aspects of the contemplative dimension of Christianity nearly thirty years ago with his bestselling books *Celebration of the Disciplines* and *Prayer: Finding the Heart's True Home*. Similarly, Dallas Willard, scholar and bestselling author of *Renovation of the Heart* and *The Divine Conspiracy*, has also played a helpful role in introducing Evangelicals to the contemplative dimensions of Christianity. Foster, Willard, and other Evangelicals have joined together to create Renovaré, an organization that draws heavily upon the Christian contemplative tradition. The mission of Renovaré is "to resource, fuel, model, and advocate more intentional living and spiritual formation among Christians and those wanting a deeper connection with God."[7]

In academic Evangelical and mainline circles, the writings of Dorothy C. Bass have reintroduced spiritual practices into the spiritual formation conversation at both the seminary and congregational levels. All of these writers follow in the footsteps of Henri Nouwen, who more than any other spiritual writer blazed the path to interior, contemplative Christianity for Evangelicals. Nouwen's most popular writings—*The Return of the Prodigal Son*, *Here and Now*, and *The Wounded Healer*—continue to be a first-stop on the spiritual path for many Christians emerging out of their doctrinal cocoons, hungry for the life-giving spiritual food of Divine healing and love.

Finally, a glance at recent titles published by the Evangelical stalwart InterVarsity Press reveals a distinct interest among Evangelicals in the contemplative path. Among these are Richard Foster and Gayle D. Beebe's *Longing for God*, which is a survey of spiritual practices as interpreted through contemplative and mystical Christian writers, such as Julian of Norwich and John of the Cross; and James Bryan Smith's *The Good and Beautiful God*, which is an Evangelical invitation to think differently about God using spiritual practices, or what Smith calls "soul training."

Inter-denominational Contemplative Expressions

One of the most compelling examples of contemplative community is Taizé in France. Taizé was begun after World War II by a Roman Catholic simply referred to as Brother Roger. Like the Christian monasteries of the past, the Taizé community was founded around a spiritual rule. Today, many Christian churches are familiar with Taizé because of its distinctive style of worship music, but worship is only one aspect of their community. What characterizes Taizé more than anything else is the intentional contemplative experience of love in community. Taizé is a community of brothers who have taken monastic-like vows, but the community is also open to visitors. Each year, thousands of guests and young people participate with the brothers in their experience of community and worship.[8]

The Taizé community is built upon a core contemplative Christian concept—the human longing for the presence of God. An essay on their view of faith puts it this way: "Right at the depth of the human condition *lies the longing for a presence*, the silent desire for a communion. Let us never forget that this simple desire for God is already the beginning of faith."[9]

Roman Catholic Expressions

While many Roman Catholic parishes and monasteries are living examples of the contemplative spiritual life, ordered around daily spiritual practices and worship, the most well-known expression of contemplative Christianity continues to be the writings of the late Thomas Merton.

In recent years, however, two other Roman Catholic monks have contributed significantly to the contemplative conversation. The works of Thomas Keating and Richard Rohr are calling a new generation of spiritual seekers hungry for a deeper life with God. Keating's *Open Mind, Open Heart*; *Invitation to Love*; and *Divine Therapy and Addiction*, and Rohr's *Radical Grace, Everything Belongs*, and *The Naked Now* have sold hundreds of thousands of copies and are getting the contemplative word out in accessible ways, helping many in their journey of discovery into the ever-present love of God.

Rohr also has a special gift for connecting with men and understands their unique spiritual journey. This is of vital importance, for men are very spiritually disadvantaged by our culture. Imprisoned in their rationality, they ache for a different way of being connected with the heart of God. Through the Center for Action and Contemplation, Rohr hosts retreats and seminars on the integral spiritual life, which unites both the contemplative and active life.

A final resource rooted in the Jesuit Roman Catholic family is the online contemplative community at www.Pray-As-You-Go.org. This resource provides daily contemplative prayers, music, scripture readings, and meditations. The quality of the content and production sets this resource apart as a leading example of the interconnected spiritual community, available online beyond the boundaries of nations and denominations.

The Church of Conscious Harmony

While none of the aforementioned models of contemplative Christian community is perfect, or captures all the dimensions of the contemplative path, one community has emerged over the last twenty years as a leading example of contemplative Christian community. The Church of Conscious Harmony (CCH) in Austin, Texas, provides a compelling case study of the fruitfulness of intentional contemplative community.

While no church community or one personal story encompasses the totality of possibilities for contemplative Christian community, CCH is one model that captures many of the previously discussed dimensions of contemplative Christian spirituality. These friendly observations are offered so that the wider Christian community can benefit from my neighbors.[10]

To the best of my knowledge, CCH is the only contemplative Christian church in the world that completely identifies itself as a contemplative Christian church founded as a school for love and transformation. CCH isn't a monastery.

Nor is it Protestant, Roman Catholic, Eastern or Russian Orthodox. It's none of these, yet it's all of them. CCH's name, while curious to some and threatening to others, is a highly intentional description that succinctly conveys its aim as a contemplative Christian community.

CCH was founded in 1988 by Tim and Barbara Cook as a "monastery without walls," and as a "five-year experiment in Christian community." The experiment appears to be working. Today, CCH provides a contemplative model for spiritual communities wishing to grow in grace together through spiritual practices beyond the walls of a monastery. While CCH is called a church, and serves all the functions and services of a traditional church, its deeper purpose is to be and become, in Tim's poetic words,

> [A]n ongoing manifestation and continuation of the flame of Christian love. In this way CCH is both a church and a school of love. As members are touched by the mystical experience of God's right-now loving presence, they join countless generations of Christians who have preceded. Feeling together the astonishing, ever increasing power of the call of God's silent, invisible, yet utterly tangible presence, CCH members are inspired to share more and more of their time, treasure and talents in the ongoing co-creation of the CCH community.
>
> The inspiration that moves them is the very same Spirit that moved the apostles and the first century Christians as they struggled together in self-transcending efforts to build their communities into homes for the spirit of love. [CCH] has inherited the blessings that have resulted from the [Apostles'] efforts and are in our own generation renewing them and participating in the continuing and ongoing evolution of the way human beings work and live together.
>
> No coercion, no visible reward, no threat of punishment inspires our community to make the tremendous efforts that go into the creation and maintenance of our Church home. Christian love does this. It may be inconceivable to those who have not experienced it, but it is perfectly obvious to those who have. It needs no explanation, no justification and no publicity. God's love is its own attraction and reward. It moves us as nothing else ever could, just as it has been moving and inspiring generation after generation of the human family for two thousand years.

What we are learning together, as we open to the contemplative level of the gospels and the Christian religion, is that Christ is far more literal, present and active than most of us had ever dreamed and that His invitation to participate in the Kingdom of God is not a promise of distant reward for good behavior but a right now experience of the utterly convincing, transforming touch of God's love.

This love is so powerful and literal that it completely outshines any shadows of our early conditioning that suggest a punishing and vengeful God. God's interest in us is in our identity, not in our behavior. God wants us to know that we human beings have been created for love and that our birthright and destiny is waiting to be discovered within us every single second. When we know what we are and who created us, harmonious actions will follow without fail.[11]

On the twentieth anniversary of CCH's founding, Tim Cook reflected on the original intention: "The church was founded to serve the human reconnection to the God who is love." The intention is visibly flourishing and the church is the vibrant embodiment of a contemplative Christian community.

The mission statement for the church's five-year experiment, written in 1988, is a declaration of intention for where Tim and Barbara Cook wanted to go and how they hoped to get there. It's also useful as a guide for others who share in their wish to experience and foster contemplative, Christian community in the Third Millennium:

> The Church of Conscious Harmony exists for the sole purpose of facilitating the spiritual journey for people who want to make God-devotion the center of their lives while living in the ordinary world without the aid of monastery walls.
>
> Our aim is to provide the focus, the teaching and the community support required for individuals to grow in self-awareness from the illusion of separate and separative existence to the fully enlightened experience of conscious union with the living God.
>
> Toward that end, we maintain within the Church, the Tenth Man School, a school of transformative spiritual psychology and practice. Our basic teaching core stands on two legs: (1) the teachings and practices of the contemplative Christian tradition, as presented by Fr. Thomas Keating and others, and (2)

the teachings and practices of the esoteric Christian Fourth Way known as the Work, as presented by Maurice Nicoll, G. I. Gurdjieff and others. Though we are firmly founded on these teachings, we are not limited by them or to them. We are free to reach deeply into all religious and spiritual traditions for insight, wisdom and inspiration; using these gifts to illumine our own religious roots and to enliven our spiritual practice.

Though we necessarily employ dogma, theology and ritual, the Church uses these tools solely as a means of assisting individuals to attain personal experiences of God's presence and activity in their lives. We encourage all people who worship or study in the Church and the Tenth Man School to engage in intentional daily spiritual practice and study, realizing these to be absolutely essential requirements for becoming aware of and receptive to God's Transforming Grace.

We also encourage loving service to our human family, reaching out and responding to those in need with inspiration, care and transformative teaching. Ultimately the Church is a community of individuals who acknowledge their absolute dependence on God and who simply wish to learn to receive and to express genuine love for God and humanity.[12]

CCH provides a compelling template for the future of contemplative Christianity. Its core beliefs, while unique, are broadly orthodox. CCH is both a church and a school, and this unique combination of contemplative Christianity is woven into their faith statement.[13]

Over the years, CCH has been noticeably shaped by an ongoing spiritual friendship and partnership with Thomas Keating. The church has also been deeply influenced by the writings and teachings of Bernadette Roberts. But beyond these two profound Christian thinkers and writers are many others who've helped form the theological and spiritual personality of the community, including Babaji Mahavatar, Wayne Teasdale, Carl Arico, Raimon Panikkar, Pierre Teilhard de Chardin, Rabbi Joseph Schultz, Ngari Rinpoche, Baba Virsa Singh, G. I. Gurdjieff, and Maurice Nicoll.

Wayne Teasdale, author, contemplative, interreligious leader, and friend to CCH, saw the unique importance of the CCH community. He wrote:

The Church of Conscious Harmony is a community of seekers who take very seriously their spiritual life both individually and in common. This ecclesial community is a brilliant example, or model, of what every church should be. It is a light for the future. It is wise, holy, deeply conscious, in touch with the Divine Source, and so able to live harmoniously with everyone else. It deserves enthusiastic support and study by other communities.[14]

We will now heed Brother Wayne's encouragement to study and explore several of the guiding principles that make CCH a model for contemplative Christian community, bearing in mind that CCH is founded upon two legs: Centering Prayer and "the Work."

A MONASTERY WITHOUT WALLS

At the heart of every monastic community are the vows taken by the community members. Such vows are not just vows for their own sake. Spiritual vows are the essence of intentional spiritual community, because vows enable a personal and corporate surrender to live under the authority of something or someone, surrendering certain freedoms to gain a certain kind of force for loving God and neighbor. Placing oneself under the authority of a teacher, teaching, community rule, or daily spiritual practice provides a "containing space" wherein one surrenders in order to gain. What one surrenders is, in Keating's terminology, the "false self." What one gains is a deeper life in God.

While many people wish to live a God-devoted life, most people don't want to take the traditional monastic vows of abstinence, poverty, chastity, and obedience. For those who *do* wish to experience long-term monastic life, but are unable to do so because of various life-circumstances such as a career or financial obligations, the idea of living the monastic life amid work and family is compelling.

To live as monks in the world and partake in a contemplative Christian community that is a monastery without walls—that is in the world, but not of it (John 17.15–18)—you must place yourself under the authority of a daily spiritual practice, or *ordo*. According to author Fred Edie, the word *ordo* has come to describe "the patterned communal way of life shaped around the practice of . . .

holy things . . . thus *ordo* 'ordered' includes not only worship life on Sundays but the entirety of the church's life before God. Patterns for worshiping became the patterns for communal living."[15]

One doesn't need to be in a monastery to live the contemplative life. One can bring the monastery into life. Cultivating spiritual practices is both an underlying foundation for spiritual renewal, and the primary way to participate and manifest the presence of God as continuing incarnations of Christ, individually and collectively.

One of the motivating factors for having a spiritual *ordo* or practice is the renewal of human community in relationship with God. Spiritual practices help people integrate bible study, theology, and personal experiences in transformative ways that glorify God and help heal humanity. Such a life is, understandably, something that many long for, and often find during brief visits to monasteries or when on spiritual retreat. But the life of worship and wholeness are not just for spiritual retreats or monasteries. Through spiritual practices such as Centering Prayer, we're nurtured deeper into the life of God right in the middle of wherever our life may be.[16]

At CCH several spiritual practices form the personal and community *ordo* to foster the right now, right here experience of God's loving presence and action. We'll consider each of them with a view to their applicability beyond the CCH community.

Worship

Worship at CCH is the heart of the community, and the heart of CCH worship is silence, scripture, and sermon. The sanctuary is a sealed chamber, with soaring beams rising up to windowed cupola. A cross hangs front and center. The sanctuary is truly that: silent and sealed off from the distractions of life. It's widely recognized as a beautiful and unique worship space, looking like a blend of the soaring ribs of a Gothic cathedral and a Native American tipi. Underneath the sanctuary is the Theosis Chapel, formed in an oval, with a lighted dome above, seating thirty people in two rows encircling the oval. The chapel is an ideal place for small gatherings for Centering Prayer.

The main worship service at CCH occurs on Sunday mornings in the sanctuary. During this service, a period of Centering Prayer occurs and the minister often invites congregational sharing. The order of worship follows a set pattern, beginning with the chant, "Come and pray in us," a quiet time that continues with "Pie Jesu," and then an opening song, "The Gospel in One Word Is Love." The main instrumentation is usually set to piano and led by a lector's singing; then follows the announcement, various readings, Centering Prayer, and the minister's message, which is succeeded by the offering and a closing song, during which the children proceed into the sanctuary in a kind of celebratory reunion. During the liturgical year, special emphasis is placed upon Advent and Lent. Likewise, contemplative special services are provided for Ash Wednesday, Good Friday, and New Year's Eve.

A shorter worship service occurs on Wednesday evenings and begins with twenty minutes of collective Centering Prayer, scripture readings, a message from the minister, and the Eucharist. The sanctuary was intentionally designed to seat approximately 365 people. This number provides a spiritual "family" feel. While all worship services are open to visitors, the church provides a two-year membership process that includes classes on Centering Prayer and "The Work."

Scripture

The written Word of God becomes personal and alive in the CCH community through the practice of *Lectio Divina*. This slow, meditative reading is often viewed as a first step toward Centering Prayer because it helps the reader/hearer descend into the heart through a "heartfulness" that moves beyond the normal critical/rational reading of scripture. *Lectio* is usually not a literal reading, but a depth reading, wherein we don't so much read the text of scripture, but rather the text reads us. This, of course, is the work of the Holy Spirit in us, using the living and active written Word of God to bring purgation, healing, insight, and illumination.

To aid the community in its scripture reading, CCH uses a popular Roman Catholic lectionary and "daily office" called Magnificat.[17] This "daily office" or *ordo* of scripture reading provides morning and evening scriptures, and a main reading usually comprised of an Old Testament, psalm, and gospel selection. CCH also will offer occasional scripture classes, with particular emphasis on the relationship of scripture to the teaching of "the Work," as interpreted through Maurice Nicoll.

CCH teaches that the impressions received on a regular basis from "digesting" the scriptures give inner food for the spiritual journey. This spiritual bread is life-giving and feeds the community "higher influences," beyond the level of life-influences from newspapers, Internet sites, and email, to name a few.

Of particular importance to the CCH community is the contemplative dimension of biblical interpretation. While the scriptures have multiple layers and meanings, highly dependent upon the psychological and spiritual state of the reader, CCH values, explores, and celebrates the inner, psychological interpretation of the scriptures. At a different time in church history, this mode of interpretation was known as the allegorical method. Today, it is spoken of as the "depth interpretation," a model that reveals more about what is occurring for the reader than the historical context. The depth method also invites the Spirit to reveal what is necessary for our own growth in grace.

This inner, contemplative method of scripture reading opens the individual and community to the vibrant presence and action of the Holy Spirit. A classic illustration of the distinction between literal and depth readings is Jesus' teaching of the Lord's Prayer in the Sermon on the Mount, particularly the phrase, "When you pray, go into your inner room and shut the door and pray to your Father who is in secret" (Matthew 6.6).

The literal reading of this text would lead one to find an actual quiet room in one's house, shut the door, and begin praying. While such a reading is appropriate, the contemplative, inner interpretation of this passage teaches that the inner room is our heart, into which we enter apart from our discursive, thinking mind. In the silence and solitude of our heart, we may experience the prayer of presence, being one with the Father through Christ by the Spirit. This leads us to the second spiritual practice at CCH: silence and Centering Prayer.

Silence

It was St. Ignatius of Antioch who wrote that God's first word was silence, from which the Word springs forth.[18] CCH believes that the gift of silence is the primary characteristic of a contemplative community. Within this silence, the heart of prayer can bloom, unleashing the life-giving presence beating in the space between all things. Silence also leads to an inner solitude, enabling a deeper consent to the presence of God who was and always is with us beyond the noise and chatter of our thinking minds. Silence is a priority for contemplative community, but it isn't "emptiness" or "apathy." The contemplative silence that births the gift of Centering Prayer is a structured silence.

CCH follows the teaching of Contemplative Outreach, whose guidelines for Centering Prayer invite one to enter into silent, meditative prayer for at least twenty minutes, twice a day, at minimum. The guidelines are simple and straightforward, yet equally profound:[19]

1. Choose a sacred word as the symbol of your intention to consent to God's presence and action within.
2. Sitting comfortably and with eyes closed, settle briefly and silently introduce the sacred word as the symbol of your consent to God's presence and action within.
3. When engaged with your thoughts, return ever so gently to the sacred word.
4. At the end of the prayer period, remain in silence with eyes closed for a couple of minutes.

The gift of silence can lead to a sacred oneness deeper than all words, funding strong bonds for human fellowship. Sitting in silence during collective Centering Prayer is intensely intimate. Bound together by the Spirit in silence, the CCH community becomes the living Body of Christ. CCH believes that just as service and mission help embody the living Christ in community, so too does silence. It is a deeply nourishing way of being Christian and creating life-giving and vulnerable community before the depth and presence of Divine love itself.

CCH celebrates the experience of this Divine love by providing a seven a.m. daily Centering Prayer service, facilitating weekly Centering Prayer groups, and hosting and leading Centering Prayer retreats for church members and the greater community. Retreats range from half-day commuter retreats to ten-day programs. The purpose of the retreats is to share in community, silence, sacrament, and Centering Prayer. Through the church's longstanding relationship with Thomas Keating, many CCH members make Centering Prayer pilgrimage retreats to St. Benedict's Monastery in Snowmass, Colorado, where Keating resides.[20]

Centering Prayer is a daily practice that helps guide those who discover in their own heart the insatiable hunger for God's loving presence in the silence of prayer, as individuals and in community.

Eucharist

The Sacrament of the Lord's Supper, or Eucharist, is offered at least weekly at CCH. The Eucharist is celebrated at CCH as the real, mystical, and living presence of Jesus Christ. The spoken intention of Jesus Christ that this is and shall be my body and blood reverberates through the centuries. Communion occurs at CCH's Wednesday contemplative worship service, which begins with twenty minutes of collective Centering Prayer, lectionary readings, a sermon, and then the Eucharistic celebration, which Tim Cook refers to as "the main event."

The vital importance of the sacrament of the Lord's Supper at CCH is best captured by reviewing CCH's liturgical Eucharistic prayers. There follows a sample Eucharistic service, which includes the offertory, invitation, Eucharistic prayer, words of institution, prayer of thanksgiving, and benediction. The service speaks for itself.[21]

Offertory

Awake now to the nearly unbearable grace of love, we dedicate these tithes and offerings to the victory of consciously chosen love, in each of our lives and on our planet, over the lie that we are separate, and our useless acting out from fear. In Christ we pray.

Invitation

Here the mystery goes on; the Spirit and matter, the form and the formless, the time bound and the eternal are meeting right here on this altar in an offering that has been continuously perpetuated since one man stood in a little room in Palestine with a dozen friends and said, "Take, eat, this is my body, here is the cup of my blood, the blood of the new covenant." What a miracle that it is still here! It is still a mystery. It is still an intimate offering of spiritual intimacy. But none of us will ever explain it; we can only participate in it.

Eucharistic Prayer

Abba. We thank You that we know You hear us now and that we know You always hear us. It's You who are giving us words. You who are teaching us to pray and You who are giving us faith to pray with, that lets us know and be certain that You always hear and answer when we ask. Abba, we ask, pour out Your spirit on these elements, that we might recognize them, receive them, and respond to them as the Body and the Blood of Your Son, Jesus Christ. Let them communicate His Body to our bodies and His Blood to our blood. Fill us with Your Holy Spirit, and transform us in Your love. We pray this in Jesus' name. Amen.

Words of Institution

During supper on the night He was betrayed, Jesus took bread, and having said the blessing, He broke it and gave it to His disciples saying: "Take this all of you and eat it. This is my Body which shall be given up for you." This is the Body of Christ. When supper was ended, He took the cup, and again He gave God thanks and praise. He gave it to His disciples saying: "Drink from it, all of you. This is the cup of my Blood, the Blood of the new and everlasting covenant; it will be shed for you and for all, so that sins may be forgiven. Whenever you do this, remember me." This is the Blood of Christ.

Prayer of Thanksgiving

Lord Jesus, living and eternal Christ. We feel Your risen presence as the very life that pervades and yet transcends our bodies and our minds. We realize You are the Way and the Truth, and we're grateful to share in Your Body and Your Blood. May our participation in these Divine Mysteries transform us into one in Your Mystical Body, the true Body of Christ. For the glory of God our Father, for the glory of His Kingdom here on Earth, and so that our joy may be complete. We pray this in Your most holy and precious name. Amen.

Benediction

May the love, the peace and the joy of our Lord Jesus Christ, be with us now and always. Amen.

Spiritual Reading

In addition to the daily reading of scripture, CCH also practices a monthly community reading. The purpose of this monthly reading is to foster spiritual growth through study. While community occurs in worship, it also occurs through the united commitment to spiritual practices, such as the monthly community reading. Together, the community is literally on the same page, growing in their knowledge through in-depth study of compelling books.[22]

Service

Service is modeled to the CCH membership by a group of eighty leaders. This group is called SEVA, which is a Sanskrit word that means "voluntary work in service to God's Creation," and which the CCH community interprets as "selfless service." The SEVA members are organized in five teams of sixteen members, with one leader for each of the five teams. Each SEVA team is assigned a week. During this week, the team serves the church by opening and closing the building, sweeping, preparing food for fellowship hour, ushering, preparing for all worship services, including preparations for the Eucharist. SEVA members embody the servant nature of Jesus and represent the serving nature of Christ to Christianity. They give of themselves in selfless service as contemplative leaders in the CCH community, holding the center of servant-leadership and Christ-like intention.

Like most churches, CCH members serve their community on various committees that support all the church's programs, such as finance, music, children's, and youth. In addition, service is grounded in CCH's commitment to "reciprocal maintenance." In this way, the CCH community gives back through financial tithes to the organizations that support and feed them spiritually, such as Contemplative Outreach. Through this relationship with Contemplative Outreach, CCH serves the greater community in Central Texas by providing many Centering Prayer workshops, retreats, and prayer groups.

Annual Aim

The annual aim is a meaningful dimension of the contemplative community life at CCH.

Each year, the leadership discerns an aim for the community that forms the matrix for further spiritual focus and practices. For example, a recent annual aim was "forgiveness." Through the use of prayer cards, the community focused monthly on different aspects of forgiveness. This particular aim was also supported by a weekend seminar on forgiveness, early in the year, grounding the aim in practical teaching. The aim is also supported in the monthly church newsletter written by both CCH ministers and various community members.

A SCHOOL FOR CONSCIOUSLY CHOSEN LOVE

Most of our review of CCH to this point has dealt with the first leg of the church. We now turn to the second leg, which is "The Work." While this may seem an unusual term, it's actually the psychological application of esoteric (or inner) Christianity.

A chant that is often sung following the sermon at CCH is, "The gospel in one word is love." While the love of God felt and shared in community is one of the marks of this contemplative community, love is not their only intention. Christianity was founded upon two commandments: love of God and love of neighbor (Matthew 22.36–40). The Christian church continues to aspire to this noble embodiment of love, summarized so beautifully by St. Paul: "These things remain, faith, hope and love, but the greatest of these is love" (1 Corinthians 13).

Yet there is a further value beyond love that inspires the CCH community, and that also differentiates it from other Christian churches. The difference is the community's awareness of and commitment to a growth in consciousness. The emphasis on consciousness is conveyed in the church's name, and was inspired by the teachings of Maurice Nicoll, whose *Psychological Commentaries* articulate a handbook for interior Christianity. The *Commentaries* address the questions: How can I be a Christian on the inside? How can I access the inner experience so that, in Jesus words, "the inside of the cup is clean?" How can I actually be whom I seem to be and actually experience life as I wish to experience it? The commentaries are tools for this process and spiritual journey, and wisdom from those who have gone before.[23]

One of the great paradoxes of the spiritual journey is that we first have to see the need for such interior transformation. So, when everything is just fine in our middle-class normality and affluence, when things are going as they should, and we're not feeling fearful or anxious, we normally have no reason to examine our life or its values. But through insights offered in the *Commentaries*, we can begin to get a glimpse into what Gurdjieff called "the terror of the situation," and what Thomas Keating calls simply, "the human condition."

The need for a psychological tool for transformation is summarized by Maurice Nicoll in his book *The Mark*, which provides a contemplative interpretation of the gospel:

> Man on Earth, from the standpoint of the gospels, is incomplete, unfinished, not perfect, and his deepest meaning lies in the fact that he is incomplete, but capable through a new understanding and a new will of reaching an inner completion. . . . The completion, the self-evolution, the rebirth, and so the fulfillment of a man can only be brought about through himself, through his own individual seeing the truth, his own understanding of it, his own desire for it, his own will applied to it. This is the supreme idea of Man on Earth, as taught by Christ.[24]

This tool for psychological transformation is sometimes called "The Work" or "The Fourth Way." The CCH community summarizes it this way:

> The Work is an ancient system of spiritual transformation, which is also referred to as the work of Christian transformation [providing the practical method to fulfill St. Paul's maxim "to work out your own salvation"]. The Work teaches that human beings are asleep to higher levels of consciousness and being, and that through effort and grace, it is possible to awaken. Moreover, The Work teaches that to awaken one must first study oneself. The teaching provides an integrated spiritual psychology and cosmology, providing a system of laws that govern creation and humanities' relationship to and within the Ray of Creation. The Work is a living tradition and useful system that helps us understand ourselves in the context of the great universe in which we live.[25]

Robin Amis, a Christian contemplative and a scholar of early Christianity, has dedicated his life to translating Orthodox monastic texts into English and teaching them. Through Amis's work with the Praxis Research Institute in England, several important books have been published, such as *A Different Christianity* and *The Gnosis* series. According to Amis, The Work is simply inner Christianity. He writes:

> [M]y observations have convinced me that . . . Christianity possesses and always has possessed an inner tradition; not a system, but what might be called a discipline . . . yet the Western churches either claim that there is no tradition or inner or esoteric knowledge, or reserve it to a clergy who themselves are not expected to give too much credence to it. This has forced countless thousands to turn to Eastern faiths for no other reason than because their inner teachings are more accessible than our own: because although Christianity has always possessed its own tradition of inner knowledge, looked at through intellectual eyes, that tradition has been relegated to the status of an intellectual curiosity. As a result some of it has been irrevocably lost, much mislaid, and the remainder has reached only a very small proportion of the population. Consequently, because knowledge acts only through being known, it has had little effect on our civilization. This is one reason why many people no longer regard ours as a Christian civilization. But the truth is not Nietzsche's "death of God," nor has Christianity failed. What actually happened was that, due to the difficulties of conveying the inner tradition through the barbarous centuries following the decline of the Roman Empire, and due to the limited classical education of most Westerners, this key element of Christian teaching has never been common knowledge in the Western world.[26]

CCH is helping reverse this situation through its school for transformation called the Tenth Man School, and its weekly Work classes.[27] The Tenth Man School exists for the sake of personal transformation as a community. The CCH description of the school reads like a dedicated spiritual corps:

> This is a sacred school for disciplined spiritual practitioners. Members of the Tenth Man School put themselves under the authority of the teachings of the Work and a teacher, with the aim of awakening into the consciousness of Christ in and as our life. The school provides the teaching, programs and focus

to help students awaken from the illusion of separation and to help them live as conscious and free beings. Joining the Tenth Man School is a serious lifelong commitment. Candidates prepare themselves with a series of classes and daily study, among other specific things. Membership is capped at seventy-two and entry is by invitation to qualified candidates.[28]

While the Tenth Man School is limited in its membership, the weekly Work class is open to everyone who wishes to explore the teachings of Maurice Nicoll's *Psychological Commentaries on the Teachings of Gurdjieff and Ouspensky*. Participants learn Work ideas that help one transform the way one experiences oneself so to include the experience of God's love as one's moment-to-moment event. Students are given homework for the week based on the application of Work ideas. Work on oneself is considered the First Line of The Work. The Second Line of The Work is considered work with and for another. This Second Line occurs at CCH through small Work groups and Work partners. Among its many benefits, The Work is most certainly the practical application of Christian ideas in the form of psychological tools that can be applied to one's everyday life, and that help one dismantle the false-self system by increasingly making the personality passive through self-observation, non-identification, and self-remembering, to name a few Work ideas.

CCH AS A COMMUNITY FOR EVERYDAY MYSTICS

The experience of God's emerging presence and love through all of creation, personally felt in the silence of the heart, is the essence of Christian mysticism. While mysticism has been widely misunderstood by the Protestant community, it's the blood beating in the heart of all personal and communal spiritual experiences. Mysticism, as the personal, immediate experience of God's loving presence and action, is both the roots of the tree of contemplative Christianity and its emerging leaves. It's really just a fancy way of talking about "abiding in Christ" (John 15.4). As Christians, contemplative Christianity is both our history and future.

Bernard McGinn, preeminent scholar on the history of mysticism, defines mysticism as an "attempt to express a direct consciousness of the presence of

God."[29] Oxford theologian Andrew Louth also characterizes mysticism as the "search for and experience of immediacy with God. The mystic is not content to know *about* God, he longs for union with God."[30]

CCH understands the role mysticism has played in the development of contemplative Christianity, and through their association with Bernadette Roberts, CCH can rightfully be known as a church for everyday mystics. While many Protestants think Christian mysticism is a contradiction in terms, the development of many of our most cherished and orthodox Christian doctrines were deeply shaped by contemplative and mystical ideas of the early church fathers.

Today more than ever, the Christian church is in need of experiencing God's loving presence and action through our union with Christ by the power of the Holy Spirit. As Tim Cook puts it, "There are two ways of knowing Christ. One can either know a lot about him or one can *know* him." Knowing and experiencing Christ is the essence of Christian mysticism and the heart of the gospel.[31]

Wayne Teasdale wrote a compelling book just prior to his untimely death called *A Monk in the World* where he outlined a way of being a contemplative Christian grounded in spiritual practices. He discovered that he was drawn into the contemplative life, not just in the monastery but as a monk in the world. He confessed that the Spirit had called him

> into the world to live a spirituality of engagement with those who suffer, and that's all of us. This call includes kinship with other species and with nature as a whole within this vast cosmos, which is our real community and certainly the context of our life on this fragile planet. I want to be in the bosom of God in the heart of the world. St. Francis of Assisi taught me when I was a child the importance of simplicity of life, what the Catholic tradition calls poverty. . . . Living as a hermit monk in the world, as a contemplative mystic working for a living, like most people, living simply and consciously, I can do the most good for others. Furthermore, I choose to be a monk living in the midst of the real world, among my brothers and sisters, because I am first of all a contemplative mystic.
>
> That is, I am anchored in deep and growing inner awareness of God's presence, of the Divine's incomparable love for each one of us. Often I feel the Divine One giving itself to me directly, in my relationships with others

and in the natural world; it is always a source of inspiration, delight, and even bliss I experience and so am aware of this Presence in some way, all the time. Often I am overwhelmed by God's love and I feel it inviting me to profound and subtler degrees of surrender, that is, of greater generosity in assenting to God's invitation. My mystical experience is emphatically and inevitably God centered.[32]

With Brother Teasdale, it's my hope that many Protestant church communities will find this everyday contemplative, mystical journey deeply enticing to heart and mind, and discover opportunities to "taste and see the Lord is good" (Psalm 34.8) in the extraordinary ordinariness of being human, in the world but not of it (John 17.17).

CCH provides a compelling model for ordinary people who wish to remain in the world but also who hunger to live in God's presence. CCH demonstrates that it's possible to build a community around a set of spiritual principles and practices, especially if there's a shared vision as to what the aim of the church is. CCH's shared vision is to be a contemplative church and a school for love and transformation. The tools of Centering Prayer, scripture, and The Work interpreted through Maurice Nicoll all help ground this spiritual intention into a lived, personal, and communal experience.

CCH is a current witness to the truth that in this era of spiritual awakening and seeking, Christianity is rediscovering its own inner, contemplative dimensions. It's evidence that the contemplative path is shaping a different kind of Christianity, one both ancient and emerging. While no church is perfect and Christianity will always be an evolving community experience, useful models are currently available to help those who long for a fuller feast of God's presence, but are dissatisfied with the fare they are finding. Robin Amis summarizes this movement in Christianity well, especially in relationship to CCH:

> For several years it has been clear to me that Austin's Church of Conscious Harmony is one of the rare churches in the Western world that makes genuine efforts to recover and then live by the healing truths that gave early Christianity its strength but have since been generally forgotten.[33]

Christianity is not a solo endeavor. It is a family journey. Even the most solitary of contemplatives is grounded in the communal love of the Triune God. This Divine community is to be modeled in our churches, contemplative and non-contemplative alike. But the unique gift of the contemplative path is to demonstrate just how personal and loving community can be as it rests in silence, consenting to God's presence and action, and applies effort and intention to personal, interior transformation.

The spiritual journey is difficult. Each of us needs the support of companions. Just as the eye cannot see itself, neither can the "I" in us see itself. It requires the reflection of friends in spiritual community to help us graciously see what we otherwise could not.

This lack of vulnerability and fear of reflection keep many church communities living on the surface of things rather than engaging the shared human struggle with the false self and all its programs for happiness. When Christian communities lose touch with this interior spiritual journey, much confusion results. The vibrant, interior spiritual life mutates into an externalized social experience governed by rules and doctrines. Many find this kind of Christianity lifeless. I wish that instead of leaving Christianity altogether, such individuals could rediscover a different kind of Christianity: *the contemplative way within Christianity, hiding in plain sight.*

SEVEN

LEAVING CHRISTIANITY FOR CHRISTIANITY

———◄○►———

*Our birthright is to live in constant awe of God, to live in constant
relationship, as his daughters and sons, not as distant knowers of a possibility
or as believers in a religious system, but as experiencers of the reality
that Jesus Christ revealed.*

—TIM COOK[1]

WITH A FEW EXCEPTIONS, most Christian communities in the West
have all but neglected the contemplative way of being Christian.
However, this is slowly changing and the contemplative way of being
Christian is a welcome discovery for those increasingly disengaging from the
Christianity they've grown up with. In this sense, the contemplative path
is bearing Christianity to Christianity, and awaits to welcome with open
arms spiritual pilgrims who find other expressions of Christianity unable
to answer their deepest questions or provide food for their increasing God-
hunger. While the reasons for the Western exodus from Christianity are both
complex and not new, several trends can be identified as to why some Christians are exploring spiritual alternatives and why some leave Christianity
altogether.

SEEKING AN EMBODIED SPIRITUALITY

Sensing this spiritual anemia in their overloaded thinking lives, but often not having words to talk about it, some Christians slip away from the church to explore other, more embodied spiritual traditions attempting to address the totality of their humanity. They are exploring, in part, because they cannot find life-giving, embodied spiritual practices in their church community that are both authentic and transforming.

SEEKING TO SQUARE THE SPIRITUAL CIRCLE

For others, it's just too difficult to square one's intellectual sensibilities with inherited, seemingly irrational religious doctrines.[2] This is all the more true for those who find their faith challenged by the confusing and controversial theological doctrines and debates seemingly disconnected from human experience and spiritual longings. Church leaders and apologists demanding people to become more doctrinally pure or repent from error don't help the situation either. In my view, we've had enough of condemning councils, marauding crusaders, and blithering bully-pulpiteers full of fire and fury signifying nothing except their own sense of power, control, and importance.

SEEKING TO FLATTEN THE VERTICAL MYSTERY OF GOD

Some also seek outside the Christian tradition because of the compelling claims of medicine, technology, and science. The challenge of these claims is that while they explain much of the universe and human existence in coherent ways, they do so in materialistic terms. The problem with materialism is that it evicts the Spirit. By doing so, these claims deflate spirituality and mute human nobility, diminishing us to what C. S. Lewis once described as "men without chests,"[3] or, as Ken Wilber suggests, we become "flatlanders."[4]

Flatlanders reduce the mystery of the human spirit and consciousness to chemical reactions of the brain. While consciousness is currently one of the most fruitful areas of inquiry shedding light on human spirituality, it's also a bit like Dorothy discovering that the Wizard of Oz is just an old man playing at levers. Flatlanders (no smear on Dorothy's Kansas) smother the vertical miracle of being human for the sake of the horizontal rationality of Western scientific thinking. Somewhere in between is the up-ending mystery of being human, a mystery Blaise Pascal consented to when he wrote that "all things cover some mystery; all things are veils which cover God."[5]

Tempted and confused by the flatlanders, rationality can drive one over the edge of doubt. If one tries to square God with all that is called scientific knowledge, one begins to feel a thinning of soul. When we ignore the contemplative inner, vertical world of intuition, poetry, and prayer, our humanity is diminished. Over time, we may lose our capacity to feel the wonder of oneness with the creation and creator. If ignored long enough, communion with God and the felt awareness of God's presence and action in our lives, numbs and, like a second language unspoken, simply slips away.[6]

I once heard an astute atheist argue on a radio program that the reason he didn't need the word "God" was because he had the word "love." Such is the way of the atheist. But something rings true in this, for God is love, and love more than anything else demonstrates the nobility of the human condition. As the phrase goes: To err is human, to love Divine. But love, though enduring in its power and glory, isn't the only game in town. Being human is indeed our glory, but it's also our undoing, and for this reason love leads us not to the end of faith but to the end of ourselves. In the moment of surrender to love, we also discover that we've somehow lost a bit of ourselves and in so doing, paradoxically, can begin to find ourselves again.

So why introduce God? One answer in line with the tendencies of the contemplative tradition is that we do so because, in addition to God being the Source of love, remaining in relationship with God is *lawful.* Whether we like it, know it, or accept it, humanity exists in a lawful relationship to the higher, vertical influences of the universe just as planet Earth exists in a lawful relationship to the higher, vertical influences of the planetary forces and celestial laws now being revealed by physics.

But unlike with Dorothy, no old man is playing at the levers. Above and beneath is the ground of being: the One and the All who is a being-in-relationship pouring forth and upon the vastness of eternity, drenching light, life, and love that simply IS. So why God? Because it's lawful, and also probably genetic. But exploring such legality and ontology any further is a task beyond the scope of this book.

SEEKING AN EXPERIENCE BEYOND
JUST INFORMATION

Today, people are attracted to different spiritual ideas beyond the Christian tradition because, in many instances, Christian leaders have failed to explain why and how the gospel message connects with the human hunger for healing and transformation. For far too long, the Christian tradition has simply proclaimed proscriptive information, such as rehearsing biblical stories and announcing that Jesus died on the cross to forgive sins. Some sermons and Christian devotional literature does this in exceptionally creative, compelling, and even therapeutic ways.

But all too often the horizon of the biblical world and its stories is limited to its literal, historical level through which life-applications are then drawn. This kind of Christianity is important, but is only one dimension of the spiritual journey. There are other ways of interpretation and application, but in my experience the only way the horizon of cultural religiosity will change is if our biblical interpretation changes. Caught in the whirl of inner development, such change takes time.

One hindrance to change is that, as Protestants, we've tried to mimic scientific rationality. While this mimicry has created robust theologians, it has also led us to demand that the Bible be literally, scientifically true. By doing so, we've tended to reduce the Christian life and its message to differing formulas and systems.[7] This rational approach to the Spirit and scriptures ultimately leads to a "disconnect" from the inner life of the human spirit. One result of this disconnect is that Protestant Christianity has increasingly isolated itself from its dominant host culture, creating its own subculture of schools, publishing houses, media outlets, music, and pop-Christian stars.[8] But the way of isolation and separation ultimately limits fecundity. And increasingly, a dissonance rings in the ears of those wondering if there's another way.[9]

As humans, we long to experience the mysterious and transforming presence of God, spirit to Spirit. Smothering this impulse by any means deeply denies our human flourishing. Christian fundamentalism and cultural evangelicalism were acutely harmful to my own flourishing. In its attempt to isolate the core truths of the faith from its perceived enemies—modernity, certain scientific developments, and the general cultural trend toward secularization—Fundamentalism made a fateful move. Shadowing the very cultural developments it feared, Christian fundamentalism turned away from its inner, experiential tradition and tried to become more scientific, going toe to toe with science, entering a ring in which Christianity was ill-equipped to fight. In my view, the fight has been bloody, clumsy, and harmful to all involved.

CONTEMPLATIVE CHRISTIANITY
FOR CHRISTIANITY

Fortunately, recent shifts in science have begun to humble the dominance of scientific rationalism. During the last hundred years, new insights have revealed the ancient wisdom of a relational reality, something the fourth-century Christians creatively grasped in their Trinitarian formulations.[10] These "new" scientific insights have revealed that physical reality is much more relational and mysterious than we modern Westerners previously thought. The quantum level discloses a highly quirky world of relationships at the deepest levels of interior reality. Even deeper, some say, is the vibrating, interrelating, perichoretic world of strings, declaring in their ancient song the octaves of creation and its creator.[11]

Rationality is very important. Science is essential. We need both for our humanity, civilization, and culture. Both are manifestations of the image of God and human genius. However, rationality is no longer the exclusive monarch of Christianity. It continues to play its vital role, but it must be supplemented by other relational/spiritual levels of being and knowing, opening the way for us to address our longing for the love at the heart of all reality, beyond our sense perceptions and differing life situations.[12] I like the way Bono puts it: "Stop helping God across the road like a little old lady."[13] God doesn't need our help or defense. God desires our love. And, back to Bono: "Love, love, love. God is love. And love is evolution's very best day."[14]

A DIFFERENT KIND OF CHRISTIANITY

The contemplative way opens up for us a different kind of Christianity—a way of being Christian that is credible, historical, and deeply integral.[15] Contemplative Christianity can be a life-giving alternative for many Christians who find the techno-scientific world of rationalism substantively unable to hold the mystery of their inner experience, or on the other hand, the heart-hardening reaction that is fundamentalism, with all its significant repressions and contortions of mystery, in the earnest effort to fit in the rational box of a few choice doctrines.

In contrast, and transcending both rationalism and fundamentalism, is the contemplative/mystical path. Overflowing all containers of mind and doctrine are the beauty, glory, and mystery of the soul's longing and experience of God in Christ by the Holy Spirit. This is the heart of contemplative Christianity and, in my vision, the future hope of the Christian church.

Take for example the pithy and popular quip of G. K. Chesterton: Christianity "has not been tried and found wanting; it has been found difficult and left untried."[16] With due respect to Chesterton, looking across the gulf that separates modernity and postmodernity, I actually think that, in the modern era, Christianity *was* extensively tried, both personally and culturally, and for many it has been found deeply wanting—at least when it comes to a particular form and expression of Christianity.

I have in mind the kind of Christianity that resists the critique of itself, but is addicted to the judgment and critique of others; that ignores new scientific realities and laws, but is obsessed with its own law of literal biblical interpretation; that disregards that its idea of salvation is built upon a ghastly and primitive presupposition and demand for blood sacrifice, and infuses this presupposition into its interpretation of the gospels using a judicial interpretation filtered through the Middle Ages.[17] The kind that thinks it's exempt from the development of religious ideas and cultural influence because it takes refuge in the doctrine of revelation, excusing it from normal rules of engagement; that forgets that its foundations rest upon an Earth-centered worldview and cosmology, yet stubbornly thinks its message and inner logic are relevant and complete as they could be, even in a universe observed by the Hubble Space Telescope (remember Galileo?). The kind that contorts itself to explain how and why people who die in non-Christian cultures go to hell, even though they could never have heard the words "accept Jesus as your personal lord and savior," much less have heard and chosen to believe something else.

These are just some of the attitudes that have been tried and found deeply wanting in certain kinds of Christian communities—and we haven't touched on attitudes regarding sexuality, stem-cell research, the expanding universe, evolutionary evidence in geological formations, or the role of biochemistry in human consciousness or DNA.[18] So, flummoxed by the frictions of faith in our postmodern world, we wonder: What would it be like to rid ourselves once and for all of this creaky faith in God? We ponder before the depths: Who would I be if I tore down the religious edifice I inhabit?

DEALING WITH THE DIFFERENCES

You may be thinking, *With a Christian friend like you, who needs an enemy?* But I love Christ and the Christian tradition deeply, and take my task to be like that of a spiritual doctor, who very much desires to rid the patient of toxins. From the contemplative perspective, the primary toxin infecting Christianity is the idol of rationality. Now, I love reason. I use it to think and write. I value its contribution to medicine, communication, nutrition, and transportation.

However, Christianity was never meant to live on the rich, heart-hardening diet of scientific-rationalism alone. It was designed to live on the rarified purity of bread and water, which is faith and experience. This is one reason why Jesus said, "I am the bread of life" (John 6.35) and "living water" (John 4.3–15). He knew the essence of Christianity would need to be an inner taste of spiritual relationship.

Jesus could have said: "I am the final proof," or "I am the cogent argument," or "I am the scientific formula," or "I am the inerrant book from heaven." But he didn't. Instead, he said: I'll give you my Spirit "who will lead you into all truth" (John 16.12–15). And this truth is personal: "I am the way, the truth and the life" (John 14.6). In other words, Christ is the "I am," a personal experience, a relationship that will lead us to participate in the Divine life of God; this, too, is the essence of contemplative Christianity.

Lately, some of Christianity's fiercest critics, such as Richard Dawkins and Christopher Hitchens, have claimed in their books[19] that the form Christianity has taken in the modern world has been tried, found wanting, and dangerous. Regardless of their bully-pulpit bile and anti-God gall, these critics are useful, because they are at least honest in their critiques. And such self-reflective honesty is something we Christians are often not very good at, even though we desperately need it for our own development.

It's true that such books are less about Christianity in particular and more about what the authors see as the most self-evident of all truths: that we no longer need God or monotheism to explain things. To them, God is just one more needless complexity in the equation. But not all of Christianity gets a critic's blood up. It's a *certain kind* of Christianity. If a criticism can be leveled at some of these recent screeds, it's that the writers tend to lump a diverse multiplicity of faith expressions into one, fundamentalist stew, which is not only bad science but worse sociology. Frankly, if Christianity were as monolithic as some atheists and cultural observers make it out to be, I'd run far and fast from the faith, too!

Thankfully, however, I know diverse forms of Christian faith very distinct from the kind these people criticize. Unfortunately, the dominant response to atheistic critiques comes from Evangelicals, who possess a strong network and even more powerful means of getting their message out through popular media outlets, blogs, and publishing houses, not to mention political clout. Take, for example, the bestselling Evangelical book, *Reason for God.*[20] The very title says everything about the book's methodology and philosophy. It tells you that Evangelicals are responding in kind, and the kind is rationalistic, intellectual, scientific.

It's my belief that the answer to the supposed irrationalism of Christianity cannot and must not be in kind—Christianity baptized in cogent rational, scientific arguments; more Athens in Jerusalem. The answer is not a retreat to a savvier and intellectually beefy fundamentalism. The academic bastions of modernity no longer need Christianity to explain anything. To them, Christianity is just one more book in the library of human development and cultural expression that ushered in the autonomous rational, scientific mind.[21]

The simple truth is that Christianity can't keep up with scientific rationalism. But then it was never meant to. Christianity's very being and essence is different. It moves beyond the rational level of consciousness that so typifies the industrialized, scientific, modern era. St. Paul said the gospel was foolishness to the Greeks—that is, to the thinkers (1 Corinthians 1.23). And St. Augustine wrote in his *Confessions* that "I had to leave the philosophers for the love of Thee."[22] In other words, Christianity is not a pre-rational faith, it is trans-rational, and that is one of Freud's fundamental errors. According to Ken Wilber, Freud confused *pre* with *trans*, something Wilber calls the "Pre–Trans Fallacy."[23] What Wilber means is that contemplative Christianity is not a return to a pre-cognitive, infantile state, but rather retains the rational and then supersedes it, moving farther into the heights of Divine being and human consciousness where we know as we are known and where it is "I, and not I but Christ in me" (Galatians 2.20).

In my opinion, therefore, Christians should resist the temptations of trying to defend their faith against science and technology. For the lack of a Christian response is only a problem if you think its one! "Rejection" and "loss of prominence" are not things we need to cry about or fight against, contrary to what so many Christian organizations and leaders tell us. *That is a mission based on a false premise that Christianity was to be the dominant cultural power. From a contemplative perspective, the Christian church is the bride of Christ, not the queen of culture.*

Furthermore, at its heart, Christianity is an inner experience of the mystery of God's loving presence and action experienced in relationship through Christ by the power of the Spirit in word, sacrament, and through the disciplines of prayer, fasting, charity, solitude, and silence—to name a few. Everything else that happened as a result of Christendom and all our cultural power during the modern era was gravy, and now the gravy train has ended.

Thankfully, history has provided stunning samples of Christian contemplatives and mystics who didn't leave Christianity and were found by God in deeper ways than they ever could have imagined. A case in point is Pascal, who at the age of thirty-one wrote in his journal on Monday, November 23, 1654:

From about half past ten in the evening until half past mid-night . . . Fire
. . . God of Abraham, God of Isaac, God of Jacob, not of philosophers and
scholars. Certitude, certainty, heartfelt joy, peace. God of Jesus Christ. God of
Jesus Christ! Joy . . . joy . . . joy, tears of joy.[24]

The experience transformed Pascal and he retreated for three weeks in solitude and prayer. He dedicated his life to spiritual writing and abandoned scientific pursuits. At his death in August 1662, family members found sewn into his
jacket a paper with the above quote. He had kept it beside his heart.

This brings us back to why I think the perspectives of contemplative Christianity can bring Christianity *to* Christianity. As restless Christians are addressed
by a different kind of Christianity—contemplative Christianity—healing will
occur. At present, many are seeking to find their way through the chaos. Some
discover Emergent churches where their former dissonance with Christianity is
eased; others journey toward Catholicism or Orthodoxy; and some simply leave
for Eastern pastures.

Like those generations who've gone before us, we too must listen to the Spirit
and discern the wisest ways in which we can continue to bear witness to the truth
that "the Lord is not here, but has risen" (Luke 24.5), and simultaneously Jesus'
entreaty to remember: "I am with you always, to the end of the age" (Matthew
28.20). The mystery is in how Christ is with us always. It lessens when we experience Christ in others and then, with holy wonder and humility, in us.

Surely, we who have at the heart of our story the confession that "the Word
became flesh" (John 1.14), should understand and embrace the human quest to
experience the presence of God. Unfortunately, many of us have neglected our
tradition's treasure—God's interior, personal presence, and our participation in
manifesting this presence in personal ways. It's neglected because we're distracted
by modernity pressing us to explain our faith in a scientific way. It's time to
release ourselves from this pressure of rationality and reclaim the story of God's
unfolding presence, which is the story of contemplative Christianity, and the
heart of God, who is All in All.

CONCLUSION

IN ALL THINGS GOD

———◄○►———

My concern is that Evangelicals have not paid anything like the necessary attention
to this major theme of Christian life and thought. As a result, Evangelicalism has become
impoverished where it ought to be rich. . . . I wish to suggest that the time has come to . . .
move toward the development and rediscovery of spiritualities that will complement the great
Evangelical emphasis of the sufficiency of scripture, the centrality of the death of Christ,
the need for personal conversion and the evangelistic imperative.

—ALISTER MCGRATH[1]

For from God and through him and to him are all things.

—ROMANS 11.36

I say, "You are gods, children of the Most High, all of you. . . ."

—PSALM 82.6

LTHOUGH WE BELIEVE that the presence of God was consummated
in a full and unique way in Jesus Christ, we also believe that the presence
of God did not stop with Jesus. The presence of God continues through
individuals who become the body of Christ in the world. We can, as relational
vessels of Spirit, manifest in word and deed the power and presence of God. To
put this as simply as possible: our spirituality is relationality.

Trinitarian relationality is the theological center and source of contemplative
Christian spirituality, and our hope for all present and future human endeavor and
relationships. It's the reason we can perceive God in all things. From the deepest

levels of quantum existence to the farthest reaches of the universe, reality is in relationship to and within itself. God is the Source of this relating, for God is the relationship of all relationships. The word "God" really means relationship. God is a relationship—Father, Son, and Spirit—and relationality is what God is and does.

The great popularity of spirituality reveals the human longing for meaning at the heart of reality, of which humanity is an exquisite participant. St. Paul illustrates this longing in his address from "Mars Hill" to the people of Athens. Athenians' spirituality was open and tolerant of many deities, even to the point of creating an altar with the inscription, "to the unknown God." During his address, Paul illuminates why the human spiritual dynamic operative in our own generation is unique and universal:

> From one ancestor, [God] made all nations to inhabit the whole Earth, and [God] allotted the times of their existence and the boundaries of the places where they would live, so that they would search for God and perhaps grope for [God] and find [God]—though indeed [God] is not far from each one of us. (Acts 17.26–27)

The crucial insight from this text is that our time (generation) and space (location) are bound up in the human search for God (relationship) and intrinsically affect the development of spirituality. Thus, every generation everywhere must realize that things are the way they are so that in each moment of history (time) and in that situation (space) humans will seek God (relationship). This insight comes with a question: What is our life-situation at the beginning of the third millennium? From a contemplative Christian perspective, our time and space are marked by a heightened interconnectivity of mediated presence.

THE AGE OF PRESENCE

Our age reveals profound relational needs and confusion: the rise of religious terrorism; the emergence of a global, technological, commercial culture and economy; the increasing complexity of a spiritually collaged culture; and the instant human connectivity through satellite and other communication networks. Are we living in an age of presence?

On the one hand, we're present to one another in immediate and virtually unrestrained ways as never before. Consequently, I believe that articulating a theology of God's presence will help us reframe our purpose, individually and in community. A theology of the presence of God can help us rethink our missional endeavors, our spiritual authenticity, and eco-ecclesiastical stewardship— in short, our apostolicity, relevancy, and integrity. On the other hand, this age of presence leaves us longing for deeper intimacy (love), for enduring community (relationships), and for meaningful legacies (purpose). Our global technological and economical connectivity has only heightened the sense of separation we feel spiritually, psychologically, socially, and environmentally.

The contemplative Christian message addresses this four-dimensional sense of separation. It teaches that the sense of separation we feel can be healed when we remember our true nature as sons and daughters of God, receive the gift demonstrated and offered by Jesus, and return home to the presence of God by the Spirit who forms Christ in us. In this journey, a powerful healing and re-ordering begins to occur in all dimensions of our humanity, so much so that God shines through us, to one another and the world, so that, in the words of St. Paul, "we may be filled with all the fullness of God" (Ephesians 3.19).

In this way, the goal of "salvation" is no longer just getting what we need to go to heaven to be with God. Rather, it's about what God has done in Christ by the Spirit to be with us. It means that God gives to us our spiritual inheritance in Christ by the Spirit, here and now. This is the God who is here by the Spirit forming Christ in us, who is our light, life, love, and Lord: "Be not afraid. I am with you to the end of the age" (John 6.20, Matthew 28.20). We consent, Lord, and with the Psalmist sing: "You show me the path of life. In your presence, is fullness of joy" (Psalm 16.11a), and this pathway is prayer.

Prayer is the uplinking of our consciousness with God. It's an organic, networked, relational reality available to humankind. In this age of presence, the unspoken language of silence in prayer might just be what unites us most deeply. Because Jesus taught us to use words to pray, we can use the matrix of the first four petitions of the Lord's Prayer to chart a contemplative interpretation for what could be an age of presence and prayer. In the following section, we proceed along four tracks: 1) centeredness and connectedness; 2) love and wholeness;

3) time and transformation; 4) attention and surrender. I mentioned earlier that the inner room Jesus invites us into in prayer is the heart, which is the center of our being. These reflections should be read in light of his idea.

CENTEREDNESS AND CONNECTEDNESS

From the Lord's Prayer taught by Jesus (Matthew 6) we discover much about our spiritual community and spiritual Source. Jesus begins his teaching very simply: when you pray, say this: "Our Father. . . ." These two profound words convey the essence of contemplative Christian community. "Our" is the circumference of community. "Father" is the *center* of being. Combined, "Our Father" is the deepest relational *connection* available to humanity.

"Our" is plural. Yet this "we" includes many individuals comprising the community. Diversity is the natural flourishing of love. Love doesn't keep to itself. In the case of the Father's love, it manifests in community, imbuing individuals with a "new life." Jesus spoke of the historical evidence of the flourishing power of Divine love as "being born from above" (John 3.3). This means that the love of God awakens us further into consciousness, which is represented by light. Thus, "the life of Christ was the light of all people. The light shines in the darkness, and the darkness has not overcome it" (John 1.4–5).

An increase of consciousness, wisdom, and meaning in our lives comes from "above"—that is, from a direct and personal communion with God who is the center of the community. Jesus demonstrated this for us and we're called to replicate it. While "our" is communal, it becomes personal in the silence of our heart's surrendered "yes" to the closeness of Divine love as manifested by Christ. Keep requesting, and the door to Divine love is opened to us, allowing the Spirit to bring the personal closeness of God. Recall that Jesus' life was changed when he received the gift of the Spirit in his baptism, at which time he also heard the life-giving words: "This is my beloved, with whom I am well pleased" (Matthew 3.17). Under this knowledge and voice of love, we too will come under different influences that will transform our life as it did Jesus'.

For many in our time the word "Father" has become problematic. In part, that difficulty is right, because God isn't a father in the classic image of an old white man with a grey beard sitting on a throne in heaven. If that *is* God the father, then I also don't want that God. Old images of God need to be released as unworkable and confusing. Thankfully, cosmology is doing just that. Images from space teach us vast information about the nature of "Father" and our relationship to and with this Source of life and light and love.

What "Father" means is better conveyed by the word *Abba*, which I take to mean "loving, personal Source." In Abba, we see the generative essence of being and becoming, and this transcends all gender. Abba is personal love, communication, and wisdom as-is and becoming what has hitherto not yet been. The universe expanding is a good image to describe the being and becoming of Abba.

In the word *Abba*, we have relationality, with its invitation to being; communication, with its invitation to love; and wisdom, with its invitation to transformation. We also have a declaration that human existence has meaning. Over against systems that ignore the vertical world and ascribe purpose only on the horizontal plane of history, and the impersonal energy of evolution as the only source of being and becoming, Abba represents the personal experience of a different kind of life available beyond just the principles of success and survival. Abba-Life offers us a community wherein we can develop together more fully in love and consciousness—not just for survival, but for the transformation of our species under the template of Christ, who calls us into his life to be "conformed to the image of the son" (Romans 8), and "participants of the divine nature" (2 Peter 1.4). When this transformation begins to take root in vast numbers of the human community, we'll start to realize the prophetic hope of "a new heavens and a new Earth" (Revelation 21.1). Thus, "thy kingdom come," actually means "thy community of consciously chosen life and love." But we're getting ahead of ourselves.

LOVE AND WHOLENESS

In a world longing for love, the community of Christ must not only have a demonstrative personality of love, but an integral, unconditional love. We often set conditions for love. The ideas we have lead to judgments, which don't lead to love, but often to fear, anger, frustration, and separation. The gospel in one word is love and this *love* can bring *wholeness*.

Unconditional love demands the release of the false self and an awakening to the Christ nature we partake in (2 Peter 1.4). The release of the false self—whether the individual or composite false self of the community—is an important part of the process as we're transformed into the image of Christ. Only God's love is without conditions and perfect, a love that casts out fear. Our task as the community of God is to seek to decondition our love. The fewer conditions we have before we love someone the more we will be the presence of God in our world.

For some, the circle is very small and few people are allowed into the circle of love. Others may have larger circles, and therefore more people are encircled as "lovable." In Christ, we're invited to expand our perimeters of love so that our love is more and more subsumed by the infinitely expanding love of God. I think this is what the Apostle John is trying to communicate when he instructed us to "love one another" (1 John 4.7–12).

But having greater love for others than for ourselves doesn't mean that love permits *anything*. We must be both loving *and* holy. Interestingly, only one adjective describing God is repeated three times in the scriptures. It's not love, but "holy, holy, holy" (Isaiah 6.3). Love brings life. Divine love is the relational action of God for our transformation into life. Holiness brings light. Divine holiness is the relational action of God for our transformation into light. Thus our God is both loving and holy simultaneously—that is, full of love and light.

The community of Christ must be at once loving and holy, never compromising the reality that we are a community of people who've been "rescued from the power of darkness and transferred into the kingdom of Christ, in whom we have redemption, the forgiveness of sins" (Colossians 1.13–14). We are a people in whom life and light have occurred by the power of God's love and holiness. This is deeply humbling and produces the fruit of humility and gentleness.

The word "holy" also conveys the idea of "wholeness." It's in this dimension where we see the healing available in our union with Christ. When we pray the Lord's Prayer and say "hallowed be thy name," we're accessing the integrating wholeness of God's life, light, and love and requesting this wholeness to be and become the overarching dynamic in our lives. As the first petition, we're placing ourselves under Divine wholeness, which will further enable us later to live into the intentions for higher influences (daily bread), release us from the law of cause and effect (forgiveness of debt), and protect us from aimless and destructive primal impulses (lead us not into temptation).

God is holy, and in this holiness we're made whole. Holiness isn't just moral sanctity; it's also psychological and spiritual completeness. As self-developing beings, we were created with the freedom to be transformed more into the image of Christ, and in this development, we literally can experience not just transformation of knowledge, but of our level of being. Many church fathers, like Irenaeus and Athanasius, summed it up nicely: "God became man, so that we might become God." Or, as St. Paul puts it: so that Christ might be "all in all" (Colossians 1.19).

For this to occur, human beings will need to experience a significant transformation of being, but not on our own. The template and path were provided by Jesus, who at each stage of his human development was faithful in his "sonship" to Abba (Luke 3.22–23).[2]

TIME AND TRANSFORMATION

The Jewish theologian Martin Buber once said he wasn't a Christian because Jesus wasn't the Messiah for whom the Jews had waited. For Jews, the final goal of the Messiah is the redemption of Israel and of the world. Buber went on to state that to accept Jesus as such would "contradict the deepest meaning of our Messianic passion. In our view redemption occurs forever, and none has yet occurred. Standing, bound and shackled, in the pillory of [humankind], we demonstrate with the bloody body of our people the unredeemedness of the world. . . ."[3]

The ongoing presence of sin, suffering, and the general unredeemed state of the world after Jesus is a serious theological problem. Clearly, Jesus' death and resurrection, while revolutionary, didn't eradicate the power and presence of sin, sickness, death, suffering, and evil. Historical evidence bears this out. So does our own personal experience of the human condition. All pontificators who speak of "living your best life now" from spires of power and privilege need to be humble. In fact, humility is daily bread for all people, pontiff or not. The kingdom of God has little to do with power, success, wealth, and glory. It is about experiencing transformation through love so as to die to self and be alive to God (Romans 6.1–10), indeed to be full of God—even if such transformation requires suffering.

Because of the reality of the unredeemedness of the world, we need to take Jesus' instructions on prayer very seriously, especially the petitions for the future, and pray "thy kingdom come" and "deliver us from evil." Jesus understood that despite the centrality of his life, death, resurrection, and ascension for humanity, his contribution, as recorded in the gospel passion stories, wouldn't eradicate the power and presence of sin. Thus, he urges us to pray for the only reality that will—the coming kingdom of God—and for protection from the dynamics that lead to evil, personally and globally.

Every time we pray "thy kingdom come" we stand with the Jews and anyone and anything that has suffered under violence, injustice, and the inescapable gravity of the world's unredeemedness. We affirm the incongruency of current affairs, but hold the indomitable hope for the Divine presence that matters to show its final hand—the Royal Flush of redemption. Jesus was certainly the ace up God's sleeve that even the finest-educated Jewish rabbis of his day didn't see coming. There's more to come as well, and this second coming through you and me will be part of the dramatic flushing out of such powers that grip the human condition and keep it enslaved to sin and sleep and "the terror of the situation."[4] And so we pray, "Lord, have mercy," and also "let the second incarnation begin—in you and me by the power of the Spirit."

The fact that we are to pray for the kingdom to come is evidence that Jesus knew he represented the kingdom's presence in part, but not in full. He understood that there was incongruency, something we explore more deeply in our next reflection, when we consider the second part of this petition: pray "thy kingdom come, thy will be done on Earth as it is in heaven."

The kingdom of God is a symbol for the "rule" or "reign" of God that will occur in its totality sometime in the future. Jesus was like the first buds of spring announcing that the fullness of summer was coming. The development of things requires *time*, which is one reason the Jewish people are still waiting. We wait with them, and we can all join in the solidarity of hope for the fruits of transformation in the future.

There's a reason God's revelation did not begin with Jesus. God began by call-ing Abraham into a people and later giving Moses the law. Surely it would have been easier to just start with the Son instead of the Law? Certainly it could have saved a lot of trouble and time. Such ideas demonstrate that a developmental process is involved, a readiness revealed in the unfolding relationship between the mind of God and humankind.

Step by step, we emerge into a deeper, fuller knowledge of the Divine plan: its relationality; its interconnectedness. It's a dance of being to Being, unfolding through the cosmos. We get so caught up in our questions about who God is that we forget what God is asking us: Who will you be? This leads us in time to *transformation.*

Who will we be? What if human beings began to wake up to the role they play in their own personal transformation? What if religion ceased being the power that divides and began to "bind" us back in the love of God and one another? What if we began to understand the gifts of "salvation" both spiritually and psychologi-cally? How many of us are mature in faith, but immature in human development? What if we began to self-observe in such a way that we saw our own patterns of negative emotions, mechanical reactivity, and unconscious appetite and passions driving us to be and do and get and have even at the expense of others or the Earth? How does that phrase go? The light shines in the darkness.

Consciousness enlightened by the ongoing reality and presence of Christ is this light. What if Christianity were less about knowing the right beliefs and more about being transformed further into and by the light of Christ? Would this not speed the evolution of human development beyond the levels of regres-sion, aggression, and division that have marked our cultural history? What does it say that Christian countries killed over one hundred million people in just two of the many wars during the twentieth century alone? What does it say that churches continue to fight, divide, and split over countless issues?

And just how might this connect with Jesus' revolutionary announcement that "the kingdom of God is within you" (Luke 17.21)? It was Rainer Maria Rilke who suggested that we think of God as a direction rather than as an object. Thinking of God as an object has been the source of much human suffering. So, too, it would be wise to think of the kingdom of God as a direction we're moving toward, yet are also within. We are spiritual pilgrims embodied on the way in this earthly experience, invited to become something more than we ever could imagine—sons and daughters of God—in a transformative surrender to ultimate love, which is and must be the standard, rule, and reign behind, beneath, and beyond all things. The experience in and of this love and justice is what we anticipate when we pray "thy kingdom come" in me and everywhere else where people stop resisting its presence and power.

ATTENTION AND SURRENDER

The third petition of the Lord's Prayer conveys the incongruence between our human condition and the Divine intention for the human dimension. This incongruence is concisely defined by Jesus: "Thy will be done on Earth as it is in heaven." If there were congruence, the petition would be unnecessary. Because the Divine will isn't naturally done on Earth by human beings, we are to pray not just that it will be done, but also that it's done on Earth as it is in heaven. We'll first explore the concept of "will" and then consider it in light of Jesus' cosmology, deepening our understanding of what is meant by the words "heaven" and "Earth."

Will occurs with the fusion of thoughts, emotions, and physical movement. When these three centers of human activity come together, the event is called willing. Our human will is what enables us to pursue what we desire and want. Desires and wants are often grounded in our emotional center, where we're attracted or repulsed by what we love, want, need, fear, or hate. This is often a response to a particular felt emotional need or situation, such as fear, lack, or longing.

For example, a famous person whom you've admired for many years sits next to your table in a restaurant. For fun, let's say it is Bono, lead singer of the band U2. You notice you have a desire to talk to Bono, but you're nervous and don't want to be rude. One part of you says, "Go for it;" another part of you says, "Don't bother Bono, he has enough on his mind." What's happening is that you're experiencing a conflict of desires, and desires can often impact you emotionally (feeling excited), intellectually (remembering all the words to your favorite song, "With or Without You"), and physically (sweating palms, nervous stomach). Curiously, whether you act on your desire or don't, both choices are actions of the will.

When we pray that God's will be done, we're both requesting and surrendering. We're requesting that God further act toward fulfilling God's desires for human flourishing. We're giving *attention* to a particular wish. We're also *surrendering* to participate in this Divine flourishing of humankind. When human beings act on their will, great things can occur. In a similar way, as spiritual beings in Christ, we're invited to surrender our will to Christ for our daily living.

We're asking God to bring our thoughts, feelings, and physicality under the attention, authority, and direction of the living Word of God, who is Christ. The living Word of God united with the human Jesus and enabled him to do the Father's will, even in the face of severe temptation and suffering. From Jesus' life, we learn that the fulfillment of the petition that "God's will be done" begins with individuals. This is a very personal surrender, and in weighty matters, requires solitude, prayer, and at times, agony (Luke 22.43).

Now, let us briefly explore Jesus' cosmology, which is summarized by the statement "on Earth as it is in heaven" (Matthew 6.11). In various ancient passages, a ladder connects heaven and Earth. This ladder is a symbol for the chain of Divine influences that have been revealed and provided to humanity for our further flourishing in the Divine desires, one of which is that we "be fruitful and multiply" (Genesis 1.28). Interpreted spiritually and psychologically, this means: You are capable of higher development—grow in the soil of grace!

Another Divine desire is "to love the Lord your God with your whole being and your neighbor as yourself" (Luke 10.27). The scriptures reveal many such Divine desires and this revelation is symbolized by the ladder from which higher influences, or grace and truth, descend upon humanity to help us in our spiritual evolution and development. The cross is the consummate ladder spanning the vertical dimension between heaven and Earth and the horizontal dimension between desires and will. After the cross, the ladder is ignited by the flames of the Spirit at Pentecost, and the spoken word becomes the primary means of linking the intentions of heaven with the conditions of Earth.

A compelling interpretation of the word "heaven" is that it refers to the highest expression of Divine intention and action: that's to say, where the presence of God is; where love, worship, community, justice, and beauty happen instinctively, naturally, and spontaneously. Psychologically, heaven and Earth aren't just physical places, but actually inner states of being. In this light, the higher state of being that is heaven reaches out in grace to the lower states of being through various means of grace and experiences, such as the Lord's Supper and Centering Prayer, to bring a greater inner correspondence between the higher and the lower: thus, the image of the ladder as a symbol of the means of grace.

Let's also remind ourselves of Jesus' nocturnal conversation with Nicodemus in the Gospel of John, where Jesus' spiritual and psychological cosmology is further revealed. Jesus instructed Nicodemus that "you must be born from above" (John 3.3). When this new, second birth occurs, a transformation of being occurs. The old person diminishes and the new person emerges. In other words, the person by higher, heavenly intentions comes into being, even to such an extent that St. Paul could declare that "the old has gone and the new has come" (2 Corinthians 5.17), meaning less Earth and more heaven—spiritually and psychologically speaking. This is the essence of inner transformation: as it is above, so let it become below.

The more aware we are of what and when we are desiring, the more clearly we'll see where we need the Holy Spirit to "create in me a clean heart, O Lord" (Psalm 51.10). This will allow us to begin to desire in ways that foster doing the Lord's will, not just our own—and being the Lord's servant, not just our own master. He taught us to pray saying, "thy will be done on Earth as it is in heaven," which is the vision for a relational/spiritual community in harmony with the Earth.

RELATIONAL, CONTEMPLATIVE CHRISTIANITY

The message of this book is an attempt to provide a compelling bridge between the doctrinal, religious Christianity of the past, and a contemplative Christian spirituality of the future.

This contemplative Christianity will be grounded in spiritual practices such as Centering Prayer, and culminate with the transformation of individuals who bear a different kind of Christianity to Christianity, through the personal experience of God's love, presence, and action in their lives and communities. The urgency for such a bridge is intensified by the global context. The increasingly interconnected web of human community and deepening awareness of our relationship to all things, especially the Earth and one another, are the primary drivers for humanity to rediscover the value of its contemplative spiritualities.

I've attempted to address what is perceived to be an increasing apprehension among Christians about how to *be* Christian. The worldwide Christian church—in all its diverse expressions and embodiments, paradoxes and problems—is the vehicle Christ is using to increasingly manifest the presence of God in our world. Yes, it's a world of pain and paradox: a world Flannery O'Connor once described as a place "we cherish at the same time struggle to endure."[5] In the midst of this world's cultures, disasters, joys, deaths, beliefs, and hymns to countless altars and nameless gods is the Christian story and community, challenged more than ever to articulate its relevancy and connectivity to the particular angst and pleasures of postmodern life. In such a world and time, it's good for us to reclaim a relational, contemplative spirituality, whereby the human community participates in God's loving presence as further incarnations of Christ by grace, through the power of the Holy Spirit to and in the world.

Relational, contemplative spirituality is grounded in the wisdom of fourth-century theologians who articulated God's relational nature, as a being-in-relationship, and the One who is in relationship to and with all that is. This ancient affirmation is now also a very postmodern insight, sustained and explained further by the new physics. The relational nature of God was demonstrated in Jesus the Christ. Jesus reminded the world that God cannot be separated from humanity, nor can humanity be separated from God. That is the essence of the story and life of Jesus. It can be our story and life, too.

There are no easy answers or relationships in our world. However, we must continue to face its tragedy with tears and sorrow, comfort and empathy; enjoy its comedy, paint its beauty, sing its glory, dance and act upon every stage we can, proclaiming in words, books, museums, universities, libraries, factories, and in towers of power that life is indeed meaningful and beautiful because of what Christ by the Spirit is continuing in and through us: redeeming, recreating, and filling us with the abundant relational life and love of God.

We must embrace the future with courage; be the church until the end of the ages. This is no time to give up or dissolve into a pop-culture fog of accommodation. Though strength and wisdom are gained from the church fathers and classics, a fearful retreat into the past is *not* the answer, either. We're called to push forward in a dynamic action of faith, learning from our past but not hiding in it. Life is pulsing forward. Faith wants to flourish! Therefore, let us be the brave people who know their vocation to be one of incarnational living—a life of consent whereby God, through Christ and by the Spirit, is here with, in, and through us individually and communally.

Let us be a courageous global community that moves into this world with deep love and awakened presence, entering into the mysterious and frightening future with all the energy of our minds, all the creativity of our imagination, and all the humility, love, hope, faith, wisdom, power, and silence of our suffering-yet-risen Lord, who remains with us by his Creation and People, Word and Sacrament, Silence and Spirit. On this journey, we hold in our hearts the vision of St. John, who saw deeply into God's future, and returned to cheer us on:

> Beloved, we are God's children now; what we will be has not yet been revealed. What we do know is this: when he is revealed, we will be like him, for we will see him as he is. (1 John 3.2)

Amen.

Appendix A

THE RELATIONALITY OF GOD

A Reflection on the Nicene Creed

————◄O►————

T THE CENTER of the Christian tradition are two confessions that, at first, seem contradictory: God was with us in history as the person of Jesus the Christ, and after Jesus' ascension God continues with us by the person and power of the Holy Spirit. The physicist Niels Bohr summarized this kind of apparent contradiction when he suggested that "[There are] two sorts of truth: trivialities, where opposites are obviously absurd, and profound truths, recognized by the fact that the opposite is also a profound truth." In the discussion of God's presence, we're dealing with a profound truth: the mystery of relationality.[1] During the last hundred years or so, new insights in cosmology, biology, ecology, psychology, neurology, philosophy, and sociology—to name a few disciplines—have expanded our understanding of our universe, ourselves, and our interconnectedness with all of reality. *The God Who Is Here* is an attempt to apply these relational insights to Christian tradition.[2]

The Christian confession, "God was with us in the person of Jesus the Christ," is only one half of the circle. The rest is that "God continues with us by the Spirit." Jesus, as Christ, was a developmental move and leap forward in the fulfillment of God's promises and plans for humanity. Jesus, as the Christ, was God with us. This was a development in our understanding of human relationships to and with God. It continues to press forward and unfold with significant consequences and insights for human self-understanding. More importantly, it set in motion a spiritual awakening and recapitulation process that has spiraled humanity forward more fully into relationship with God.[3]

Who was Jesus the Christ, and to what degree was God present in and through him? These primary questions lie behind the claim that in Jesus the Christ dwelt the fullness of God. Furthermore, is Jesus just one among many others with the same capacity for Divine infusion, or is he somehow unique, in a different order or category? Although we're now adopted as children of God and heirs of Christ, does this mean that we share in his divinity?

At the beginning of the third millennium of Christian faith, the temptations and threats to distort the creedal assertion that Jesus was "very God of very God" abound, just as they did in the time of Arius, a presbyter of Alexandria (c. 256–336).[4] The issue now as then is whether Jesus the Christ is truly Lord and God, or only a created intermediary between God and human beings, a religious leader whose example we are to follow and adapt. At stake is the cohesion of Trinitarian faith.

Deconstructing the divinity of Jesus the Christ is intrinsically an assault on Trinitarian faith. Father, Son, and Spirit are not just linguistic expressions of the "One, true God," or metaphors that attempt to communicate the unknowable. Rather, they are revealed names that communicate the content, history, and relationality of who God has been, is, and will be for us and our salvation. At a time when the Christian community could be resourcing its Trinitarian faith for relevant connections with a spiritually curious culture, Christian churches remain functionally unitarian in practice, mission, language, and liturgy.[5]

We're not Trinitarian Christians because it's a convenient theological structure or easy to understand; nor because interesting Trinitarian analogies abound in human experience (Augustine's Love, Loved, Loving, etc).[6] We're Trinitarian Christians because Jesus the Christ, our Lord and Savior, reveals to us the intrinsic Triune relationality that God the Father, through Christ the Son in the power of the Holy Spirit, are one being-in-relationship. We're Trinitarian Christians because the witness of scripture again and again bears forth the reality that only paradoxical language can describe: that God is "one being, in three persons."[7]

Trinitarian paradoxical language bloomed during the great theological debates of the fourth century. From the crucible of these theological (and often political) debates, the Nicene Creed (325) emerged as the preeminent expression of Trinitarian orthodoxy. Although from time to time, alternative understandings and beliefs threatened the widespread acceptance of the Nicene Creed, Trinitarian orthodoxy prevailed, so that today the Nicene is the most ecumenical of Christian creeds. With the exception of Eastern Orthodoxy's rejection of the *filioque* clause (the Spirit proceeds from the Father *and the Son*), the Nicene Creed is accepted and confessed by Roman Catholics, Eastern Orthodox, and most Protestant Christian traditions.[8]

As early as the third century, the theologian Tertullian (c.160–c.225) coined the phrase, "three persons, one substance" in an attempt to convey the fullness of the gospel of Jesus Christ, and to protect it from Gnosticism and Marcionism—philosophical and theological movements that distended the relationship between God the Father and Jesus Christ.[9]

The debate, however, is rooted in the ideas of Arius. Arius asserted that Jesus Christ, the Word of God, was *not* coeternal with God the Father, as the Arian motto summed up: "There was a time when [Christ] was not." At stake was the very divinity of Christ. Was Christ a mere creation, albeit a primary and preeminent creation, yet nonetheless the first-born of creation? Or was Christ, as Athanasius (d. 373), Bishop of Alexandria, countered, truly Divine, uncreated and coeternal with God the Father? Arius' argument was logical: if Christ was also divine, then there were two gods, making Christians polytheists. Yet from the time of the Apostles, the church had confessed and worshiped Christ as God.

Bishop Athanasius condemned Arius' position. In response, Arius solicited other bishops and congregations, and soon gained enough support to stimulate public protests and letters to Constantine (306–337), the pseudo-Christian emperor. By 325, the theological conflict had polarized the region, threatening political and ecclesiastical stability. A council was called for in Nicaea, forty miles southeast of Constantinople. The council didn't solve all the problems. Further tensions emerged, and by 381 it was apparent another council was needed. This council convened in Constantinople, ultimately the capital of Byzantine culture and commerce. There, the divines finalized the confession's form. They anathematized Arius and his position and agreed with Athanasius. Thus, the Nicene Creed developed in two stages, first at the Council of Nicaea, where the basic structure was formulated in response to Arius' theological proposals, and second, at the Council of Constantinople, where further theological and pastoral insights clarified the orthodox position.[10]

The Nicene Creed declares and embodies the Christian understanding of the triune God: "We believe in God the Father, in One Lord Jesus Christ and in the Holy Spirit." It is structured in a Trinitarian way: three paragraphs, one confession. The entire confession begins and is propelled by a verb of faith, "We believe. . . ." *We* represents the community of faith, the people of God. It embodies the ecumenical reality of this creed in particular and Christian faith in general. "We believe" embodies both the community and the individual. The *I* is bound up in the historic confession of the *We* that was proclaimed and received by the *We*.

From *We to We*, the gospel is articulated and the church lives on. Within the *We* is the *I*, and so out of the many, there is one, and in the one there are many. The paradoxical *We* in *I*, and *I* in *We* bears witness to the inner reality of God: that God is three persons, one being: Father, Son, and Holy Spirit. *We*, the people of God, the body of Christ are *We*, yet *I*; *I*, yet *We*, and as a *We*, we believe, first together, bound up with those who have confessed and believed before us as the "cloud of witnesses," and then as an *I*.

We *believe*: the *ipsissima verba*. Belief is what the Christian community does. We believe the gospel of Jesus Christ proclaimed from *We* to *We* and *I* to *I*. We don't invent, sell, deny, distort, or dilute it. We must believe it. We're believers in God the Father, Christ the Son, and the Holy Spirit. The fullness of the gospel and the fullness of the truth are connected and organically intertwined with the intrinsic logic of the word "and": We believe in God the Father . . . *and* in one Lord Jesus Christ . . . *and* in the Holy Spirit. Bound together in a Möbius strip, a self-returning and interrelating reciprocity, God is Father, Son, and Spirit, confessed and reflected upon through the inner logic of language.[11] Note the binding and open connectivity of the word "and," coupled with and explained by the nuanced personality of prepositions: *in* God, *through* Christ, *by* the Spirit; or, *with* God the father, *through* Christ the Son, *in* the fellowship of the Holy Spirit. Such language points toward the three-in-oneness of God, and in doing so the One who is revealed is simultaneously the revealer.

Such rubrics of faith are rooted in the inner coherence of language and the logic of the Spirit. The latter, structured in language allows grammar the freedom to shape, embody, and articulate theological truths. The articulation is not invention, but reflection on the word of God. The results of prayerful and Spirit-reciprocated reflection are insights, which flow out from reflection upon the witness of scripture, and subsequently disclose the revelation of God in history, preeminently in Jesus the Christ. The Nicene confession is an extended insight embodying diverse themes and concepts from within the scriptures. "We believe" is nothing without the witness of scripture or reflection of those who've preceded us, or without the faith of the great "cloud of witnesses." In the service of insight and clarification, we believe what we confess: the Holy Spirit, the giver of life, is thrown back within the reflecting and articulating process.

The Holy Spirit is not only "confessed," but is intrinsically within the process of creating the confession. Our faith and confession are inextricably bound up within whom we confess. We confess the Father because the Father is in our confessing. We confess the Son because the Son is in our confessing. We confess the Spirit because the Spirit is in our confessing. We confess the Trinity, because the Trinity is within our confessing, and has led us, by God the Spirit, to do so.

The Nicene Creed insightfully communicates three essential theological realities of Christian faith:

- Because the Divine truly united with the human, God is truly known in the person Jesus Christ.
- Because the human was truly united with the Divine, humanity is truly healed in the person Jesus Christ.
- Because the Holy Spirit is truly Divine, humanity is lifted up into Christ by the presence and action of the Holy Spirit.

These three hinges of the confession point to the logic of the process: because Jesus is one in being with God the Father, and because the Spirit proceeds from both the Father and the Son, who God is in God-self is what God is toward us in history—eternally Father, Son, and Holy Spirit. Simply put: God is whom we experience God to be: Father, Son, and Holy Spirit.

TRINITARIAN RELATIONALITY: (I–THOU–WE)

The history of the Triune God is the history of relationality, of God in relationship with and for us. God is the God for us. We haven't willed or deserved this, but only find ourselves here and now in this relationality. To know, speak, and think of—and believe in—this God is to know, speak, think of—and believe in—the God who has been, is now, and will be in relation to us. Not because we deserve it, but because God has in freedom and in love willed this to be so.

To know God is to know the God of relationality with His creation in three dimensions: Time–Space–Relationship. To know God is not to speculate on the origin or destiny of God, nor hypothesize His activities, but to experience the God who interrelates with His creation.[12] We know no other God because there is no other God than this God who created the heavens and the Earth and all who dwell therein (Isaiah 42.5, Acts 17.24).

In the history of salvation, as revealed in, through, by, and with the written word of God, we encounter the God who is for us as the Triune God. Thus, the beginning of Christian knowledge and experience is a relationship with the Trinity of God, that is God's relationality expressed primarily in the personal touch of Divine love.[13] The relationality of God with contingent beings and creation is rooted in the Trinitarian being of God Himself. We know relationality through the Trinity and Trinity through relationality. The relationality of God is preeminently revealed through and in Jesus the Christ. The logic learned from Scripture, and interpreted throughout the years after the resurrection and ascension of Jesus the Christ, is part of a salvation history, whose beginning is rooted in the love of God for the world, expressed through the choosing of Abraham and the people of Israel. Salvation history articulates who God is to us: Father, Son, and Holy Spirit.

When Jesus said, "and if I go and prepare a place for you, I will come again and will take you to myself so where I am, there you may be also" (John 14.2–3), he wasn't speaking in terms of this world but of another world outside this one—a spiritual world where, when asked how to get there Jesus responded, "I am the way, and the truth and the life. No one comes to the Father except through me" (John 14.6). This is a radical proposition, for it links God the Father to us by means of a relationship. Jesus the Son breaks into our world as incarnation and brings God to us by the promised Spirit.

The gospel is presence and relationship and spirituality. It's not just about "getting saved" or being "declared righteous" by a "heavenly judge." At its core, the gospel is the answer to the question, Where is God? It doesn't end at Jesus' resurrection. It transitions there, and is taken to new levels of relevance and relationship with the arrival of the Spirit at Pentecost. The corollary questions are: How does the gospel become presence? How does the gospel extend into Pentecost, and therefore presence? The answer: Through our personal and communal understanding of and experience of the Trinity.

A BRIEF HISTORY OF CHRISTIAN MYSTICISM

————◇————

I
N THE BIBLICAL TRADITION, human communication with God begins in the book of Genesis in a paradisiacal garden where Adam and Eve are in direct contact with God. After the fall, and Adam and Eve's expulsion from the garden, God continues to interact with certain human beings, often giving instruction, guidance, commands, warning, and comfort. Noah is instructed to build an Ark (Genesis 6.13); Abraham talks constantly with God, and is promised a multitude of heirs (Genesis 15.2); God directly answers Rebekah's prayer (Genesis 25.23); Jacob has a vision-dream and is addressed by God during his ascent of the ladder (Genesis 28.13); God calls Moses from the fire of a burning bush (Exodus 3.4); on Mt. Sinai, Moses speaks with God and receives knowledge directly, but only sees God's backside (Exodus 33:34).

When Moses returned to his people, they thought he'd had a facial—his face is shining (Exodus 34.29)! After Moses, prophets and kings also heard from the Lord and experienced deep states of prayer. But during these years, Israel slid into idolatry, and after the Babylonians took the Israelites into captivity in 586 BCE it became rare for God to speak. So the priests turned to the writing and reading of the scriptures.

During the three hundred years preceding the birth of Christ, Judaism was profoundly shaped by Hellenism—an influence that led to new perspectives on how Jews related to God and the cosmos, and the means by which God communicated with humanity. The first new perspective was the recognition of a text as sacred. The evolution to written communication was a later development in Judaism, occurring after a long dependence upon the oral tradition and the spoken word of God. As religious texts were written and the oral tradition was codified in writing during the two hundred years before Jesus' birth, the reading and study of these sacred texts became a primary focus for spiritual formation and religious obedience. The emergence of the sacred text and the importance of interpretation for spiritual formation led to the rise of a powerful social class: learned scholars and interpreters of scripture distinct from the priesthood. We know them by their biblical name—*the scribes.*

The notion of "deeper meanings" in Jewish sacred texts was influenced by the Greek practice of seeking mystical or allegorical meanings in poems and mythic stories. This kind of interpretation in due course influenced early Christian interpretations of scripture. By the second century CE, Christian teachers such as Origen wrote of "deeper" interpretations of the Hebrew scriptures, and called them "spiritual."

The second new perspective in Judaism was the emergence of apocalyptic literature. Prior to the third and second centuries BCE, Judaism had no apocalyptic literature. A primary example is the fourteenth chapter of 1 Enoch, written in the third century BCE, in which Enoch (Genesis 5.24) tells of his ascent to heaven. According to Genesis, Enoch "walked with God," then disappeared because "God took him." What follows is the first account of a bodily ascension into heaven in Jewish literature:

> And behold I saw the clouds: And they were calling me in a vision; and the fogs were calling me; and the course of the stars and the lightnings were rushing me and causing me to desire; and in the vision, the winds were causing me to fly and rushing me high up into heaven. . . . And I observed and saw inside it [the second heavenly house] a lofty throne—its appearance was like a crystal and its wheels like the shining sun; and I heard the voice of the cherubim; and from beneath the throne were issuing streams of flaming fire. It was difficult to look at it. And the Great Glory was sitting upon it—as for his gown, which was shining more brightly than the sun, it was whiter than any snow. None of

the angels were able to come in and see the face of the Excellent and Glorious One; and no one of flesh can see him. . . . And the Lord called me with his own mouth and said to me, "Come near to me Enoch, and to my holy Word." And he lifted me up and brought me near to the gate, but I continued to look down with my face." (1 Enoch 14.8, 18–21, 24–25)[1]

This text, like the visions of Daniel and Isaiah, was, according to Bernard McGinn, "part of a wide range of revelatory literature that proliferated in the Hellenistic world at a time when traditional means of access to the will of God or the gods seem to have become problematic to many."[2] The heavenly journey of the soul and its encounter with God's voice or presence in a heavenly realm were new phenomena in the Jewish tradition. Hitherto, the Jews had answered the question of where God was found with the declaration: "In the temple!"[3]

However, when the Israelite Temple was destroyed by the Babylonians in 587 BCE, within two hundred years new Jewish concepts of both communicating with God and experiencing God's presence had emerged, replacing the older, cultic understanding of God's presence dwelling with them in the Holy of Holies of the Temple, which now lay in ruins.

Elijah (1 Kings 19, 2 Kings 2), Isaiah (Isaiah 6), and Ezekiel all had significant mystical visions. While in exile in Babylon, Ezekiel reported this vision:

There the hand of Yahweh came upon me. I looked; a stormy wind blew from north, a great cloud with light around it, a fire from which flashes of lightning darted, and in the center a sheen like bronze at the heart of the fire. In the center I saw what seemed like four animals. (Ezekiel 1.4–5)

This vision has inspired Jewish and Christian mystics throughout history and clearly influenced the imagery of the Apostle John's mystical experience, which we know as the Apocalypse of John, or Book of Revelation. What's important to notice here in connection with Ezekiel's vision is that the destruction of the Temple in McGinn's words, "paved the way for a new situation in which Ezekiel was able to experience the Divine presence in all its majesty independently of Jerusalem"[4] or the Temple. This would be the first of many significant adaptations within the evolving Jewish understanding of where God was and how one related to God.

Within four hundred years of Ezekiel's vision, another Jewish prophet would reveal even more radical concepts about how to experience God's presence. Jesus said, "I am the way, the truth and the life, no one comes to the Father except through me" (John 14.7), and "You know God, because he abides with you, and he will be in you" (John 14.17). Texts such as these led St. Paul to question, "Do you not know that you are God's temple and that God's Spirit dwells in you" (1 Corinthians 3.16)?

Even a cursory overview of the Jewish background to Christian mysticism reveals that Jewish faith and understanding were continuously evolving. Moses could never have imagined the sacrificial cult of Solomon's temple, nor could Ezekiel have imagined Jesus' radical teaching. Each unfolded, one from other, as if in sequential stages, just as a Russian nesting doll contains more than meets the eye. Judaism continuously adapted its spirituality in response to historical and cultural experiences, whether it be the influence of cultural Hellenism or the tragic and violent destruction of Solomon's Temple in 587 BCE and again, for the final time, in 70 CE. Both events radically shaped and shocked the spiritual expression and experience of Judaism and, in logical succession, Christian mysticism itself. In summary: Judaism provided fertile soil from which Christian mysticism could emerge.

Judaism and Christian mysticism are organically related to one another in at least two ways: first, through the cultivation of a sacred set of scriptures and the interpretive tools and techniques for rendering them continuously alive for the faith community; and second, through mystical ascents into heaven where prophets beheld the vision of God.[5]

We now turn to Platonism. (An extensive account here is not possible, but it's necessary to offer a basic overview of Platonism's key ideas that influenced Christian mysticism.) The Platonists believed that the soul was unbegotten and immortal, naturally Divine, and as such, the goal of life was to return to God through purification and contemplation.

Plato (420–347 BCE) viewed the soul as a searcher, restless until it permanently possessed the Absolute Good. Such possession occurred through *theoria*, or contemplation, which is the fruit of an ascending purification (*askesis*) of both love and knowledge.

Christian mysticism differs from Platonism is four major ways:

- First, the concept of God. Platonism refers to the Absolute or the Good. It doesn't have a relational God who loves humanity and offers grace to redeem us by entering into our broken human condition.
- Second, Christianity modifies the relationship of the soul to God. In Platonism, the soul ascends through contemplation and *askesis* to realize its innate divinity. In Christianity, the soul is created by God and has a kinship with the *logos* in Christ and through relationship or union with Christ, who descended to us, in order to ascend with us to the Father. In so doing, we can become participants of the Divine nature.
- Third, the understanding of the moral virtues. In Platonism, the moral virtues help purify and control the body. In Christianity, they are the fruit of the Spirit and the evidence of the indwelling union with Christ.
- Fourth, the love of Christ and the communion of the saints. In Christianity, contemplation and action are held together by love. Christian love is the love of Christ, which unites us to him and through him to one another. In Platonism, the elite philosopher pursues intellectual purification. It is the flight of the alone to the Alone. In Christianity, the final vision of the Bible is this: "And lo I beheld a great multitude" (Revelation 7.9). The communion of saints that is the church is the body of Christ.

In addition to Plato, two other thinkers also influenced the development of Christian mysticism: Philo of Alexandria (c.25 BCE–c.50 CE) and Plotinus (c. 204–270). This is a cursory overview of some of the key distinctions between Platonism and Christian mysticism. Certainly, Platonism deeply influenced the early church fathers, but they revised many of the Greek concepts in light of their experience of, relationship with, and wisdom in Christ.

From the Greek context of Plato, we turn now to the matrix of the gospels, especially Mary's personal mystical experiences as the mother of Jesus, and Jesus' own sense of God's presence. Mary has a vision-like experience, where the Angel

Gabriel converses with her, instructing her that she will have a personal encounter with the Holy Spirit who will "come upon you and the power of the Most High will overshadow you, therefore the child to be born will be holy and will be called Son of God" (Luke 1.35). Mary's special relationship with her son endured for the rest of her life, and her devotion inspired many of Jesus' earliest followers.

Jesus' public ministry begins with a mystical event at the river Jordan. At his baptism is an auditory and visual theophany: "And the Holy Spirit descended upon him in bodily form like a dove. And a voice came from heaven, you are my son, the beloved, with you I am well pleased" (Luke 3.22). Many of Jesus' miracles demonstrate his mystical relationship with God and manifest this reality in all his relationships with God, humanity, and nature.

Before we move on from Jesus, we must consider one final mystical event, and that is the Transfiguration (Matthew 17.1–8). A select group of three, Peter, James, and John, ascend a mountain to pray with Jesus and see him glorified, blazing white, talking with Moses and Elijah, overshadowed with the cloud (similar to Moses' experience on Mt. Sinai), and hear the voice again say, "This is my son, the beloved" (Matthew 11.5). These are some examples from the many mystical elements the gospels record, proving that mysticism—the immediate encounter/relationship with God manifested in trans-normal ways—is at the very foundation of Christianity.

And it continues in Jesus' disciples' lives. Consider John and Paul. John's theology, not to mention his apocalyptic visions and journeys, are profoundly mystical. John alone speaks of our relationship with Jesus in the terms, "God is love" (1 John 4.8), the *logos* made visible in creation and in Jesus (John 1.1–4). Thus, we are to love one another and "abide in Christ" (John 15.1–12). These deeply moving and mystical texts are edifying because of the inner, spiritual relationship with Christ that they convey, such as the metaphor of remaining in Christ like a branch abides in a vine. John also speaks of Jesus as the light of the world, bread of life, living water, and in the book of Revelation he gives the Christian tradition its first apocalyptic text. Like Jewish prophets before him, he ascends into heaven and sees terrifying, glorious, and unspeakable holy things.

The Apostle Paul was born Saul, and his conversion began as a mystical experience (Acts 9). En route to persecute Christians, Saul sees a blinding light, falls from his horse, and hears the voice of Jesus. The experience changes Saul's life, mission, and name: Paul. Like John, Paul has a spiritual, mystical vision, being caught up to the third heaven (2 Corinthians 12.2). His theology of union with Christ or being in Christ (1 Thessalonians 4.17, Philippians 1.23) is also deeply mystical, and of course his hymn to love in 1 Corinthians 13 is at the heart of his own experience of God's love for him in Christ. Paul is the first theologian to begin speaking consistently of God as the Father, and Christ as the Son, and also talking about the Holy Spirit and the Spirit's ongoing relationship with the believer.

These are just some of the high points of Christian mysticism in the primary players of the New Testament. I leave you with the summation of mysticism in the words of Paul from Galatians 2.19: "I have been crucified with Christ, and I live now not with my own life but with the life of Christ in me. I, not I, but Christ in me."

From the gospels and apostles, we turn to the early church fathers, beginning with Origen (ca. 185–253), who was probably the greatest figure of the third-century church. Origen believed that the purpose of the Christian life was the immediate knowledge of God by the believer, a goal hampered by the natural inability of humans to comprehend God. Nonetheless, Origen noted, God sent the *logos*, his son, as a mediator to teach us knowledge in Divine matters. For the mystics, the scriptures are an introduction to the knowledge of God. One must go above scripture and ascend to Jesus for further immediate knowledge. Ascetical practice was vitally important to aid in one's ascent. After Christianity became the officially sponsored religion of the Roman Empire after Constantine became Roman Emperor in 324 CE, Christians began fleeing to the desert wilderness where they began the first monastic communities in order to struggle to overcome the body and its passions and appetites. These Christians wanted to be God's athletes in training, focusing their entire lives on the price of knowing God, while battling temptations through buffeting the body with fasting and solitude.

Thanks to St. Athanasius's biography, *The Life of Anthony*, which greatly influenced the spread of Christian mysticism and monastic desert spirituality, St. Anthony the Great (251–356) became the most famous desert monk. An Egyptian from a wealthy, but uneducated family, Anthony sold all his possessions, gave the money to the poor, and devoted his life to spiritual discipline. After twenty years, he was led into the Divine mysteries and inspired by God. He was given Divine gifts: visions, the ability to know the future, clairvoyance, discernment, and healing powers. Many came to Anthony for help and counsel.

Augustine (354–430) was probably the most important theologian/mystic of the late church fathers. Born to a wealthy family in what is now Algeria, Augustine was educated at the Harvard of his day and was by all accounts a brilliant scholar. He was also a religious seeker. Drawn to spiritual realities early in his life, he became a Manichean, then a Neoplatonist, and then near midlife, finally converted to Christianity. Augustine was, at heart, a monastic and mystic. His spiritual autobiography, *The Confessions*, describes many of his mystical experiences, as for example, in book seven:

> With you [God] as my guide I entered into my innermost citadel, and was given power to do so because you had become my helper. I entered with my soul's eye, such as it was, saw above that same eye of my soul the immutable light higher than my mind, not the light of very day, obvious to anyone, nor a larger version of the same kind which would, as it were, have given out a much brighter light and filled everything with its magnitude. It was not that light, but a different thing, utterly different from all our kinds of light. It transcended my mind, not in the way that oil floats on water, nor as heaven is above Earth. It was superior because it made me, and I was inferior because I was made by it. The person who knows the truth knows it, and he who knows it knows eternity. Love knows it. Eternal truth and true love and beloved eternity: you are my God. To you I sigh "day and night." When I first came to know you, you raised me up to make me see that what I saw is Being, and that I who saw am not yet Being. And you gave a shock to the weakness of my sight by the strong radiance of your rays, and I trembled with love and awe. And I found myself far from you "in the region of dissimilarity," and heard as it were your voice from on high: "I am the food of the fully grown; grow and you will feed on me. And you will not change me into you like the food your flesh eats, but you will be changed into me." . . . [A]nd you cried from far away: "now, I am who I am" (Exodus 3.14). I heard in the way one hears within the heart, and all doubt left me.[6]

Tomas Spidlik insightfully reminds us in his book *Prayer: The Spirituality of the Christian East* that, when it comes to the role of personal experience and truth, Pavel Florensky, a Russian scholar, analyzed the word "truth" and made several insightful observations:

> The same Sanskrit word *var* lies at the origin of the Latin word for truth, *veritas*, the German verb *wehren* (to defend), the Slavonic *vera* (faith), and the Greek noun *eorte*, a festival, as something venerable, hence forbidden to some; comparable to the Latin *reverendus*, awe-inspiring, and *verenda* (to be feared). Thus, knowledge bears witness to an immediate contact with the mystery, with religion, with worship. The Hebrew noun for truth, *'emeth*, has the same root as the verb *aman* (to support or believe), i.e. Amen. Truth then would be defined as a revealed word, the object of faith. The Slavonic term for truth, *istina* (Sanskrit *asmi*, *asti* and the German verb *atmen*, to breath, to live) expresses contact with a living reality known in a personal relationship. The Greek word for truth, *aletheia*, is entirely different. It is formed of the negative *a*, "not," and of *lethos* or *lathos*, a forgetting, oblivion, to be hidden and to sleep. Truth, then, is that which is no longer hidden, which is known, that which has been uncovered.[7]

The Greeks believed that philosophers, using reason and contemplation, could uncover the truth. But this high view of human reason diminished in late Antiquity and over time, in Spidlik's view,

> an entire class of sages repudiated reason and turned toward the irrational, toward mystery. . . . According to St. Paul, a "mystery" is the fulfillment in Christ of a divine plan which was first hidden, then revealed to human persons. The contrast between the two aspects "hidden-revealed" (or also "shrouded" in silence "announced and revealed") is essential to the concept of mystery. This contrast is indicated by the element of time (once hidden, now made manifest) but it also transcends time: even when known, the mystery always remains partly veiled.[8]

There is a perennial tension at the heart of the spiritual journey, especially between the nature of revelation, personal spiritual experience, and truth. What can be known of God is less important to the Christian mystic because the knowing is inferior to first experiencing and participating in God's life and love in union with Christ by the Spirit. While God always remains the holy and veiled "I Am," God's being of love draws humankind into God's Triune life of love so that "we also shall be." Our being is forever grounded in the human–Divine union in the one being Jesus Christ, which is the theological basis for St. Paul's extraordinary declaration that we have made so much of in this book: "For I am convinced that nothing can separate us from the love of God in Christ" (Romans 8.28).

Appendix C

CONTEMPLATIVE PRACTICES AND THE APOSTOLIC CHURCH

L ET US LOOK at each of the apostolic practices listed in Acts 2.42 through a contemplative lens for the purpose of further manifesting the presence of God through Christian contemplative community.[1]

TEACHING

The teaching has a predicate: it's the *apostles'* teaching. What this means for us is that we source our faith and understanding from the witness of scripture. Within the boundaries of Christian community and tradition we believe that the scriptures bear witness to the community's life with, and experience of, God.[2] The goal of dedicating ourselves to the apostles' teaching is to appropriate the message of God's presence in Jesus the Christ: to feel, think, and live differently. In other words, we dedicate ourselves to the interpretation of Christian scriptures, which leads to our transformation further in Christ. When the church gathers, we do so to read and reflect upon scripture, the prismatic revelation of God.

But the drumbeat of God's message is also beating beyond the pages of scripture. The Spirit is still speaking to us, just as music still lingers in the heart long after the symphony ends. It's the echo of God's voice as deep calls to deep. It's unmistakable, undeniable, and all who are in union with Christ know this to be true. God is still speaking in words recorded long ago, and in words whispered in the still place of the soul right now.

Illumination and inspiration are never limited to scripture or past revelation, but always available relationally with Christ by the Spirit here and now. This is the miracle of God's light, life, and love among us by the Spirit, and no religious authority or theological system can cease the Spirit's free flow to and through us bringing wisdom and truth. It is lawful. Truth permeates the cosmos and is available in the knowledge incarnated in the living and written word of God.

While teaching is rooted in scripture, it's also holistic. The interpretation and application of the scriptures need to have an intellectual, emotional, and physical dimension. Holistic, balanced teaching brings wisdom, emotional healing, and physical transformation. The wisdom and truth of the tradition have the capacity to re-order our thinking, feeling, and doing.

We recognize there are multiple readings of scripture: some reveal historical and cultural details, such as the social meaning of foot-washing; others convey spiritual depth under and beyond the literal meanings of the surface, such as the allegorical meaning of cleansing the influences of life that we encounter during our daily interactions in the world. In the latter reading, our feet are the lowest level of our humanity and represent the place where we "meet the world," so they must be cleansed. All this is psychological and spiritual and not literal.

But what, you ask, is the truth? Truth is God's love and non-truth is everything that distorts and separates us from this love. Thus, truth is our identity as a participant of Divine nature, a being of inestimable beauty and value. Non-truth is our false identity that has forgotten the truth of our being. But we can remember and awaken to who we really are, and the truth that, through our union with Christ, God is always available and present to us by the Spirit.

The opposite of truth is not error, but fear; because fear is the opposite of love. Why? Because "perfect love casts out fear" (1 John 4.18), and fear distorts the love of God and the deep truth that all things are in relationship to and with God. Thus, the deepest awakening truth is this: *God so loved the world that he has given Christ the Son to demonstrate that whosoever might remember and believe in Christ will not experience a meaningless life, but will live in the bliss of God's love and presence experiencing the true purpose of life, to know God and enjoy God forever. And this love will not disappoint us, for it can free us from all that hinders, and heal us from all that is wounded.*

The contemplative use of the tradition and scriptures relies upon an attentive listening for the text's inner or hidden meaning. We study the text for depth-understanding and personal, psychological transformation, not just for historical information or edifying life-application. It's important to remember that there's not just one meaning to the text. Meaning is multiple and is related to our interpretive lenses and level of being. The one who reads (subject) can never be separated from that which is read (object). There's a deep interplay between the two, an example of which is the allegorical or spiritual method of interpretation.

THE ALLEGORICAL TRADITION

Throughout the Christian tradition, church fathers and biblical interpreters have found the allegorical method of interpretation useful for spiritual transformation. A famous example of this is the theologian and church father, Origen. Origen believed that the purpose of the Christian life was the immediate knowledge of God by the believer, a goal hampered by the inability of humans to comprehend God. Nonetheless, because God sent the *logos* as a mediator to teach us knowledge in Divine matters, our minds can be healed and transformed to see and experience God.

For Origen, the study and interpretation of scripture are just introductions to the knowledge of God. One must go above scripture and ascend to Jesus for further immediate knowledge. Ascetical practice was vitally important to aid in one's ascent, and Origen took this seriously, castrating himself in order to more easily fight off the beclouding passions of the flesh. (This extreme measure is viewed today as inappropriate and harmful for spiritual development.) Despite this, Origen made significant theological and mystical contributions to the development of Christianity, such as his elaborate and distinctly Christian *Commentary on the Song of Songs*, which he took as a mystical journey of the soul's longing and union with God, and which set the standard for the mystical interpretation of scriptures in the ensuing Christian era.

Through the "soul's eye" or the "eye of the heart," we can perceive things beyond the mind—an important principle of contemplative biblical interpreta-tion. Through the "eye of the heart," we're led inward by the Spirit, and in this interiority see and hear, taste and experience a "light higher than the mind"—that is to say, wisdom, revelation, and Divine encounter. Origen is a pillar of allegorical biblical interpretation in service of psychological and spiritual trans-formation in Christ. There are many others, including the modern examples of the two Thomases—Merton and Keating—both of whom have provided extensive models in their writings of spiritual interpretation that nurtures the contemplative Christian dimension.[3]

The apostolic church gives us a picture of a community gathered around the written text but also the spoken word interpreting that text in ways that foster spiritual knowledge and psychological transformation in union with Christ. At the beginning, the text the community gathered around was the Hebrew scrip-tures read in light of their experience with Jesus. *This experiential reading under the guidance of the Holy Spirit became the touchstone of the contemplative reading and interpretation of the scriptures.* Such interpretation is God-directed in that it leads us further into communion with, and in the life of, the Trinity, which ultimately leads us into life in loving community, one for the other, especially the least of us. In this way, we're led into the second aspect of the apostolic community: fellowship.

FELLOWSHIP

The meaning of this word is very rich. One way of defining fellowship is a state of relationship that demonstrates unity through sharing with others. This can be as simple as sharing your joys or sorrows, or as complex as distributing your wealth. Fellowship is the outcome of love in relationship, and the counterpoint to all the isolation, independence, and loneliness that characterizes much of our urban and suburban life experience.

Fellowship is crucial for the Christian community. It's central to the life we share in Christ and participate in by the Spirit, and a visible demonstration of the relationship we share with God through Christ by the Spirit with one another. It's the essence of our spiritual communion: a mutual indwelling with

God and with one another as sisters and brothers in Christ. The church is not the building. It is a nexus of relationships where love can be expressed and God can appear through us, for us, and with us. Fellowship is the external demonstration of the internal reality of the relationship we share in Christ.

Because of the human condition, fellowship in a community is easily disrupted. The human condition, even for Christians, is problematic because it's a constant gravitational force toward self-interest versus care for one another. The gravitational power of the human condition is rooted in our unconscious. We tend to sleepwalk through life, unaware of our emotional negativity and mechanical reactivity. Thus, we need grace to wake us up and draw us further into the light of consciously chosen love, which invites its own force that neutralizes the gravity of unconsciousness.

The future of the church and humanity hinges upon the increased awakening of individuals into the light of consciousness. The scriptures speak of this in terms of being "raised from the dead," which is not just an individual event, but an experience of the community. Nowhere is this more powerfully conveyed than in Ephesians 2.4–10, which I adapt in a contemplative way:

> But God, who is rich in mercy, out of the great love which he loved us even when we were dead through our trespasses [sleepwalking], made us alive together with Christ—by grace you have been saved [awakened]—and raised us up [further into consciousness] with him. . . . For by grace you have been saved [awakened] through faith, and this is not your own doing; it is the gift of God—not the result of works, so that no one may boast. For we are what he has made us, created in Christ Jesus for good works [consciously chosen love in human community], which God prepared beforehand to be our way of life.

The writings of Ken Wilber further illuminate how this spiritual process of awakening is happening. Divine grace is calling to humanity to awaken from its fears and regressions rooted in separateness. Through grace, the spirit of wisdom is inviting us to cease our sense of separateness from one another and rise to more connected, relational ways of being. Awakening further into love and consciousness is the key to the future of community and fellowship. Wilber has synthesized a vast amount of literature for a popular audience, and by doing so has mapped the levels of consciousness. One of the reasons fellowship is so challenging is because people are at different levels of consciousness. They are seeing the world from very different perspectives.[4]

The Christ-consciousness that grace is awakening and calling us to is the level of the transpersonal, or in the language of St. Paul, the level of "I, not I, but Christ in me" (Galatians 2.20). The future of human civilization is opening up to this level of selfhood in community and beyond.

As the communities of Earth continue to interconnect, we're confronted with a new reality: we must learn to live together bearing each other's presence in unprecedented proximity. Our population has grown to such an extent that we *must* learn how to have meaningful fellowship—one rooted in our mutual recognition of oneness, which can only occur through love. The "other" is worthy of being here just as you are, while we may not understand one another or even approach life from the same faith perspective, we are one human species, sharing in the gift of life together. Meaningful fellowship has several requirements:

- **Unity within the community**: In contrast to the division and disunity that characterizes much of the religious community in general.
- **Love as the predominant personality of the community**: In contrast to the weakness and inability to love others due to not living in the present, and a lack of attention to the real and present needs of others.
- **Selflessness and humility on behalf of each individual member of the community**: In contrast to the prevalence of indifferent, self-centered lifestyles.
- **Remain and abide together**: In contrast to the transience and speed of our culture; uprooting from place to place, and relating long distance through technology and transportation.

Recognizing that religion and religious communities will need to play a leading role in implementing such a vision, an international, interreligious call summarizes how humankind can live in community. The call is entitled the *Charter for Compassion*:

> **The principle of compassion** lies at the heart of all religious, ethical and spiritual traditions, calling us always to treat all others as we wish to be treated ourselves. Compassion impels us to work tirelessly to alleviate the suffering of our fellow creatures, to dethrone ourselves from the centre of our world and put another there, and to honor the inviolable sanctity of every single human being, treating everybody, without exception, with absolute justice, equity and respect.

> **It is also necessary** in both public and private life to refrain consistently and empathically from inflicting pain. To act or speak violently out of spite, chauvinism, or self-interest, to impoverish, exploit or deny basic rights to anybody, and to incite hatred by denigrating others—even our enemies—is a denial of our common humanity. We acknowledge that we have failed to live compassionately and that some have even increased the sum of human misery in the name of religion.

> **We therefore call upon all men and women**—to restore compassion to the centre of morality and religion—to return to the ancient principle that any interpretation of scripture that breeds violence, hatred or disdain is illegitimate—to ensure that youth are given accurate and respectful information about other traditions, religions and cultures—to encourage a positive appreciation of cultural and religious diversity—to cultivate an informed empathy with the suffering of all human beings—even those regarded as enemies.

> **We urgently need** to make compassion a clear, luminous and dynamic force in our polarized world. Rooted in a principled determination to transcend selfishness, compassion can break down political, dogmatic, ideological and religious boundaries. Born of our deep inter-dependence, compassion is essential to human relationships and to a fulfilled humanity. It is the path to enlighten-

ment, and indispensible to the creation of a just economy and a peaceful global com- munity.[5]

In light of such urgent and compelling words, we say *Amen*, and from fellowship and compassion we turn now to its inevitable fruit: worship.

WORSHIP

For many, worship is reverence. The presence of God in the incarnation dramatically shifts this perspective. In the incarnation, the ineffable comes close, and we're moved in adoration of the grace that brings God to and with humankind in Jesus. Incarnation is the antithesis of the old transcendent aloofness of the ancient conceptions of the "sky God." Incarnation announces that God is a relational being. God was fleshly, real, knowable, touchable. God chose to come among us as one of us, for us and our salvation. But this incarnation can spiritually continue through worship. Indeed, the early Christian community dedicated themselves to the "breaking of bread." I take this to mean one of the twin functions of the worshiping church: the ministry of the table (communion) and the ministry of the word (the sermon).

Worship is the axis whereby the life of Christ enters the life of the community and brings a foretaste of the kingdom of God. The kingdom of God is anticipated in hope, but experienced in the gathered community at worship. We know from experience that the worship of the community of Christ is as equally diverse as it is different. But what unites us is the reality of the One who calls us, the One who has our attention and to whom we offer our reverence and adoration. The worship of God is embraced in the body and blood of Christ, where we interact and link with the historic dialogue of faith and the hosannas of the forgiven.

Worship is the act of contemplating God. St. Paul experienced it as a contemplative and community event. One passage conveys the extraordinary dimensions involved in worship and our participation in it: "And we, with unveiled faces reflecting like mirrors the brightness of the Lord, all grow brighter as we are turned into that image that we reflect" (2 Corinthians 3.18). Bernard McGinn comments that "the word translated as 'reflecting' was often understood as 'gazing' or 'contemplating.' . . . Thus, the text could be read to mean that it is by contemplation of the glory of the risen Christ that the image of God in us is being conformed to the Word."[6] In other words, worship adores God and transforms us.

There is great hope in the church at worship, for it looks beyond the promises of this world—with its politics and persuasions—to the hope of the One who is "the same yesterday, today, and forever" (Hebrews 13.8), ever intending that the community of Christ grow "into a dwelling place for God" (2 Corinthians 6.16). This, I think, is the central reality of our worship: *God is with us as the gathered community of Christ, and the goal of the church is to be a people of praise whose songs and creativity demonstrate to all that there is a certain selflessness to all our existence, and a worship that engages the whole person: mind, heart, and body.* This is a worship inspired by the faithfulness of those who have cherished and anticipated the presence of their God, such as the Psalmist, who declared:

> Praise the Lord! Praise God in his sanctuary; praise him in his mighty firma-
> ment! Praise him for his mighty deeds; praise him according to his surpass-
> ing greatness! Praise him with trumpet sound; praise him with lute and harp!
> Praise him with tambourine and dance; praise him with clanging cymbals;
> praise him with loud clashing cymbals! Let everything that breathes praise the
> Lord! Praise the Lord!" (Psalm 150)

In a world preoccupied with itself, fearful of potential tragedies and tempted by ephemeral pleasures, worship is our enduring ballast, inspiration, and antici-pation. Worship lifts us away from our navel-gazing and self-adoration to con-template the glory of God as an infinite outpouring of light, life, and love.

PRAYER

The apostolic church was a community of prayer. If worship is looking into the face of God in Christ, then prayer is wordless communion. Yet prayer isn't just silence. It's also a conversation, sometimes conveyed with tears, anguish, and holy fury. Such is the nature of prayers of intercession. But what does intercession look like? It's the Spirit-inhabited community groaning inwardly with the suffering and pain permeating the human condition. There's something deep and enigmatic about this reciprocal relationship we have with the Spirit who both

> helps us in our weakness; for we do not know how to pray as we ought, but that very Spirit intercedes with sighs too deep for words. And God, who searches the heart, knows what is the mind of the Spirit, because the Spirit intercedes for the saints according to the will of God. (Romans 8.26–27)

Could it be that what Paul is getting at here is a certain mystery about being human? It's the privilege of a Spirit-infused community to have the Spirit who not only searches us, but intercedes on our behalf in this mysterious interaction between the human spirit and the mind of God. Our role is to take the suffering and injustice we encounter in ourselves and the external world and groan inwardly, transferring the requests of the world from our own minds to the mind of the Spirit who understands our empathy and co-suffering.

Could it be that we're organically designed vessels of intercession? Could it be that our mind has the capacity to interact with the material world in a way that we become conveyors of the Divine healing power available to humanity when we activate our intercessory prayer centers appropriately? Such, I think, are the insights the quantum world unveils to a spirituality of prayer. We become a conduit through which the unspoken requests of a world in pain are pleaded to and with God. Dietrich Bonhoeffer once wrote that "intercession is not general and vague but very concrete; a matter of definite person and definite petitions. The more definite my intercession becomes, the more promising it is."[7]

The community of Christ must learn again the art of interceding and praying in particular, for it's the Spirit who interprets the particulars to God even if we don't understand the particulars of each situation. Our hope and confidence is not in our own efforts of intercession, but in the relational intercession with and in the Spirit who "helps us in our weakness" with understanding and ability.

A second way of prayer beyond intercession is the prayer of transformation. Prayer is the means by which God moves in this world and in us. One glance at the pattern of scripture shows us that prayer occurred prior to the crucifixion (Luke 22.39–46, Mark 14.32–42, Matthew 26.36–46); there was prayer before

Pentecost (Acts 2); there was prayer before the Gentiles began to be incorporated into the fulfillment of the Spirit with salvation (Acts 10–11). Thus, the pattern is clear: prayer precedes spiritual transformation.

Centering Prayer

Centering Prayer is a method of prayer rooted in the Christian tradition that also leads one to the experience of transformation and, over time, beyond transformation, to the non-dual, unitive state. The theology and practice of Centering Prayer can be traced to the anonymous fourteenth-century *Cloud of Unknowing*, and the writings of St. John of the Cross and St. Teresa of Avila. Modern Benedictine monks interpreted these writings in light of psychological insights and developed the method of Centering Prayer.

Centering Prayer prepares one for contemplative prayer and is a spiritual practice that helps us experience more contemplative states. While Centering Prayer has emerged quite recently as a preparatory step toward contemplation, throughout church history various forms of contemplative prayer have found expression in both the Eastern and Western churches. For example, in the Eastern churches such as the Russian and Eastern Orthodox communities, a kind of contemplative prayer known as *hesychia*, the prayer of stillness or quiet, was developed using the simple phrase, "Lord Jesus Christ have mercy upon me a sinner."[8] It was believed that through the renunciation of the passions (anger, lust, greed), one could begin to experience inner stillness and silence (*hesychia*) where one could be united with God. This bears striking similarity to Centering Prayer, which emerged within the Roman Catholic tradition.

The basic definition of Centering Prayer from the writings of Thomas Keating and summarized by Contemplative Outreach gives a good idea of what is meant by this practice:

> Centering Prayer is a method of silent prayer that prepares us to receive the gift of contemplative prayer, prayer in which we experience God's presence within us, closer than breathing, closer than thinking, closer than consciousness itself. This method of prayer is both a relationship with God and a discipline to foster that relationship. Centering Prayer is not meant to replace other

kinds of prayer. Rather, it adds depth of meaning to all prayer and facilitates the movement from more active modes of prayer—verbal, mental or affective prayer—into a receptive prayer of resting in God. Centering Prayer emphasizes prayer as a personal relationship with God and as a movement beyond conversation with Christ to communion with Him. The source of Centering Prayer, as in all methods leading to contemplative prayer, is the Indwelling Trinity: Father, Son, and Holy Spirit. The focus of Centering Prayer is the deepening of our relationship with the living Christ. The effects of Centering Prayer are ecclesial, as the prayer tends to build communities of faith and bond the members together in mutual friendship and love.[9]

The Centering Prayer movement began in a Cistercian Catholic order at St. Joseph's Abbey in Spencer, Massachusetts in the early 1960s. From 1961 to 1981, Father Keating was abbot of the community and began to dialogue with other monks, including Thomas Merton and monks from the Hindu and Buddhist traditions. They discussed both formally and informally the nature of the spiritual life, and in particular the importance of meditative prayer for one's spiritual growth. Keating was curious how to harmonize the wisdom of the East with the Christian contemplative tradition. Up until this time of exploration and inter-religious dialogue, the Cistercian and Benedictine monks were primarily using the meditative practice of *Lectio Divina*, an ancient way of reading scripture with a deepening prayerful awareness that moves one toward contemplation. In 1975, William Meninger, a monk at St. Joseph's, using *The Cloud of Unknowing* as a guide, developed a method of Christian meditation, which he called, "the prayer of *The Cloud*." He started teaching the method to priests and visitors at the Abbey's retreat house.

The method distilled by Father Meninger used a single word such as "God," "Love," or "Jesus" to express one's desire to be with God. At one retreat in 1976, Basil Pennington, also a monk at St. Joseph's, taught Father Meninger's method. During this retreat, the participants suggested the name "Centering Prayer" to describe this meditative prayer-practice. Thomas Merton also speaks of meditative prayer as "Centering Prayer" in his writings. Father Keating also began teaching Centering Prayer at the Abbey, and later at St. Benedict's Monastery in

Snowmass, Colorado, where he moved in 1982. Through Keating's teachings and writings, a movement began to teach the Centering Prayer method to laypeople. The positive response from Keating's talks, retreats, and books also led to the creation of the Contemplative Outreach organization, a nonprofit ministry that teaches and supports Centering Prayer.

Centering Prayer is a Christian practice grounded in God's love and life. According to Keating's writings, Centering Prayer is possible because of our relationship with the Trinity.[10] The Trinity is an ever-flowing personal stream of Divine life, light, and love, which constantly pours forth from the Father to the Son, through the Spirit to humanity. God deeply desires to be in relationship with us, and as God pursues humanity, the life, light, and love within the Trinity begins to spill over into our lives. This Divine "spilling-over" is called "grace," and God's benevolent gift transforms our life. As we surrender to God's promptings of grace and follow our God-quickened longings, we begin to experience the presence, action, and healing of God.

The inner relationship with the Trinity is not theoretical or merely poetic sentiment. It was made visible and available to us in the life of Jesus Christ who was Emmanuel—God with us—mighty demonstrator of divinity among and for human beings. As the Lord of Life, Jesus Christ is also "living water," "light of the world," and "everlasting love" to and for humanity. Our journey back to God begins with a relationship with Christ, and this interior spiritual relationship starts to activate several processes in our life, one of which is the cleansing of the negative emotions and what Keating calls the "unloading of the unconscious," which can be a difficult time of purgation that ultimately leads one to a deeper awareness of God's loving presence and purpose for one's life.

Like the story of the prodigal son (Luke 15), Centering Prayer can lead to an increased awareness of one's condition and often, by grace, the gift of change— *metanoia*. The prodigal "comes to his senses," remembers whose he was, and returns to the father. This inner action leads to a loosening of encrusted psychic/spiritual energies, which often begin to "come up" and be purged. Keating refers to this as Divine therapy. As purgation continues, a noticeable attraction to and desire for the study of scripture, prayer, and worship begin. This idea connects with the classic, threefold Catholic teaching of the spiritual path of transformation: purgation, illumination, and union. For Keating, following in the long line of Catholic mystics, Centering Prayer involves all three; but one of its gifts, not goals, is the unitive experience, something not everyone may experience or at least know they're experiencing it.

From a Reformed Protestant perspective, the contemplative, mystical path has always taken a backseat to the emphasis on justification through faith, especially through the faithfulness of Jesus Christ and his work on the cross.[11] However, Calvin does deal with this subject matter, although he uses different presuppositions and terminology than Keating. For Calvin, any transformation we experience is grounded in the secret working of the Spirit who mediates God's presence and healing in us, always through our union with Christ. By faith and baptism, we're plunged into the loving and living waters of God. This is what it means to be "baptized by the Spirit," a life-giving and transforming infusion of Divine life, light, and love in us. We know that this transforming infusion occurs because we begin to increasingly long for a deeper, fuller, more immediate experience with God. The longing is compelling evidence that the gift of God's presence and action is "spilling over" into our hearts and minds, and quickening us to love, serve, worship, and seek after God in prayer and action.

For Protestants, union with God is made possible through union with Christ. So what does "union with Christ" mean? It means that we know who God is by what God does, and God has been doing quite a bit of revelation. To the best of our knowledge, God has chosen to be a relationship as Father–Son–Spirit, and to send forth to humanity the Son, who is Jesus Christ, to be for us and our salvation the very manifestation of God among us. This Son, Jesus, would himself show us (reveal) who God is and teach us the way to know and experience God. Jesus taught us to change our way of life and to believe in him; that to know him was to know the Father. By surrendering to Christ, one could receive the gift of his Spirit and thereby be united to God through Christ the Son by the power of the Spirit.

Prayer, worship, and creativity go hand in hand. I long for this era of Christian community to be less reactive and defensive, and more creative and prayerful, so our time will rise to the excellence of other great movements in our past: such as the Anglican Psalter, Bach's sacred music, the frescos of Michelangelo, or the literary legacy of Augustine himself. Prayer is a crucial axis that forms the pattern of the community of Christ's relational way of life.[12]

The contemplative church is captivated by the vocation of prayer. For it's the community of prayer that will act as an informed advocate on behalf of the suffering world before God, and as an activist for the sake of those without voice who are often violated by injustices. The community of Christ stands in a unique position to co-suffer with the people of this world, as well as plead as ones living in this world as God's continuing incarnational presence through prayer. In a world so preoccupied with its own systems of survival and success, prayer counters self-autonomy.[13]

A PROBLEM WITH PRAYING

For all the promise and power potentially available through prayer, many of us struggle to pray. I've been a pastor for ten years and during this time I've heard many parishioners share that they don't have time to pray, and that if they did, they wouldn't know how to. On the flip side, I've also heard parishioners wonder why, when they do pray, their prayers seem dull and disconnected from God. They wonder why their prayers don't have more of an effect on their behavior and emotions, and, poignantly, why God doesn't seem to hear or answer them. I've listened in empathy as they question why their prayer life doesn't help them better handle their negative emotions, such as anger, or improve such moods as sadness or depression, and why even after much prayer they still experience a sense of spiritual stagnation or dullness.[14]

These reports and questions are worrying because prayer is one of the most important spiritual remedies for the spectrum of diseases we experience in life—physical, spiritual, and psychological. This isn't just theoretical: I have personally experienced that prayer practices can be very effective in helping one encounter the complexities of the human condition, and as a pastoral caregiver, I want everyone to share in this kind of transformative and helpful experience in prayer, especially Centering Prayer.

Prayer is the birthright of humanity, or in biblical terms, an extension of our relationality as ones created in the image of God. Prayer shouldn't be so difficult, and that it seems to be so for many Christians is quite puzzling. In actuality, the problem isn't with prayer itself, but with our conceptions about prayer, humanity, and God. Prayer is a deep thread, woven together with wonder, running through everything that exists. Prayer can hold, help, and heal our lives, making a broken world whole. So why might our experience with prayer be to the contrary?

A PROBLEM WITH THINKING

One reason it may be so difficult to pray, and why some may feel disconnected spiritually in their prayers, is because of the gravitational pull of cultural history. Modern Christians have been swamped by scientific and technological modernity—using the term "modernity" as a catchall for the many intellectual and cultural developments following the scientific revolution.[15] Modernity flattened out much of the inner mystery of spirituality and prayer in Western Christianity, resulting in a diminishment of the value of intuition, mystery, and immanence, and a simultaneous valorization of the clean lines of dogmatic rationality, pragmatism, and transcendence.[16] Knowledge of God was rational, tending toward measurable results, and, cosmologically speaking, God remained fixed "up there" somewhere in a royal realm far, far away. Is it any wonder that the tradition built upon the revolutionary claim that "the Word became flesh and dwelt among us" (John 1.14), and whose master once said "the kingdom of God is within you" (Luke 17.21), became confused as to the purpose and practice of praying?

It now appears that the church forgot a spiritual treasure of the premodern tradition: meditative prayer, or what was described above as Centering Prayer.[17] Thankfully, as also detailed above, this treasure has been rediscovered by the Western church, Catholic and Protestant alike, in the last forty years. This has occurred, in part, because of an interesting cultural and philosophical backlash. Just when modernity seemed to have reached its zenith, a new ethos emerged that sustained a revival of less rational spiritualities, including a deepening dialogue with Eastern meditative traditions and other more esoteric forms of spirituality.

The result of modernity upon Christian spirituality is an enduring and complicated legacy. One of the more negative results is that in forgetting our own inner, contemplative spiritual practices, the Protestant church has focused on discursive prayers, such as intercession and petition, including the majestically humble Lord's Prayer. Discursive, intercessory prayer is very helpful and appropriate, and will always have its place in the spectrum of prayer, but it's only one dimension and expression of Christian prayer![18]

Consider the example of the very successful book, *The Prayer of Jabez.* It represents the essence of what I call "discursive scientific prayer," that is, proscriptive, verbal cause-and-effect praying: *If* you pray this, *then* you will get that. While I don't aim to critique other prayer methods such as taught by *The Prayer of Jabez*, I do want to note the impact modernity and scientific rationality have had upon spirituality in general and Protestant prayer practices in particular.

A further reason why some struggle to pray and feel frustrated is because they conceive of God "up there" or "out there," and who listens to audible prayer requests. Many Christians conceive of God as a being far away whose in-box of prayers is constantly overflowing and only those who are holy or good enough or pray in just the right way will be heard at all. A result of this conception is that many don't feel inspired or nourished in spirit by reciting needs or requests, or think that by telling a "professional" such as their minister or priest, their prayers will have a better chance of being answered. Another consequence of the "up-there" God is the prevalence of rote prayers. Such prayers may bring a feeling of familiar comfort, but often don't lead to a sense of transformation or spiritual growth. And without a sense of spiritual growth or a feeling that prayers have been answered, one tires of this kind of praying quickly.

A great need exists to find methods and practices that authentically connect with spiritual stagnation, frustration with prayer in general, and our desire to become more spiritually mature. The church needs to identify methods that promote long-term spiritual growth, rather than short-term consumer gratification. To put it simply: Give someone a fish and you feed them; teach them how to fish, and you transform their life.

The church and its leaders must rediscover and teach meditative prayer practices to help people "catch God" themselves. For the record, I'm still casting my prayers as well. Every day in the morning light, I wade through the river of life, hoping to catch the big one. Or maybe it's the other way around. Maybe that big, elusive whale in the darkness will swallow me whole. There's nothing fancy about it. It's simply a daily discipline of surrender and trust in the God who's already with us, if only we let go of what Thomas Keating calls our programs for survival and security, power and control, affection and esteem.[19] This dovetails with the human condition, or what I call our way of being.

A PROBLEM WITH BEING

Prayer and our humanity are inseparably interwoven. This important insight is illustrated by the folk wisdom known to every carpenter: you never pick up a board you're standing on. If you try, you either break the board or your back. Instead, you must step off the board. Trying to change one's behavior without changing one's being is similarly futile. Something is going to break. To put it another way, your level of prayer corresponds to your level of being. Thankfully, the latter can change and grow. This change occurs through the union of grace and intentional spiritual practices, especially through Centering Prayer. This requires further knowledge, which is summarized below.

First, you may be surprised to hear there are different levels of being. Developmental psychologists have helped us understand this.[20] They have delineated that within each human lifespan one passes through certain definite markers or levels.[21] However, there's more to levels of being than just our normal human development; there's also the inner development of our being. This process can be described in various ways. In the Christian biblical tradition, it's explained like this: "And all of us . . . are being transformed from one degree of glory to another; for this comes from the Lord, the Spirit" (2 Corinthians 3.18), and "I am again in labor pains until Christ is formed in you" (Galatians 4.19).

The Christian theological tradition conveys the concept of different levels of being through the doctrine of sanctification. Depending upon one's theological orientation, this could mean anything from *theosis, divinization,* or simply *holy living.* The point here is that just as the universe and creation has a certain ascending order, so too an ascending order of being is available to humanity.

The Christian view is that Jesus Christ was the fullest expression of the highest level of being, which the Nicene Creed describes as "fully God and fully man, *of one being* with the Father." Jesus the Christ demonstrates what the highest, maximum level of being looks like, and invites us into that being, or in the language of St. Paul, to be "united with Christ" (Romans 6.1–14). Likewise, as St. Peter teaches, we can become "participants of the divine nature" (2 Peter 1.4), and "have the mind of Christ" (1 Corinthians 2.16). This is also the inner meaning of Jesus' own teaching about the vine and the branches, where we "abide in him" (John 15.1–8). We abide in order to grow in being, which is ultimately a restoration of the Divine likeness in us.

That there are different levels of being is one reason why St. Paul instructed different styles of teaching for different levels of being, milk for the lower levels and meat for the higher ones (1 Corinthians 4.15), and why St. Peter urged believers to crave the spiritual milk that would enable them to "grow into salvation" (1 Peter 2.1–3). All of which begins to make the connection between our thinking and being or our consciousness and being, which is one reason why St. Paul urges Christians to "be transformed by the renewing of your minds" (Romans 12.2).

Ken Wilber's writings have helped frame this concept of different levels of being, or in his language, *consciousness*, in an integrated, comprehensive way, and most importantly chart and define exactly the different levels of being. Although Wilber's concept is of marginal significance for this book, it's extremely important to grasp the conceptual gravity of his work in relationship to the purpose of prayer. That is, to what end do we pray? We pray to experience a transformation of our being, from one level to the next, or to be more fully and completely united into the being of Christ.[22] Indeed, as St. Paul put it: "When I was a child I spoke like a child, I thought like a child . . . but when I became an adult, I put an end to childish ways" (1 Corinthians 13.11).

Centering Prayer helps us engage the dimensions of ourselves we normally don't use. Consequently, we're in need of practice, and with practice, we can become quite good at "praying" in the right direction. Thomas Keating summarizes the way in which certain prayer practices, especially contemplative prayer, address all three aforementioned problems in his classic work on Centering Prayer, *Open Mind, Open Heart*:

> Contemplative Prayer is a process of interior transformation, a conversion initiated by God and leading, if we consent, to divine union. One's way of

seeing reality changes in this process. A restructuring of consciousness takes place which empowers one to perceive, relate, and respond to everyday life with increasing sensitivity to the divine presence in, through, and beyond every-thing.[23]

PRAYER AS A CLUE TO THE MEANING OF OUR EXISTENCE

As people of the Spirit, a crucial role we play is to offer ourselves as living locations of the Spirit on behalf of others, where we become places of prayer. Romans 8 teaches us that, in Christ, we can offer ourselves as the location of a mystical communion between our human spirit and the Holy Spirit. In the words of Teresa of Avila, in prayer we enter the interior castle of our being, where mind and spirit meet. In this place, by the Spirit, we become living temples where empathetic, meditative, intercessory prayers occur.[24]

It's crucial to notice the connection and logical flow from suffering to prayer. Both are rooted in the Spirit who now aids us in our endeavor to be human and spiritual in the midst of suffering. Listen to Paul's beautiful declaration of a new spiritual reality. In his vision, we now have the potential to access that reality when we live life according to the Spirit. He writes:

> Likewise the Spirit helps us in our weakness; for we do not know how to pray as we ought, but that very Spirit intercedes with sighs too deep for words. (Romans 8.26)

While we are vulnerable in this world to suffering and weakness, this weakness can lead us to an even deeper vulnerability of spirit to Spirit. So often in the face of our personal suffering and weakness, we attempt to overcome our difficulties with an autonomous strength of will. This isn't the way of the Spirit for our own lives or for those we'd minister to. In the face of suffering we are to remain vulnerable to the Spirit and consent to the Spirit's work in us even as we experience a diminishment of energy through intercession.

In the midst of tragedy and pain, words fail more often than they succeed. Oftentimes, we're stunned into silence at the prevalence and power of suffering in life. In such situations, our response is a vulnerability to the Spirit to be the presence of God to and in us, whereby God is the one "who searches the heart, knows what is the mind of the Spirit, because the Spirit intercedes for the saints according to the will of God" (Romans 8.27).

We remain vulnerable to the Spirit in our weakness, and allow our empathetic prayers to·be embodied by the Spirit's empathetic "groaning," interpreting our prayers to the mind of God according to the purposes of God. Our confidence is that God searches, knows, and interrelates with us. God is not systematic, but relational, and open to hearing the interpretation of our prayers through the intercession of the Spirit who is God with us.

Let us conclude St. Paul's flow of spiritual logic completely. Notice that chapter 8 of Romans begins with the potential of living in two directions, the flesh and the Spirit. Paul then develops suffering and prayer as two spiritual realities that can be transformed in the Christian by the Spirit. But the apex of Paul's argument is in verses 28–39, which represent a majestic crescendo giving meaning to what often seems meaningless. Listen to his conclusion and notice how it grows with the reality of spiritual transformation into the image of Christ, or more clearly, the reality that Christ is here in those who are being made like him by the Spirit. This spiritual transformation is the purpose of life, and gives meaning to the suffering we so often experience. Because we're being formed into the image of Christ, by the Spirit through suffering,

> we know that all things work together for good for those who love God, who are called according to his purpose. For those whom he foreknew he also predestined to be conformed to the image of his Son, in order that he might be the firstborn within a large family. (Romans 8.28–29)

Thus, with St. Paul we can concur:

> What are we to say about these things? If God is for us, who is against us? He who did not withhold his own son, but gave him up for all of us, will he not

with him also give us everything else?·... Who is to condemn? It is Christ Jesus, who died, yes, who was raised, who is at the right hand of God, who is indeed interceding for us. Who will separate us from the love of Christ? Will hardship, or distress, or persecution, or famine, or nakedness, or peril, or sword? ... No, in all these things we are more than conquerors through him who loved us. For I am convinced that neither death, nor life, nor angels, nor rulers, nor things present, nor things to come, nor powers, nor height, nor depth, nor anything else in all creation, will separate us from the love of God in Christ Jesus our Lord. (Romans 8.31–39)

This is a declaration of the Spirit's revolution in our lives and the reality that awaits those who live according to the Spirit even in the face of the "all things." It's a warning against our fearful retreating, managing, or manipulation of life for our sole pleasure and happiness. Christian spirituality doesn't promise freedom from the suffering of this world, only a means of moving through and in it. For the Christian, the Spirit way of life is the means of living in the mist of suffering defined passionately by Paul's list of experiences that ultimately won't conquer us, contrary to all appearances at the time of deepest pain and doubt.

This is indeed the power and the beauty of the Spirit, who enables intercessory, interior transforming prayer whereby God is here in and through us. Because of the indwelling Spirit, Christians are "in process." We are becoming like Christ, dying to self and living to God, bearing the qualities produced by the Spirit and anticipating a different world to come even in the midst of suffering. While we wait, we pray, remaining vulnerable to the Spirit in our weakness and ignorance of what to pray. We pray as the suffering world spins around us in a whirl of pain and at times, immense joy, consenting into the grace of silence where everything is already all right.

Appendix D

ANSWERING IMPORTANT QUESTIONS

———◦———

QUESTION #1: CAN GOD REALLY BE HERE?

The words *hereness* and *thereness* summarize human conceptions of God's activity to humanity throughout history. Such conceptions, to various degrees, are described in the story line of scripture. This story line declares that God is God, beyond us, yet also personally with us. Another way of saying this is that we're viewing from a non-dual or integral perspective.

For example, God is the One who "dwells in unapproachable light, whom no one has ever seen or can see" (1 Timothy 6.16), which is what we might call God's *thereness*, God's inaccessibility. Although no one has ever seen God, Jesus the Christ, "has made God known" (John 1.18), and through Christ we have seen God's glory and Christ has dwelt among us (John 1.14). This is what we might call God's *hereness*, God's accessibility. This means that Jesus the Christ demonstrated for us who God is and what God desires. The terminology used by theologians in describing these biblical realities is *immanence* for God's hereness, and *transcendence* for God's thereness.[1]

When we remember that we are sons and daughters of God, and return home to God's presence, we too, in the words of Jesus, may experience God's loving presence in us (John 17.26). This is God's gift. God desires to be in relationship with us, as demonstrated by Jesus the Christ. Our remembering is quickened by the Spirit. The gift of relationship is unrestricted by race, gender, ethnicity, or culture. It's accessed when one remembers and receives the relationship. "Remembering" and "receiving" are words that help to unpack the word "faith." Faith extends beyond the thinking mind, revealing a relational logic unto itself: the logic of the Spirit, which is a spiritual logic of love. This love-logic was summarized by St. Paul with these famous words:

> For I am convinced that neither death, nor life . . . nor things present, nor things to come . . . nor heights, nor depth, nor anything else in all creation, will be able to separate us from the love of God in Christ Jesus our Lord. (Romans 8.38–39)

QUESTION #2: EXISTENCE OR PRESENCE?

The longing for God's *presence* and our experience of Divine *absence* is often at the root of our questions regarding God's *existence.* But who needs proofs for God's existence when one is experiencing God's presence? You may not be able to describe your experience or convince others of its rational veracity, but you know in an interior way that you've experienced a different level of being. The knowing is different, too. It's more intuitive, impressionistic, poetic, profound, transcendent, subjective, luminous, and sublime—all this and more is the way of faith and the participation of our being with the Divine.

In an era of confusion about how to be Christian and how to "do" church, we should recall that the Bible isn't the foundation of Christian faith. The foundation—or in biblical terms "the cornerstone" of Christian faith—is a person: Jesus Christ, who himself embodied the presence of God on the human stage (Ephesians 2.20). Thus, our faith-foundation is ultimately relational and interior, for the known and the knower meet within one's personal field of consciousness. Personal knowledge is the priceless privilege of being human. Jesus didn't write a thing, and nothing he said can be verified independently of the gospels. We trust others' personal knowledge and experience of Jesus passed down in written form.

Furthermore, our personal knowledge isn't limited to scripture or creedal assent. Beneath such vital anchors of faith is the presence of God in Christ by the Spirit permeating from Pentecost, unyielding through the ages, and unhindered by chaos, or power. In this time, with hindsight, we're beginning to understand that not one of us (neither king nor pope, prophet or priest, politician or professor) can limit the Divine One's intention to love and draw close with humankind. We are God's beloved. We've no idea what God is up to or where this is going. Some poets and prophets have tried to describe it, but they come out sounding dizzy, stretching language till it bursts. Try reading the books of Isaiah or Revelation without scratching your head or laughing in wonder!

Clearly, there's more to those texts than we can imagine. What we do know is that the Bible, for all its complexities, begins and ends with God dwelling with human beings, first in a garden then in a city. In between is Christ: rising again and again in and to his people, showing us what it looks like for God to be Emmanuel.[2]

QUESTION #3: CAN THIS HAPPEN TO ME? AND IS IT CHRISTIAN?

It's important to realize that the experience of God's presence is not just for monks, nuns, and other assorted mystical types. It's not even just for Buddhists, Hindus, Yogis, or New Age gurus. As startling at it may first sound, the Christian tradition has its own way of awakening to *and* participating in the presence of God. Yet, over the course of centuries, and in particular in the wake of the Reformation and the Enlightenment, this Christian way has often been forgotten.[3]

Excitingly, many Christians are now seeking out what's been lost. Many have found amazing, hidden treasures of our own tradition in all sorts of surprising places: Eastern Orthodoxy, New Monasticism, urban ministry, Centering Prayer, labyrinths, spiritual direction, Gregorian chanting, the Renovaré movement, Pray-As-You-Go.org.[4] This rediscovery is happening right now and will change the face of Christianity. Contemplative Christian experience is our ordinary, extraordinary birthright.

Every blessing in God's love to you on your journey.

But what is a human being? What are we intended to be? Intrinsically—that is to say, in our essence—we are an aspect of divine being, whose purpose is to manifest itself in us and through us. For each of us, our essential being is the medium through which we participate in Divine Being. It may also be said to be the means by which Divine Being strives through us to manifest itself in the world—not as something apart from the world, a mere spiritual inwardness, but as a bodily presence.[1]

CONTEMPLATIVE
CHRISTIAN RESOURCES

—◁◦▷—

www.ContemplativeOutreach.org

www.ConsciousHarmony.org

www.ContemplativeChristians.com

Join the group: "Contemplative Christianity" at www.Facebook.com

NOTES

⊷⟨○⟩⊶

Opening Quotation

1 While some translations avoid the "inner" dimension of contemplative Christianity in Jesus' teaching by mistranslating the Greek preposition "among" or "with," I along with others find "in" a perfectly justifiable translation.

Preface

1 The title *The God Who Is Here* seeks to address the widespread social and spiritual shifts since the publication of Francis Schaeffer's *The God Who Is There* in 1968. Schaeffer (1912–1984) was a popular and influential evangelical pastor, prophet, and theologian during the last half of the twentieth century. Through books, lectures, movies, and especially through the community of L'Abri, Schaeffer and his wife Edith sought to articulate the propositional truth of God's existence, and the personal, communal, and moral implications of this propositional truth. Schaeffer thought and wrote at the confluence of two massive cultural streams (periods), what we now speak of as the modern and the postmodern periods.

Although there's still disagreement about what comprises each of these periods, and when the modern ended and the postmodern began, widespread agreement exists that a massive cultural shift occurred during the last half of the twentieth century, and is still happening today, especially in the Western Christian Church. Much of Schaeffer's passionate articulation and frustration was a result of his keen observations of Western culture, even as the tectonic plates of society moved beneath him. In the areas of philosophy, art, music, and theology, Schaeffer saw a negative, downward move in Western culture generally, and Christian theology specifically, until Western culture had crossed what Schaeffer termed, "the line of despair."

According to Schaeffer, this line was crossed over a period of time, beginning in Europe in the 1890s and culminating in America in 1913. Again, there's widespread disagreement upon the dates of the shift from the modern to the postmodern; but generally speaking, Schaeffer was describing, unknown to him at the time, what we now take for granted: that Christendom as we know it was ending, and truth was moving from the objective to the subjective, from the universal to the personal, or in Schaeffer's words, from capital—T—Truth, to little—t—truth. In addition to relativism, pluralism took the place of the Western imperial concepts of cultural dominance, as globalization continued to take shape, culminating in what we experience today as a highly interconnected worldwide economy, made possible by global communication and transportation networks that connect culture, commerce, people, and power, thus inaugurating what I refer to as the *age of presence*. Whereas Schaeffer's reading of philosophy, theology, and culture led him to uniquely reassert the reality and need of God's existence (thereness), and the practical, personal implications of this rational (intellectual) proposition, I'm concerned with uniquely reclaiming the reality and need of God's presence (hereness) along with the practical, personal, and communal implications of this mystical and contemplative confession. I trust this fuller circle of truth is drawn and, most importantly, experienced.

Thus, *The God Who Is Here* seeks to unfold and take seriously the radical biblical image and confession of God's continuing, post-incarnational presence through Christ by the power of the Holy Spirit, indwelling and transforming individuals and communities. Like Schaeffer, I share the observation that some sort of intellectual shift has occurred, apparently philosophically irreversible, especially in the area of how we know (epistemology), and how we interpret what we know (hermeneutics). I don't claim to know what this shift will ultimately mean for the Christian tradition. However, whereas Schaeffer bemoaned its arrival, I believe that the new mood of being and understanding of reality open up new ways of holding conversations about the meaningfulness of our personal and communal experience(s) of God's loving-kindness and faithfulness experientially, which, in my opinion, is far closer to the actual biblical witness of how faith was passed along generation by generation, and is in part, the embodiment of contemplative Christianity.

Thus, the sphere of truth is completed antithetically: God is here, yet paradoxically also there; God is there, but paradoxically also here. The paradox of God's presence is rooted in God's being as the Trinity. *The God Who Is Here* is an extended reflection and application of the doctrine of the Trinity to the Christian community, and draws to conclusion a radical idea: at the edge theologically, and after two thousand years of Christian history, we're reaching the realization that in the words of St. Paul there is "nothing that can separate us from the love of God in Christ Jesus" (Romans 8.39). The question is whether we'll understand and surrender to the gift.

Introduction: A Contemplative Bridge

1 Bernard McGinn, *The Presence of God: A History of Western Christian Mysticism, Vol. 1, The Foundations of Mysticism: Origins to the Fifth Century* (New York: Crossroad Publishing, 1997) xvii.

2 Biblically, two scriptures are useful to frame and expand the conversation regarding the contemplative Christian experience of God's presence and absence: "Why, O Lord, do you stand far off? Why do you hide yourself in times of trouble?" (Psalm 10.1) and, "For as yet there was no Spirit, because Jesus was not yet glorified" (John 7.39). These passages link human suffering with the perennial question of God's presence and reveal the possible connection of the Holy Spirit to our human experience with God's presence in times of trouble.

3 For an exceptional review of how ancient and modern science and philosophy have contributed to the difficulty with belief and Christian theology, see Nancey Murphy, *Beyond Liberalism and Fundamentalism: How Modern and Postmodern Philosophy Set the Theological Agenda* (Harrisburg, Penn.: Trinity Press International, 1996).

4 Such an evolution of faith is no different from what we know about our own human development. For example, as we grow from childhood to adulthood, we don't throw away our earlier forms of being, but we at once incorporate and transcend them. In this way, we are layered beings, one day upon another, until years pass and we discover that our life is a woven wonder, one stage upon another recollected in memory and remembered in the depths of tissues. Ken Wilber suggests that a simple example of this developmental dimension of incorporating, but also moving beyond, the earlier forms is the way alphabet letters become words, which become sentences, which become paragraphs, which become books. The book is at once both just letters and also something much more. It's transcended a simple letter through a process of development to become a complex whole, yet retaining all its individual parts.

5 Christian mystic Bernadette Roberts can, however, and does in *The Experience of No-Self: A Contemplative Journey* (Albany: State University of New York Press, 1993).

6 For example, Sam Harris, *The End of Faith: Religion, Terror and the Future of Reason* (New York: W. W. Norton, 2004), or Richard Dawkins, *The God Delusion* (New York: Houghton Mifflin Company, 2008) and Victor J. Stenger, *The New Atheism: Taking a Stand for Science and Reason* (Amherst, N.Y.: Prometheus Books, 2009).

7 The weak spots of the Christian tradition don't mean we should jettison the entire Christian narrative structure. It means, I believe, that we bring our insights to bear upon the ancient tradition, and bring the essence of the story again and again to bear upon our present time in the most authentic and meaningful ways possible. Jesus the Christ bore witness to and lived the reality of God's light, life, and love with us, and it's the reality, presence, and universal availability of God's light, life, and love with us experienced in contemplative relationship that are the most important dimensions and contributions of the Christian claim emerging from the ancient soil of the Abrahamic-Mosaic tradition.

8 For a basic overview of the contemplative dimension in the Christian tradition see Thomas Keating, *Open Mind, Open Heart* (New York: Continuum, 2007) 140–157, and also Carl Arico, *A Taste of Silence: A Guide to the Fundamentals of Centering Prayer* (New York: Continuum, 1999).

9 Such as theological scholasticism, Christian colonialism, the Social Gospel, revivalism, and the current consumerism of the Christian subculture, selling everything from Christian self-help books to music, to enhancement programs for leadership, finances, marriage, and parenting.

10 For further evidence of the contemplative dimensions in the world's religions see, Wayne Teasdale, *Mystic Heart: Discovering a Universal Spirituality in the World's Religions* (Novato, Calif.: New World Library, 1999).

11 For a classic definition of contemplative Christianity see Thomas Merton, *New Seeds of Contemplation* (Boston: Shambhala, 2003).

12 For example, Ken Wilber, *No Boundary: Eastern and Western Approaches to Personal Growth* (Boston: Shambhala, 2001) or David Loy, *Nonduality: A Study in Comparative Philosophy* (New Haven: Yale University Press, 1988).

13 Such as Ken Wilber, *Sex, Ecology, Spirituality: The Spirit of Evolution* (Boston: Shambhala, 2000); Michael Washburn, *The Ego and the Dynamic Ground: A Transpersonal Theory of Human Development* (Albany: State University of New York Press, 1988); the more personal account by Jim Marion, *Putting on the Mind of Christ: The Inner Work of Christian Spirituality* (Charlotte, Va.: Hampton Roads, 2000); Richard Rohr, *The Naked Now: Learning to See as the Mystics See* (New York: Crossroad, 2009).

14 Laura Ellen Truelove, a contemplative Christian writer, sums up the contemplative life and its relationship to Jesus. She writes: "Contemplative Christianity makes use of silence and solitude where our restless hearts and minds find their true home in Jesus. Jesus spent forty days in silence and solitude before beginning His ministry. During His ministry, He often went apart to spend time with His Father. He needed to hear His Father's voice and to receive His empowering Spirit. Likewise, in silence and solitude our relationship with God is deepened, and we learn how to be fully present to God in each moment." Personal email correspondence, edited and used with permission.

15 Contemplative Emily Nielsen Jones broadly and brilliantly summarizes several emerging hallmarks of contemplative Christianity as:
- A theological recovery of the "Word (*logos*) of God" as the means by which personal revelation continues. God is still speaking through scripture, the natural world, and in the still, small voice within the heart, because Christ as *logos* is all in all.
- Salvation as a "journey" of increasing "union" with Christ, increasing the "vision of God," and stimulating a lifelong process of creation/restoration into the image of God; a present but never fully realized reality ("heaven of the heart").
- A recovery of the doctrine of grace, i.e. God is reaching out and speaking to all people, manifested in a universal spiritual yearning for and capacity to experience God.
- A recovery of spiritual practices to quiet the mind and listen with the heart.
- A renewed emphasis on the "hypostatic union" of Christ's human and divine natures (Council of Chalcedon, 451 CE). As "fully human," Jesus is an archetype of what we can become, i.e., an "image of the invisible God" (Colossians 1:1), and "participants

of the divine nature" (2 Peter 1.4). Through union with Christ, the divine image that
was marred in "the Fall" is restored into increasing likeness to Christ.

- A renewed discovery of reading scripture with the heart, engaging the imagination
and transforming the will, i.e. *Lectio Divina*.
- A return of the premodern view of the cosmos as a dynamic, integrated whole,
seen and unseen, infused and held together by God's loving and creative energy.
- A view of the human person—body, mind, and spirit—as an integrated whole, fallen
yet created in "original goodness" in the image of God. Adapted from the essay "The
post-modern move to center": <www.imagodeifund.org/postmodern.html>

16 The theology of Augustine is saturated with his understanding of God's love. See for
example St. Augustine, *On the Trinity* (Cambridge: Cambridge University Press, 2002).

17 See for example John D. Zizioulas, *Being As Communion* (Crestwood, N.Y.: St. Vladimir's
Seminary Press, 2002).

18 For a useful overview of what is known as the shifts in the "axial ages," see Karen Armstrong, *The Case for God* (New York: Alfred A. Knopf, 2009). Quantum physics and String
Theory are two examples of new ideas filtering into the consciousness of mainstream
culture.

19 See NASA's picture of the day at: <http://apod.nasa.gov/apod/>

20 I recommend three extraordinary books on the role of new cosmology, religion, and
Christianity: Ilia Delio, *Christ in Evolution* (Maryknoll, N.Y.: Orbis, 2008); Beatrice Bru-
teau, *God's Ecstasy: The Creation of a Self-Creating World* (New York: Crossroad, 1997), and
Cletus Wessels, *Jesus in the New Universe Story* (Maryknoll, N.Y.: Orbis, 2003).

21 For example, Amit Goswami, *The Self-Aware Universe: How Consciousness Creates the Material
World* (New York: Tarcher/Penguin, 1995).

22 One of the implications of this shift in cosmology upon the historical monotheistic
religions has been an increased demand for the traditions to adapt. Some expressions
of Judaism, Islam, and Christianity haven't found a way to do so. Much of the frustration within fundamentalist monotheism finds its source not in materialistic, secular,
"immoral" culture, but rather in an inability to shift the thought forms and presuppositions from a transcendent to an immanent cosmology. However, the contemplative
streams within these larger traditions have provided a third way, beyond fundamentalism
and secularism.

23 Flannery O'Connor, *Mystery and Manners: Occasional Prose*, edited by Sally and Robert
Fitzgerald (New York: Farrar, Straus & Giroux, 1989), 144, citing Msgr. Romano Guar-
dini.

24 In Matthew 5, Jesus unveils nine spiritual truths that help us map the stages of our growth
in Christ. These spiritual truths are often called "the beatitudes," meaning, "good" or
"blessed," and sometimes even translated as "happy." The "Sermon on the Mount" is
Jesus' pathway to the good and happy life. To see God is to experience supreme happiness, which the Lord taught us long ago during his seaside mountain sermon: "Blessed

are the pure in heart for they shall see God" (Matthew 5.8). To contemplate is to *see*. In this present life, absorbed with its trials and temptations, we cannot clearly see God. Yet, a way exists in this life to *consider with attentive presence*, i.e., to *see*. God, and the one who *sees* God, is the one through whom God is seen. This seeing is certainly not with the physical eyes. It's with the "eyes" of our emotional center. The heart is this center. Purity of heart occurs through the cleansing of the emotions.

As our emotional being is cleansed, we may experience an increasing intuitive aware-ness. This intuitive knowing is beyond our thinking, imagination, and sense-based rationality. Contemplation enables us to respond to others and life from a different per-spective than we normally do, that is, we begin to *see*, *think*, *feel*, *speak*, and *act* differently. The difference is in the quality or kind of thoughts and feelings that occur. This is the essence of inner transformation further into Christ. Our emotional level of being needs cleansing from a lifetime of accumulated emotional pain, trauma, mechanical reactivity, energetic knots in the body, and self-absorbed behavior, to name a few.

A simple example is the powerful emotion of anger. Sometimes we feel this emo-tion overtaking us, spilling out from our tensed body and muscles. We may raise our voice or strike out physically. Road-rage is good example. It shows up in arguments with loved ones, where our "love" and our unconscious negative emotions rising up from the depths unannounced contradict each other. So how do we experience the cleansing of our emotions? First, by becoming more aware we're having a negative emotion. This requires self-observation. Second, the wisdom of the contemplative tradition has always conveyed that a meditative practice of prayer is essential to obtaining purity of heart, because in meditative prayer the grace of God's healing presence and action can begin to loosen up the encrustations of negative emotional energy and replace that negative encrustation with the gifts and fruits of the Holy Spirit, such as love and peace.

Thus, for each negative emotion, there is a fruit of the Spirit. The pure in heart are happy because they're not so entrapped by their own emotional reactivity. There are clarity and peacefulness in the emotional center and they begin to provide one with a new perspective, one which Jesus calls being able "to see God." The vision of God that Jesus has in mind is not actually to see the Divine Being, for this is impossible for humans, but for us to see God in others, ourselves, and the creation. Francis of Assisi is a prime example of this transformation. But we don't have to be saints to experience this. Many are used to seeing only emotional provocations, but now we see spiritual opportunities. We used to see a jerk cutting in front of us on the highway; now we find an opportunity to practice love, empathy, and forgiveness. We used to see every detail wrong with our spouse or child; now we can see our own negativity, anger, or fear. We observe our self-reacting versus blaming the other person for being someone our personality objects to. So let us surrender to God's healing work in us as we're united further with Christ by the power of the Holy Spirit who'll lead us deeper into the truth, clothing us further with the raiment of Christ's blazing, pure holiness and love so we can discover that God has been here with us all along. We just didn't have the eyes to see.

25 T. E. Lawrence, *Seven Pillars of Wisdom: A Triumph* (New York: Doubleday, 1991). In my pastoral work, I've learned that many people kneel under the weight of life, crying for help with a pain too big to put into prayer, aching for a miracle in the moment from the One whom they sense is somehow both "up there" and "in here," as close as breath.

26 For a wonderful treatment of this, see Ronald Rolheiser, *The Holy Longing: The Search for a Christian Spirituality* (New York: Doubleday, 1999).

27 For a helpful theological overview of how the image of God is restored in our relationship with Christ, and its implications for the creation, see Colin Gunton, *Christ and Creation: The Didsbury Lectures* (Carlisle, U.K.: Paternoster Press, 1992).

ONE *Here With God*

1 Vishvasara Tantra; trans. Arthur Avalon, *The Serpent's Power* (London, 1919) 72.

2 See Bernadette Roberts, *What Is Self?: A Study of the Spiritual Journey in Terms of Consciousness* (Boulder, Colo.: Sentient Publications, 2005).

3 Thomas Keating, *Open Mind, Open Heart* (New York: Continuum, 2007) 2.

4 *The Selected Poems of Emily Dickinson*, "A Route of Evanescence." #1463 (New York: Modern Library, 2000).

5 *Theosis* is the process of participating further in the divine nature and communing with God face to face. For a very helpful resource see Archimandrite George, *Theosis: The True Purpose of Human Life* (Mount Athos: The Holy Monastery of Saint Gregorios, 2006).

6 Colossians 1.17. The Latin liturgy conveys this well: *"Per ipsum, cum ipso, in ipso"* ("through him, with him, in him").

7 Classically defined by John of the Cross, Teresa of Avila, and the anonymous author of *The Cloud of Unknowing*. See *The Collected Works of St. John of the Cross*, trans. Kieran Kavanaugh, OCD and Otilio Rodriguez, OCD (Washington, D.C.: ICS Publications, 1979); Teresa of Avila, *The Interior Castle* in the *Classics of Western Spirituality*, trans. Kieran Kavanaugh, OCD and Otilio Rodriguez, OCD (Mahwah: N.J.: Paulist Press, 1979); *The Cloud of Unknowing*, trans. Ira Progoff (New York: The Julian Press, 1957).

8 I am indebted to Tim Cook for sharing this parable with me.

9 Bernard McGinn, *The Foundations of Mysticism, Vol. 1, The Presence of God: A History of Western Christian Mysticism* (New York: Crossroad, 1991).

10 Peter Senge, et al., *Presence: An Exploration of Profound Change in People, Organizations and Society* (New York: Doubleday, 2005) and C. Otto Scharmer, *Theory U: Leading from the Future as it Emerges* (San Francisco: Barrett-Koehler Publishers, 2009). Scharmer and Otto invite humanity to see the world in new ways. Fundamental problems, as Einstein once noted, cannot be solved at the same level of thought that created them. What we pay attention to, and how we pay attention—both individually and collectively—are key to what we

create. What often prevents us from "attending" is what Scharmer calls our "blind spot," the inner place from which each of us operates. Learning to become aware of our blind spot is critical to bringing forth the profound systemic changes so needed in business and society today. Through "presencing," a term coined by Scharmer that combines the words "present" and "sensing," we can see our "own blind spot and pay attention in a way that allows us to experience the opening of our minds, our hearts, and our wills. This holistic opening constitutes a shift in awareness that allows us to learn from the future as it emerges, and to realize that future in the world." (See <www.presencing.com>.)

11 The Hebrew conception of God involves at least four affirmations.

First affirmation: God is invisible. This seems self-evident, but we must clearly state that although God often manifested in various forms, God is primarily unseen and exists in a different way and dimension than the physical world and corporeal bodies. God exists beyond the quantum. This idea of an invisible God was not antithetical in the Near-Eastern context. Israel was surrounded with religions that depicted their deities as idols in the shape of animals or other objects of nature. The Canaanites, whom Israel drove from their promised land, portrayed their god, Baal, as a young bull that symbolized life and sexual fruitfulness. The Egyptians also had symbols and names to represent their many gods. Such an environment was challenging for a people who worshiped one who could not be seen.

The most famous instance of this idolatrousness—the making seen of the unseen— took place as Moses was on Mt. Sinai receiving the law and experiencing the God of heaven on Earth. The people gathered their jewelry to make a golden calf to worship (Exodus 32.1). The temptation to create an image of the invisible is evident in the Second Commandment, which prohibits the making of idols or any graven image (Exodus 20.4–5). Such a command would be difficult for Israel to keep, producing a history of idolatry that would be the root of much of their suffering and devastation (Isaiah 44.9–20). Just because the God of the Hebrew scriptures was invisible didn't make God a natural force or energy. The Canaanites tempted Israel to view various gods and goddesses as controlling the seasons of nature, which misunderstood the very character of God. Although God is described using imagery from creation, such as being wrapped in light as with a garment (Psalm 104.2), fire (Ezekiel 1.27), or thunder (Exodus 19.18), God is always separate from such natural forces as creator and sustainer, although God sometimes interacts with it. Such natural descriptions are necessary linguistically not theologically. God must use the language of accommodation in revelation because humanity can only describe and understand the unknown from the known.

Second affirmation: God is personal. God discusses with Abraham the final fate of Sodom and Gomorrah and God apparently changes his mind (Genesis 18.16ff). God is also described anthropomorphically: as having hands, eyes, ears, and a face (1 Samuel 5.11). God laughs, smells, even whistles (Psalm 24), and has human emotions (Deuteronomy 16.22). That God shares his name suggests a personal being: God is like a father, mother, and a shepherd to his people (Hosea 2.14). Although these images are human, we must remember that any description of a being who is essentially indescribable can never fully encompass that being and therefore these anthropomorphisms provide only an element of who God is and was to his people. God accommodates to God's people, but God isn't a projection. The Hebrew scriptures recognize God as invisible and distinct from the world and yet portray God in a personal way, interacting with his people.

Third affirmation: God is active. This affirms that God has worked in and throughout history. For Israel, life wasn't a cycle of meaningless existence, but had a beginning and an end. Events that took place weren't ordered by fate, but were part of a design that found its inception in the very character of God. God actively chose Abraham, subsequently establishing a people and a nation that provided the framework for viewing God's activity in history on behalf of his people, leading them eventually to the Promised Land. The Psalms provide songs of Israel's history as they reflected upon their past, with all its joy and suffering (Psalm. 106). The point of this affirmation is that the God of the Hebrew scriptures is a God who acts in history. But how was God made present to his people? Here we move to our fourth and final affirmation.

Fourth affirmation: God is spiritual (John 4.24), essentially of a different dimension than our corporeal (physical) existence. Yet God chooses in love to manifest among us, doing it in five major ways throughout the Hebrew scriptures: the Angel of the Lord, in the Shekhinah Glory, in natural elements like fire or wind, by revealing his name, and by speaking his word(s) through various people, such as the prophets.

12　Such appearances are often called a "theophany." For a useful overview of this process, see Richard Elliott Friedman, *The Disappearance of God: A Divine Mystery* (Boston: Little, Brown, 1995) and Jack Miles, *God: A Biography* (New York: Vintage, 1995).

TWO　*Here by the Spirit*

1　1 Corinthians 2.10.

2　Karl Barth, *Epistle to the Romans* (Oxford: Oxford University Press, 1933).

3　James E. Loder and W. Jim Neidhardt, *The Knight's Move: The Relational Logic of the Spirit in Theology and Science* (Colorado Springs, Colo.: Helmers and Howard, 1992) 23.

4　This ancient esoteric Christian saying conveys the unity, Trinity, and relationality of God. That is, God is simultaneously one, three, and the Source of life, which is, in essence, the chain of being of which humankind is one dimension or level.

5　1 John is one of the primary texts that illustrate the developmental shift within segments of monotheistic Judaism in first-century Palestine following the ministry and teaching of Jesus of Nazareth. The shift represents an extraordinary unfolding of Israel's ancient faith in God's continuous guardianship and presence, to the presence of God with them in the teaching, power, and person of Jesus the Christ. The result of this shift and understanding was the emergence of a distinct faith-expression and community built upon the foundation of the Jewish tradition, but moving beyond it in form, content, and name.

6 The gospels of Matthew, Mark, and Luke also convey the essential message of God's fullness in Christ in a similar way. For instance, the birth narratives in Matthew and Luke importantly demonstrate the theological connection to the Jewish tradition, especially to the ancient Abrahamic, Davidic, and other prophetic promises, so the unique Christian fulfillment to such promises can be drawn forth. Matthew's narrative interprets and applies the prophet Isaiah in the context of Jesus' birth in a dialogue between Joseph and an angel. Joseph is not only told the name the child will be given—Jesus—he is also told why: for he (Jesus) will save his people from their sins, both to fulfill what has been spoken by the prophet Isaiah who wrote, "Look, the Virgin shall conceive and bear a son and they shall name him Emmanuel, which means God is with us" (Isaiah 7.14). The Christian claim connecting the anticipatory promise described by Isaiah for an heir to King David with the life and ministry of Jesus the Christ is a revolutionary hermeneutical and theological move within Judaism, both birthing new foundational stories for the Christian movement, and inevitably splitting away from the dominant Jewish tradition(s) of Jesus' day.

7 Ignatius of Loyola, *The Spiritual Exercises and Selected Works*, edited by George E. Ganss (Mahwah, N.J.: Paulist Press, 1991) 353.

8 John Calvin, *The Institutes of the Christian Religion* (Philadelphia: The Westminster Press, 1960) Vol. 2, III.1.1.

9 Gordon Fraser, ed., *The New Physics: For the 21ˢᵗ century* (Cambridge: Cambridge University Press, 2006). See also James E. Loder and W. Jim Neidhardt, *The Knight's Move: The Relational Logic of the Spirit in Theology and Science* (Colorado Springs, Colo.: Helmers and Howard, 1992).

10 See the spectrum of life exhibit at the Frederick Phineas and Sandra Priest Rose Center for Earth and Space in the Museum of Natural History in New York City.

11 Please bear in mind that the English word "God" is just a translation of the common Greek word for the divine one, *Theos* (Latin: *Deus*). Neither of these terms in English, Latin, or Greek are the actual name of God; this is unknown and is represented by the Hebrew word "YHWH." The word "God" is therefore more like a title of reference, like the word "President," as in the President of the United States, which doesn't reveal the president's actual name, but simply represents the person of the president and the powers of the office.

12 John 14.6.

13 Pierre Teilhard de Chardin, *Reconciliation in Christ: Selected Spiritual Writings*, edited by Jean Maalouf (New York: New City Press, 2002).

14 Thomas Keating, *Open Mind, Open Heart* (New York: Continuum, 2007).

15 The Eastern Orthodox tradition calls this process "divinization." It's closely related to *theosis*, or the renewal of our minds.

16 To put it differently: Christians claim that Jesus the Christ embodied the presence of God in such a way that a return to God for all of humanity was demonstrated and made available relationally and spiritually, rather than exclusively ethnically or ritually.

17 To be reconciled means both to remember that one comes from God, and that one can return to God in right relationship. Through this return, healing often occurs, spiritually and psychologically. See for example, John 14.

18 See Bernadette Roberts, *What Is Self? A Study of the Spiritual Journey in Terms of Consciousness* (Boulder, Colo.: Sentient Publications, 2005). This word *Christ* literally means "the anointed one" and was used in reference to the Jewish hope for a messiah who would liberate Israel from its political and social oppression to bring about the kingdom of God. Jesus, as the Christ, did bring the kingdom of God, but it appeared in the most unexpected ways. As a result, one of the earliest dilemmas of the followers of Jesus' was, "How did a Jewish hope become a Gentile blessing?" This question remains at the root of our current interreligious tensions. With many others, I believe there is a way forward celebrating the mystery and reality of God's presence to all humankind now by the Spirit, but it requires an open mind and heart.

19 J. I. Packer, *Keep in Step with the Spirit* (Grand Rapids, Mich.: Baker Books) 57.

20 *The Theological Dictionary of New Testament Theology*, edited by Gerhard Kittel, trans. Geoffrey W. Bromiley (Grand Rapids, Mich.: Eerdmans Publishing, 1999) Vol. 6.

21 The word "spirit" comes from the Greek word *pneuma* and the Hebrew *ruah*. Three basic ideas are conveyed by the word: 1) the Divine spirit, invisible and personal, like breath; 2) consciousness; 3) the whirling wind, such as when leaves are stirred up on a blustery day. The theme is developed by St. Paul to the church at Corinth regarding the new covenant that's been "written not with ink but with the Spirit of the living God, not on tablets of stone but on tablets of human hearts" (2 Corinthians 3.1–6). This fulfills God's promise to Jeremiah that one day he'd replace the heart of stone with a new heart—a heart of flesh (Jeremiah 31.31–33).

22 Cosmologists and the new physics are also speaking of this reality. See for example, Ilya Prigogine, *Order out of Chaos* (reissued edition, New York: Bantam Books, 1984) and Mark William Worthing, *God, Creation and Contemporary Physics* (Minneapolis: Fortress, 1996).

23 For a comprehensive work on this subject see Gordon D. Fee, *God's Empowering Presence: The Holy Spirit in the Letters of Paul* (Nashville, Tenn.: Hendrickson Publishers, 1994).

24 See Galatians 3.5, 1 Thessalonians 5–6, 1 Corinthians 2.1–3, 2.4–5, 2 Corinthians 12.7–10.

25 Notice this pattern in the life of Jesus, who summarized in his prayer in the Garden of Gethsemane, "Yet not what I want, but what you want" (Matthew 26.39). See also 2 Corinthians 4.7–5.15.

26 See Philippians 2.1–11.

27 See Ephesians 6.10–20.

28 See such texts as 1 Corinthians 2.11–12, 2 Corinthians 13.13, Ephesians 4.30. The Spirit also does things that are true of persons: speaks (John 16), guides (Acts 8.29), teaches (John

14.26), convicts (John 16), and prays (Romans 8). The Spirit engages in relationship: see Acts 5 where the Spirit is "lied to."

29   A further analogy might be helpful in conveying these ideas: the Spirit manifesting Divine presence is like the experience of standing on a train surrounded by people who speak a different language. You cannot understand them; an interpreter is needed; a connecting influence is required. This is the role of the third person of the Trinity—the Holy Spirit. Pressing the analogy further, it's even closer to reality to say that not only are we standing next to others, but that we and the crowd of strangers are actually one; our rational minds just can't comprehend it. We are humanness manifesting in multiplicity. Applying the analogy to our relationship with God, our separate sense of self keeps us thinking that we're separate from God, and therefore that God is somehow not present. But in Christ by the Spirit nothing can separate us from God, which leads us to the role of the Spirit as presence.

30   See 1 Corinthians 12, 15.

31   Both Galatians 5 and Colossians 3 detail such spiritual qualities (or fruits).

32   Pierre Teilhard de Chardin, *Hymn of the Universe*, trans. Simon Bartholomew (New York: Harper & Row, 1965) 29.

33   The promise–fulfillment structure has been variously conceptualized and articulated by others such as C. H. Dodd, Ernst Kasemann, and N. T. Wright.

34   John 13–17.

35   For an exceptional discussion of John Calvin's view of the mystical union, see Dennis E. Tamburello, *Union with Christ: John Calvin and the Mysticism of St. Bernard* (Louisville, Ky.: Westminster/John Knox, 1994). For an equally exceptional treatment of Karl Barth's views of union with Christ see Adam Neder, *Participation in Christ: An Entry into Karl Barth's Church Dogmatics* (Louisville, Ky.: Westminster/John Knox, 2009).

36   Romans 8.10, Ephesians 1.3ff.

37   The Spirit of Christ and the Holy Spirit are synonymous. See Romans 8.9–11. I'm not saying that Christ and the Spirit are the same, nor am I advocating a theological sloppiness. When it comes to discerning how exactly God dwells within the Christian, we must acknowledge a certain degree of ignorance. We stand in awe (and a little confusion) when we read Paul's fluctuating language. When he refers to the Spirit, the Spirit of God, the Spirit of Christ who dwells within you, and the Spirit of him who raised Jesus from the dead dwelling within the Christian, I think we must admit a degree of mystery. Essentially, we agree with the position that takes the Spirit of Christ not to be literally Jesus Christ, but the third person of the Trinity whom we know as the Holy Spirit to bear within us the fruits of Christ-likeness, so in this way we agree that "Christ is in us by the Holy Spirit."

38   However, we mustn't forget that this redemptive promise is rooted in God's promise to Abraham (Genesis 12.3, 15.5–6). In Christ, this promise is now being fulfilled, for those who would hear and believe the Gospel are united to God in Christ, heirs of the promise (Ephesians 1.13–14), and in Christ "all are children of God through faith . . . and if we

belong to Christ, they [we] are Abraham's offspring, heirs according to the promise" (Galatians 3.29). The promise is completed by the Spirit. St. Paul declares that it is only "when the fullness of time has come, [that] God sent his son, born of a woman, born under the law, in order to redeem those who were under the law, so that we might receive adoption as children; and because you are children, God has sent the Spirit of his Son into our hearts, crying, Abba! Father!" (Galatians 4.4)

39 *The Experience of No-Self: A Contemplative Journey* (Albany: State University of New York Press, 1993).

40 Hans Küng, *On Being a Christian* (New York: Pocket Books, 1978) 469.

41 Hebrews 11.1.

42 It's interesting to note something of a parallel Pentecost between Acts 2 and 11.

43 Christophany is a term coined by theologian Raimon Panikkar in his book *Christophany: The Fullness of Man* (Maryknoll, N.Y.: Orbis, 2004), where we find this helpful definition and distinction: "If Christology focuses on the doctrines that are developed on the basis of the words that speak of the experience of Jesus, *Christophany* is the opening of the third eye, which brings one in touch with the experience that the Christological doctrines refer to. Christophany does not separate philosophy from theology. That is why it does not reject Christology but goes beyond it in much the same way that it does not neglect or ignore the reason or the critical function when it employs the language of symbol and metaphor." Panikkar illustrates the mystical language of the Christophanic experience with the help of a poem of St. Teresa of Avila. The message she hears is dual: "seek for yourself *in me*; seek for me, in *yourself!*" Panikkar is keen on showing that mystical language of this kind is "neither simply human nor purely divine but theandric . . ." (*Christophany*, xiii). More to the point, Panikkar writes that, "I take the word 'Christophany' to signify a Christian reflection that is to be elaborated in the third millennium. . . . Christophany simply intends to offer an image of Christ that all people are capable of believing in, especially those contemporaries who, while wishing to remain open and tolerant, think they have no need of either diluting their 'Christianity' or of damaging their fidelity to Christ. And Christophany offers the same experience to all those who nourish an interest in that Man who lived some twenty centuries ago but still seems, to many people, to live" (*Christophany*, 9).

THREE *Here in You*

1 J. Oswald Sanders, *Spiritual Leadership* (Chicago: Moody Press, 1989) 42.

2 John 17.21.

3 Quoted in Bishop Kallistos Ware, *The Inner Kingdom* (Crestwood, N.Y.: St. Vladimir's Seminary Press, 2000) xi.

4 For a comprehensive theological survey of this process, known as *theosis*, see Norman Russell, *The Doctrine of Deification in the Greek Patristic Tradition* (Oxford: Oxford University Press, 2004).

5 Riches hidden in Christ Jesus (Ephesians 3.1–13).

6 The theological term for this is *ousios* and the important theological word for Christ's human and divine natures is *homoousios* (i.e., the same).

7 It's important to understand the relationship between the human person and the Holy Spirit. In Hebrew and Christian anthropology, the human person is comprised of a physical body/flesh (*sarx*) and soul-spirit (*psyche-pneuma*). The soul is comprised of mind–will–emotions. Sometimes, theologians and the Bible separate the soul and the spirit (1 Thessalonians 5.23, Hebrews 4.12), but there's good reason to take them as synonyms. The soul/spirit is created by God, and is the aspect of the human being that relates to God and is the ultimate expression of the *imago dei* in the human. The soul is often thought to be immortal. The flesh can be resurrected/transformed. Essence/being (*ousia*) is synonymous with the soul/spirit. Consciousness is an activity/state distinct from the soul/spirit, but interrelated with the soul/spirit of the human being.

8 Let us pose the question a little differently: How can we reconcile the message that the Word was with us in the person of Jesus (the incarnation), with the similarly intense confession that Jesus ascended into heaven and sits at the right hand of God the Father (the ascension), and still claim that God is personally present with us? Do the opening lines of the Gospel of John refer to a one-time event of God's presence in Jesus Christ as the incarnate Word? If so, just how is it possible for Christians to claim that Christ is still with humanity here and now?

9 The "transfer" does not diminish Christ nor make us divine on our own, but it does "link" or "connect" us into the humanity and divinity of Jesus Christ, for he is the new Adam and the representative new human being through whom we receive new life. Like open-source code and cloud-computing, Jesus Christ is the cloud and the main server to whom we are reconnected by faith and spiritual surrender.

10 Raimon Panikkar, *Christophany: The Fullness of Man* (Maryknoll, N.Y.: Orbis, 2004) xvi.

11 The most important spiritual writing I can commend is one that is anonymous. It was first published in 1980. I am indebted to the *Meditations* for this insight and return again and again to this profound book for inspiration. *Meditations: A Journey into Christian Hermeticisim*, trans. Robert Powell (New York: Jeremy P. Tarcher/Putnam, 2002) 151.

12 These ideas were hashed out during the first centuries of the Christian church. In particular, this issue was addressed at the Council of Chalcedon (October 8–November 1, 451 CE) in Asia Minor, near what is today Istanbul. The bishops and pastors gathered at this church council agreed that Jesus had two natures, human and divine. In the creed, they envisioned that Jesus was "one person, with two natures": equally and fully both human and divine. They used the Greek word *hypostasis* to capture this idea, and since then theologians have called this the "hypostatic union." The hypostatic idea was essential for the development of the doctrines of the Trinity and salvation—so essential, indeed, that the fourth-century theologian Athanasius once said, regarding the union of Jesus' human

and divine nature, "that which was unassumed, was unhealed." This means that Jesus was fully human, so that in the hypostatic union his divinity could fully heal our humanity.

For Athanasius, and many other church fathers, the whole purpose of the story of Jesus was explained by the phrase, "he became man, so that we might become God." By "God" they didn't mean that the creature became the creator, but that human nature was returned to God, and in this return a healing occurred to such an extent that the likeness of God that was lost or forgotten in "the Fall" was restored in Jesus and made available again to humanity through our union with Christ. Through this union, human life was no longer just an end in itself, full of sound and fury, but could become a "means to an end," one whose destiny was the conscious return to God, just as a wave returns to the sea. See *On the Incarnation* 54.3, in Archibald Robertson, ed., *Select Writings and Letters of Athanasius, Bishop of Alexandria: Nicene and Post-Nicene Fathers, Second series, Volume IV* (Grand Rapids, Mich.: Eerdmans, 1957) 65.

13 See above note. Here is a section of the creed: "We, then, following the holy Fathers, all with one consent, teach men to confess one and the same Son, our Lord Jesus Christ, the same perfect in Godhead and also perfect in manhood; truly God and truly man, of a reasonable [rational] soul and body; consubstantial [co-essential] with the Father according to the Godhead, and consubstantial with us according to the Manhood; in all things like unto us, without sin; begotten before all ages of the Father according to the Godhead, and in these latter days, for us and for our salvation, born of the Virgin Mary, the Mother of God, according to the Manhood; one and the same Christ, Son, Lord, only begotten, to be acknowledged in two natures, inconfusedly, unchangeably, indivisibly, inseparably; the distinction of natures being by no means taken away by the union, but rather the property of each nature being preserved, and concurring in one Person and one Subsistence, not parted or divided into two persons, but one and the same Son, and only begotten, God the Word, the Lord Jesus Christ; as the prophets from the beginning [have declared] concerning Him, and the Lord Jesus Christ Himself has taught us, and the Creed of the holy Fathers has handed down to us." The text can be found on my websites, but a helpful resource for the study of early Christian documents is <www.ccel.org>.

14 Theologians refer to this view of Christology as the "ontological" theory. One of the most accessible resources that conveys this idea is James Torrance, *Worship, Community and the Triune God of Grace* (Downers Grove, Ill.: InterVarsity Press, 1996).

15 For an exceptional and nourishing resource on the name of Jesus Christ, see Irénée Hausherr, *The Name of Jesus* (Kalamazoo, Mich.: Cistercian Publications, Inc., 1978).

16 The important theological Eastern Orthodox collection of writings known as the *Philokalia* reflect the significance of Jesus' name and the relationship of Jesus and Christ to our spiritual growth by the power of the Holy Spirit: "Be watchful as you travel each day the narrow but joyous and exhilarating road of the mind, keeping your attention humbly in thinking of your death and invoking Jesus Christ. You will then attain a vision of the Holy of Holies and be illumined by Christ with deep mysteries. For in Christ 'the trea-

sures of wisdom and knowledge' are hidden, and in Him 'the fullness of the Godhead dwells bodily' (Colossians 2.3, 9). In the presence of Christ you will feel the Holy Spirit spring up within your soul. It is the Spirit who initiates [humankind's] intellect, so that that it can see with 'unveiled face' (2 Corinthians 3.18). For 'no one can say "Lord Jesus" except by the Holy Spirit' (1 Corinthians 12.3). *In other words, it is the Spirit who mystically confirms Christ's presence in us.*" From *The Philokalia: The Complete Text*, compiled by St. Nikodimos of the Holy Mountain and St. Makarios of Corinth, trans. G. E. H. Palmer, *et al.*, (London: Faber and Faber, 1979) Vol. 1, 166–167. My emphasis.

17 In biblical times, it was normal to use a name to refer to the whole person, thus "Christ" would have referred to the whole person Jesus Christ.

18 For a detailed history of the doctrines of the Trinity and Christology, see Jaroslav Jan Pelikan, *The Christian Tradition: A History of the Development of Doctrine, Vol. 1*, (Chicago: University of Chicago Press, 1971–1989).

19 John Calvin, *Institutes of the Christian Religion*, edited by John T. McNeill, trans. Ford Lewis Battles, 3.11.10 (Philadelphia: The Westminster Press, 1960).

20 Because Christianity has been the dominant narrative in Western culture, the essence of these deeply important theological ideas has often been watered down and suppressed. On the one hand, the Evangelical movements of the modern era gave us a "pop-Jesus" who "saves you from your sins." On the other, the academic and social movements of the same period have increasingly undermined the historicity of Jesus and the relevance of his claims, especially in light of Western culture's increasing religious plurality.

21 Moses experienced the sense of God's distance when he waited on Mt. Sinai for God. He basked in God's presence, which I take as an expression of divine light, life, and love (Exodus 24.15–18).

22 For a helpful survey of a mystical approach to Christ see Andrew Harvey, *Son of Man: The Mystical Path to Christ* (New York: Tarcher/Penguin, 1998).

23 See Jim Marion, *Putting on the Mind of Christ: The Inner Work of Christian Spirituality* (Charlotte, Va.: Hampton Roads, 2000), Thomas Merton, *New Seeds of Contemplation* (Boston: Shambhala, 2003), or the writings of P. D. Ouspensky, G. I. Gurdjieff, and Ken Wilber.

24 St. Irenaeus of Lyons, *Against the Heresies* (Mahwah, N.J.: Paulist Press, 1991), Ancient Christian Writers Series, Vol. 1.

25 For the classic treatment of the hierarchical view of spiritual reality, see Pseudo-Dionysius *The Ecclesiastical Hierarchy* in *Pseudo-Dionysius: The Complete Works*. Classics of Western Spirituality series trans. Colm Luibheid (New York: Paulist Press, 1987).

26 Ephesians 1.13; my translation.

27 Martin Luther, *Commentary on Galatians* (Grand Rapids, Mich.: Kregel Books, 1978).

28 Ibid.

29 John 5.19–20.

30 M. Scott Peck, *The Road Less Traveled: A New Psychology of Love, Traditional Values and Spiritual Growth* (New York: Simon & Schuster, 1978).

31 See Bernadette Roberts, *The Experience of No Self: A Contemplative Journey* (Albany: State University of New York, 1993); revised edition, *The Path to No Self: Life at the Center* (Albany: State University of New York, 1991).

32 Bernadette Roberts, *op. cit.* 163.

33 1091 John 1.4–6.

34 Matthew 5.15.

35 2 Corinthians 7.17–20.

36 Romans 8.15c–17b.

37 Dietrich Bonhoeffer, *Letters from Prison* (New York: Macmillan, 1971) 367.

FOUR *Here through Us*

1 M. Scott Peck, *A Different Drum: Community Making and Peace* (New York: Touchstone, 1988).

2 John Calvin, *Institutes of the Christian Religion* (Philadelphia: The Westminster Press, 1960) I.xiii.14, 139.

3 <www.un.org/esa/population/publications/WPP2004/World_Population_2004_chart>.

4 C. Otto Scharmer, *Theory U: Leading from the Future as it Emerges* (San Francisco: Barrett-Koehler Publishers, 2009), 4.

5 By initiatives, I mean something akin to what Miroslav Volf refers to as "right communal doing." See Miroslav Volf, "Theology for a Way of Life," in *Practicing Theology: Beliefs and Practices in Christian Life*, edited by Miroslav Volf and Dorothy C. Bass (Grand Rapids, Mich.: Eerdmans Publishing, 2002), 257.

6 Jeremy Rifkin has cast a compelling vision for empathy and its role in the future of our species in his book *The Empathic Civilization: The Race to Global Consciousness in a World in Crisis* (New York: Tarcher/Penguin, 2010).

7 I think the most helpful book encouraging the church to this ministry from our own wounds is Henri Nouwen, *The Wounded Healer: Ministry in Contemporary Society* (New York: Doubleday, 1979).

8 It is interesting to note that the Spanish word for wait, *esperar*, also means "to hope."

9 Anselm of Canterbury, *Proslogion*, trans. M. J. Charlesworth in *The Major Works*, edited by Brian Davies and G. R. Evans (New York: Oxford University Press, 1998), 87.

10 Prince Myshkin in Fyodor Dostoevsky's novel *The Idiot.*

11 Marko Ivan Rupnik, *In the Fire of the Burning Bush: An Initiation to the Spiritual Life*, trans. Susan Dawson Vasquez (Grand Rapids, Mich.: Eerdmans Publishing Company, 2004) 59.

12 Acts 2.43.

13 David Steindl-Rast, *A Listening Heart: The Spirituality of Sacred Sensuousness* (New York: Crossroad, 1999) 1. Also, for an enriching survey of the role of pursuing wisdom in the contemplative Christian tradition see Christopher Bamford, *An Endless Trace: The Passionate Pursuit of Wisdom in the West* (New Paltz, N.Y.: Codhill Press Inc., 2003).

14 James W. Fowler, *Stages of Faith: The Psychology of Human Development and the Quest for Meaning* (New York: HarperSanFrancisco, 1995) 185.

15 For a unique perspective on the intelligence of the heart, visit www.heartmath.org.

16 See for example, Francis Crick, *The Astonishing Hypothesis: The Scientific Search for the Soul* (London: Simon & Schuster, 1994); David Chalmers, *The Conscious Mind: In Search of a Fundamental Theory* (Oxford: Oxford University Press, 1996); John H. Crook, *The Evolution of Human Consciousness* (Oxford: Clarendon Press, 1980); Daniel Dennett, *Consciousness Explained* (London: Little, Brown, 1991); and Matt Daniel, *God and the Big Bang: Discovering Harmony between Science and Spirituality* (Woodstock, Vt.: Jewish Lights, 1998). For an exceptional overview of the role of consciousness in the contemplative and esoteric spiritual traditions, see Gary Lachman, *A Secret History of Consciousness* (Great Barrington, Mass.: Lindisfarne Books, 2003).

17 Daily Prayer for December 16, 2009 at <www.ContemplativeChristians.com>.

18 The Canticle of Creation is found in many forms on the Internet. For a good theological resource on St. Francis see, *The Classics of Western Spirituality: Francis and Clare* (Mahwah, N.J.: Paulist Press, 1982).

19 Two examples of this kind of intentional Christian community are the Jesus People USA in Chicago, Ill. <www.jpusa.org> and the New Monasticism movement <www.newmonasticism.org/>.

20 There are many such communities, many related to the permaculture movement. Here is a sampling of links: <www.findhorn.com>, <www.earthaven.org>, <www.transition-towns.org>, <www.ecovillage.org>.

21 Such city planners and architects are referred to as "new-urbanists." Representatives of this new initiative in design are Miami-based Andrés Duany and California-based Peter Calthorpe. Both are seeking to re-create such pedestrian-friendly towns as Princeton, New Jersey; Annapolis, Maryland; and Savannah, Georgia—towns more reminiscent of the "old" America. For an excellent invitation to building spiritual community in one place from a contemplative lay monk and activist see Jonathan Wilson-Hartgrove, *The Wisdom of Stability: Rooting Faith in a Mobile Culture* (Brewster, Mass.: Paraclete Press, 2010).

22 George Hunsberger and Craig Van Gelder, *The Church between Gospel and Culture: The Emerging Mission in North America* (Grand Rapids, Mich.: Eerdmans, 1995).

23 See Marva J. Dawn, *Keeping the Sabbath Wholly: Ceasing, Resting, Embracing, Feasting* (Grand Rapids, Mich.: Eerdmans Publishing, 2001).

24 M. Scott Peck, *The Different Drum: Community Making and Peace* (New York: Touchstone, 1987) 59.

25 See Robert Banks, *Paul's Ideas of Community: The Early House Churches* (Nashville: Hendrickson, 1994) 38. Banks argues that Paul's use of *"en Christo"* refers to the individual, not the church itself.

26 Ephesians 1.13, adapted.

27 See Michael Frost and Alan Hirsch, *The Shaping of Things to Come: Innovation and Mission in the 21ˢᵗ Century Church* (Peabody, Mass.: Hendrickson Publishers, 2006).

28 Dietrich Bonhoeffer, *The Cost of Discipleship* (New York: Macmillan, 1963).

29 C. S. Lewis, *Mere Christianity* (New York: Touchstone, 1996).

30 Thus the presence of God continues through the community of Christ in our function, form, and flow.

31 Notice the thematic development throughout Ephesians: church as Christ's body (1.23); church as Christ's building rising to become a holy temple being built to be a dwelling place for God (2.21); church as means by which God's wisdom is made visible and known to rulers and authorities in heavenly realms (3.10).

32 Ephesians 1.14.

33 The Heidelberg Catechism from the *Book of Confessions* (Louisville, Ky.: Office of the General Assembly, 1996).

34 Ephesians 1.22–23.

35 1 Corinthians 12.27.

36 Dietrich Bonhoeffer, *The Cost of Discipleship* (New York: Macmillan, 1963) 271–272.

37 1 Corinthians 12.12–13.

38 Texts such as Exodus 29.44–46, 33.14–16, and Psalm 114.2 testify to this assumption.

39 Joel 2.28–32, Isaiah 44.3–5, Ezekiel 36.27–28, and 37.14. In these texts God promises a day when the Spirit will dwell within them as individuals.

40 2 Corinthians 6:16–18.

41 Bernard McGinn, *The Foundations of Mysticism, Vol. 1: The Presence of God: A History of Western Christian Mysticism* (New York: Crossroad, 1991) 6.

42 Teilhard de Chardin, puts it this way: "Is it not a positive fact that thousands of mystics, for twenty centuries, have drawn from its flame a passionate fervor that outstrips by far in brightness and purity the urge and devotion of any human love? Is it not also a fact that, having once experienced it, further thousands of men and women are daily renouncing every other ambition and every other joy save that of abandoning themselves to it and laboring within it more and more completely? Lastly, is it not a fact, as I can warrant that if the love of God were extinguished in the souls of the faithful, the enormous edifice of rites, of hierarchy and the doctrines that comprise the Church would instantly revert to the dust from which it arose?" Pierre Teilhard de Chardin, *Reconciliation in Christ: Selected Spiritual Writings*, edited by Jean Maalouf (New York: New City Press, 2003) 32.

43 David G. Myers, *The Pursuit of Happiness: Spiritual Hunger in an Age of Plenty* (New Haven: Yale University Press, 2000).

44 Jay Michaelson, *Everything Is God: The Radical Path of Non-dual Judaism* (Boston: Trumpeter, 2009).

45 There are theological risks in speaking of God's "hereness." Many heresies throughout church history and tradition are rooted in a fundamental misconception that God is not God, but something less: a dualistic being (Manicheanism); a psychological projection

(Feuerbach, Freud); a process of spiritual evolution (Hegel, Whitehead), to name a few. My intention in speaking of God's hereness is to remind the Christian community and tradition that by reclaiming the hereness of God, we confess that God is the God who interrelates with the creation—or lives in relationship with humans and the universe, including the Earth—yet simultaneously is *not* the creation. Thus God is differentiated from us and the creation, and we're individuated from one another and from God, and from the creation. But in Christ, humanity is with God and God is with humanity and we are with one another. Such individuality retains the gift of the personal, while at the same time retaining the gift of the universal (Genesis 1, Exodus 15.1–18, Psalm 19, 150). If a subsuming of the personal does occur, it's along the lines of St. Paul's conception, "I, not I, but Christ in me" (Galatians 2.2). A simple example of this is the sphere. All points simultaneously touch each other on the surface of a sphere through each other; yet they remain unique. Two poles on a sphere appear to be separate on the surface, but can be connected within and through the sphere itself. The water filling an empty sphere touches the entire surface of the interior of the sphere simultaneously as it touches each unique point of the surface of the sphere.

The insight we're highlighting is a renewed emphasis and understanding of God's relationality to and with us, even as God as Trinity interrelates with God-self and with us in ways we may not fully understand, particularly as God the Holy Spirit (John 3.8). Neither does the hereness of God mean that the mystery and majesty of God is diminished in any way. We only testify to what we read in scripture and experience in our lives: that God is the God who interrelates with all that is (Ephesians 1.3–14, 2 Corinthians 5.17–19). Yet we don't mean that human imagination or experience confuses our knowledge of God as God. Our knowledge is grounded in the testimony of scripture that culminates in Jesus the Christ as God with us in history, and expands in the sending of the Holy Spirit at Pentecost as God with us in the present, and it's this dual dance with Christ and Spirit wherein we experience the presence of God (1 Corinthians 15.3ff, 2 Timothy 3.16–17, Acts 2).

FIVE　*Personal Awakenings*

1　P. D. Ouspensky, *The Psychology of Man's Possible Evolution and the Cosmology of Man's Possible Evolution* (Roberts Bridge, East Sussex, England: Agora Books, 1989).

2　Of importance to this conversation are the dynamic relationships of the human condition: the relationship of soul to God; the relationship of one person to another; the relationship of humankind to Earth; the relationship between here and there; I and thou; longing and fulfillment; old and the new; life and death. This is a relationship between spiritual development and human transformation not just for egocentric or ethnocentric purposes, but for the future of our combined and cherished civilization and communities, and, most of all, for our continued flourishing with this gorgeous home we call earth.

3　Contemplative Christianity is both a journey backward and a path forward. In a sense, it's both the means and the ends. For example, Brian McLaren, *Finding Our Way Again: The Return of the Ancient Practices* (Nashville, Tenn.: Thomas Nelson, 2008) and the Renovaré movement, resourced by Richard Foster, Dallas Willard, and Eugene Peterson, and others.

4 For an extraordinary view of this see Jack Miles, *Christ: A Crisis in the Life of God* (New York: Vintage, 2001). A more thoroughgoing scholarly resource that explores this inner development is N. T. Wright, *The New Testament and the People of God* (Minneapolis: Fortress, 1992).

5 Caught in the friction between faith and reason, many Christians try to shove the rock of faith through the hard place of reason. In my experience, this can lead to a mutation of faith or its loss altogether. Thankfully, there's another way: the way of relationship and relationality is the way of the contemplative journey. We wonder: "How can I integrate my spiritual life with my thoughts, emotions, and physicality?" We ponder: "Is my Christian faith more than believing information about who Jesus is and what he did?" Confused by religious doctrines that feel disconnected from reality, Christians often compartmentalize their personal faith. The contemplative path can lead to integration and wholeness. It can be a bridge for a way forward both in faith and for the sake of faith.

6 St. Augustine, *The Confessions*, trans. Henry Chadwick (Oxford: Oxford University Press, Oxford, 1992) 3.

7 This is the theological meaning of the word "sanctification," but there's much more to the process than simply being made holy. Indeed, the theological concept of *theosis* conveys more of what we're envisioning. *Theosis*, in sum, is that through our union with Christ by the power of the Spirit we become participants of the divine nature, and through this process we work not for our salvation but for our transformation, which is the increasing embodiment of Christ in our human particularity and uniqueness.

8 Personal email correspondence, March 13, 2009, shared with permission.

9 The language of "awakening" is an important spiritual concept in the Jewish and Christian scriptures. Adam "awakes" out of a deep sleep into a new relational reality (Genesis 2.21). Jesus speaks of parables of watching, praying, and "staying awake" (Luke 21.25–36). Jesus urges his disciples to "stay awake" and pray with him in the Garden of Gethsemane (Luke 22.39–46) and St. Paul urges the Thessalonians to "not sleep" (1 Thessalonians 5.6). The idea of awakening is similar to the concept of *metanoia*, which in the Greek literally means to "change the direction of thinking," or in the words of St. Paul, to "be transformed by the renewing of your mind" (Romans 12.1). James Loder uses the phrase "transforming moment" to describe something of the spiritual and psychological dynamics involved in how I'm using the "awakening" concept.

In his book *The Transforming Moment: Understanding Convictional Experiences* (Colorado Springs, Colo.: Helmers and Howard, 1989) Loder defines a transforming moment as one that links with the work of the Holy Spirit and discerns a five-fold patterning: transformation "tends to accentuate the dual unity of the self by holding transcendence and immanence together and apart at the same time. Essential to the spirit's nature is its wind-like quality; it often takes us by surprise and leads us where we would not otherwise go. Its deeper characteristic, however, is its integrity in driving toward meaning and wholeness in every complex and variegated context. Thus, in an understanding of the spirit, continuity and discontinuity must be combined in a patterned process that does justice to both in the context of a single act or event. This study proposes to show how they are combined in what will be called the logic of transformation. The steps of this logic are as follows: 1). Conflict-in-context. 2). Interlude for scanning. 3). Insights felt with intuitive force. 4). Release and repatterning. 5). Interpretation and verification. These five steps, in their systematic interconnectedness, constitute the logic of transformation inherent in the human spirit. Here it is important to understand that transformation is not merely a synonym for positive change. Rather it occurs whenever, within a given frame of reference or experience, hidden orders of coherence and meaning emerge to alter the axioms of the given frame and reorder its elements accordingly" (*The Transforming Moment*, 3–4).

From the esoteric Christian tradition, awakening has played an important role in the story of human "growth" and "evolution." Maurice Nicoll summarizes the situation like this: "This work, if you will listen to it and hear it in your hearts, is the most beautiful thing you could possibly hear. It speaks not of sin, but of being asleep, just as the Gospels do not really speak of sin, but only of *missing the mark*—the Greek word means that": from Maurice Nicoll, *Psychological Commentaries* (Boston: Weiser Books, 1996), Vol. 1.

Nicoll talks of two ancient parables. The first speaks of human beings as prisoners that need to be liberated from our prisons—the prison of human condition. It tells of a person who'd been locked in prison for many years who sees a stranger enter the prison and offer him a key. But the prisoner refuses because he's acquired prison habits, prison thoughts. He's become a prison person—forgetting his true origin and purpose. The second ancient parable tells of a person lying fast asleep on the ground and next to the person is a ladder stretching from the ground to heaven. On this ladder are angels, blowing the trumpets, which come very close to the sleeper's ear. Still, the sleeper sleeps. Perhaps the sleeper is a CEO, a parent, or a teacher—it doesn't really matter. The person is asleep in their life, unaware of the influences coming from higher levels to awaken them to the possibilities of who they could be.

These parables provide insight to gospel stories such as the one conveyed by Luke: Peter and his companions were very sleepy, but when they became fully awake, they saw his glory and the two men standing with him (Luke 9.32), and the story of the prodigal son who "came to his senses" (Luke 15.17). See also Maurice Nicoll, *Simple Explanation of Work Ideas* (Utrecht, Netherlands: Eureka Editions, 1993).

10 Not only does Jesus demonstrate this interior union in his very being as fully God and fully man, he hints of this inner dimension when he says, tantalizingly, that "the Kingdom of God is within you" (Luke 17.21).

11 My awakening in the Tetons was essentially a solitary experience. I wasn't in community. The only "congregation" was the towering mountains and lodge-pole pines. My community was the beauty, grandeur, and silence of the mountain wilderness. But the tradition of the Christian community was present with me in word, wisdom, and power through Deneen's spiritual counsel and in the healing energy conveyed through her to me. She'd received this gift through her own spiritual formation under the authority of other teachers. She was conveying to me the knowledge and formation she obtained from her community. But that community was unseen to me, and my experience seemed to be solitary. Thus, although my experience was transformative, it wasn't the fullness of transformation.

12 At the time, I didn't understand everything that occurred in my encounter with this Deneen. I didn't even understand the fullness of her message. I've been living into her words and the healing that's unfolded in me since. What I do know is that through her energetic healing work with my body, my head and heart were reconnected in a way that continues to provide abundant fruitfulness. It seems some sort of "blockage" had developed in my body, which, at its root, was energetic—what we in Western Christianity might call "spiritual." With the pathway cleared of debris, my thinking–feeling–moving being began to function more holistically and balanced in its God-intended destiny. Years of negative thinking had created constricted emotions, and rather than living in the joyful freedom of God's love, I was drowning in my own pain and longings. The pain manifested in my physical body for over a decade. I suffered from chronic acid reflux disease and severe back pain. I was lonely. As I described, I sought love in romance, and when I found romance, I often self-sabotaged with unhealed, unconscious patterns of self-centered behavior.

13 <www.casadeluz.org>.

14 Carl Arico, talk on forgiveness at The Church of Conscious Harmony, January, 2009.

15 For example, Christian masters such as Origen, Evagrius, Pseudo-Dionysius, John Climacus, the writer of *The Cloud of Unknowing*, St. Teresa, St. John of the Cross, Thomas Merton, and Thomas Keating have conveyed in their writings the importance of practices such as fasting, *Lectio Divina*, and meditative prayer—Centering Prayer and the prayer of the heart, "Lord Jesus Christ, have mercy upon me." Through such spiritual practices we participate in the renewal of the divine image in us (the *Imago Dei*) that is driving God's presence and action in Christ by the Spirit to and with us in faith.

16 The emergence of the Internet, email, instant messaging, cell phones, and an increasingly unified global culture and marketplace has fueled and intensified the paradox of presence and absence—one that has also ushered in a new confusion and contortion of reality and relationality, spiritually, psychologically, socially, and environmentally.

17 While many Evangelicals believe that Jesus' death and resurrection changed the world, we are still in need of a spiritual pathway that applies what Jesus demonstrated to our

lived existence. The "born again" experience is one way of talking about how the gospel events apply to our personal lives, but in my experience the born-again language needs to be understood within the interior dimension of human transformation and not just the acceptance of external doctrines about who Jesus is and what he did, especially when they are soaked in premodern concepts that no longer feel relevant to anyone, such as the idea of being cleansed by the "blood of Christ."

18 See also Ephesians 4.22–24, Galatians 2.9–10.

SIX *A Monastery without Walls*

1 Thomas Keating, *Open Heart, Open Mind* (New York: Continuum, 2008): 161st and 22nd guideline for Christian life, growth and transformation.

2 For a very useful resource on the shift from monastic life to common life in the world, see the extraordinary book by Ross Fuller, *The Brotherhood of the Common Life and Its Influence* (Albany: N.Y., State University of New York Press, 1995).

3 <http://gamc.pcusa.org/ministries/spiritualformation/>

4 Brian McLaren, *A Generous Orthodoxy: Why I Am a Missional, Evangelical, Post/Protestant, Liberal/ Conservative, Mystical/Poetic, Biblical, Charismatic/Contemplative, Fundamentalist/Calvinist, Anabaptist/Anglican, Methodist, Catholic, Green, Incarnational, Depressed-yet-Hopeful, Emergent, Unfinished CHRISTIAN* (Grand Rapids, Mich.: Zondervan, 2004) 151.

5 Rob Bell, *Velvet Jesus: Repainting the Christian Faith* (Grand Rapids, Mich.: Zondervan, 2005) 78.

6 <www.emotionallyhealthy.org/resources/contemplative.asp>

7 <www.renovare.us/WHOWEARE/WhatisRenovaré/tabid/2475/Default.aspx>

8 For an exceptional firsthand account of the Taizé community, see Jason Brian Santos, *A Community Called Taizé: A Story of Prayer, Worship and Reconciliation* (Downers Grove, Ill.: Inter-Varsity Press, 2008).

9 <www.taize.fr/en_article1000.html>

10 As a caveat, I'm personally acquainted with this community. While I'm honored to serve at Westlake Hills Presbyterian Church, I'm also inspired by this neighboring spiritual community. I've found it uniquely providential that I live in a town that provides such a compelling model of contemplative Christianity.

11 Tim Cook, "The Mark," October, 2009. The Church of Conscious Harmony, Austin, Texas.

12 The Bylaws of The Church of Conscious Harmony, Austin, Texas, Article 1.

13 <www.consciousharmony.org/who_we_are/beliefs.htm>:

   • God is One, eternally present in the Trinity of Father, Son, and Holy Spirit, active within us, as us.

- Jesus Christ is the Son of God, eternally present as the Logos.
- We are all One in the Body of Christ.
- Humanity is asleep and called to awaken.
- Self-knowledge and daily spiritual practice are necessary for those who wish to awaken.
- Transformation into conscious unity with The Living God is possible in this life.
- Transformation is only possible through the power and grace of the Holy Spirit.
- Man is created in the image and likeness of God. Man's basic nature, like God's nature, is absolute good.
- Jesus Christ is the coming of the Divine Light to the world.
- God is Love and His Love is eternally present.
- Love bears all.

14 <www.consciousharmony.org/who_we_are/testimonies.htm>

15 Fred Edie, *Book, Bath, Table, and Time: Christian Worship as a Source and Resource for Youth Ministry* (Cleveland: The Pilgrim Press, 2008). For a more historic perspective on a daily *ordo* or rule, see *The Rule of Saint Augustine: with Introduction and Commentary* (Kalamazoo, Mich.: Cistercian Publications, 1996).

16 For example, <www.emotionallyhealthy.org>. The renewal of the spiritual practices is also occurring through the pioneering work of Protestant minister Peter Scazzero, who is shaping the spiritual practices movement in local Protestant churches through his relationship with the Willow Creek Association. Through his books/DVDs—*The Emotionally Healthy Church: A Strategy for Discipleship that Actually Changes Lives* (Grand Rapids, Mich.: Zondervan, 2003) and *Emotionally Healthy Spirituality: Unleash the Power of Life in Christ* (Nashville, Tenn.: Thomas Nelson, 2006)—Scazzero has reincorporated the Ignatian Daily Rule back into the Protestant community. Similar books have appeared recently, such as from the Emergent church visionary Brian McLaren, who has written a compelling volume entitled, *Finding Our Way Again: The Return of the Ancient Practices* (Nashville: Thomas Nelson, 2008). McLaren's book is part of a larger series edited by Dorothy Bass designed to make the spiritual practices accessible to a lay audience. Her work is having a significant impact on the Protestant scholarly conversation, especially her Practicing the Faith Series and her recent collaboration with Craig Dykstra, *For Life Abundant: Practical Theology, Theological Education and Christian Ministry* (Grand Rapids, Mich.: Eerdmans Publishing Company, 2008). Bass and her colleagues have presented a strong case for revitalizing spiritual practices to create healthy Christian community. Beyond the academic circles, Bass is writing amid a renaissance in popular spiritual practices in the Evangelical community, especially through the Renovaré movement. Other spiritual leaders such as Richard Rohr are making an impact through teaching people how to integrate their spiritual life with their everyday life.

17 See <www.Magnificat.com>.

18 *Ad Magnesians* VIII, 1, in *Ancient Christian Writers: The Epistles of St. Clement of Rome and St. Ignatius of Antioch* (Mahwah: N.J., Paulist Press, 1946).

19 <www.contemplativeoutreach.org/site/DocServer/MethodCP2008.pdf?docID=121>

20 See www.snowmass.org. The community life at St. Benedict's provides a model for a daily *ordo* of life and prayer:

Daily Schedule at St. Benedict's Monastery

4:30 Vigils (quiet community prayer of listening to scripture and other readings)

5:30 Community meditation

6:30 Personal time

7:30 Lauds (morning prayer) and Mass

8:30 Work

12:25 Sext (short midday prayer) and dinner

1:20 None (short afternoon prayer)

1:30 Free time

2:30 Work

4:30 Lectio

6:00 Meditation

7:00 Vespers and Compline (evening prayer)

7:30 Silence until after Mass next morning

The daily duties of family and work prevent most people and CCH members from keeping such a daily schedule literally, but the spirit of the *ordo* is kept within the silence of the heart, if not *in toto* then certainly in part.

21 The service is taken from a CD recording of a Wednesday evening worship service led by Tim Cook, May 20, 2009, at the Church of Conscious Harmony, Austin, Texas.

22 A small sampling of community reading books includes Houston Smith, *Why Religion Matters: The Fate of the Human Spirit in an Age of Disbelief* (New York: Harper Collins, 2001) and Beatrice Bruteau, *God's Ecstasy: The Creation of a Self-Creating World* (New York: Crossroad, 1997).

23 In some respects, the *Commentaries* are a more detailed presentation of the same ideas Dallas Willard's book *Renovation of the Heart: Putting On the Character of Christ* seeks to convey, yet without the depth of understanding provided by Maurice Nicoll.

24 Maurice Nicoll, *The Mark* (Utrecht, Netherlands: Eureka Editions, 1998).

25 Adapted from <www.consciousharmony.org/who_we_are/teachings.htm>.

26 Robin Amis, *A Different Christianity* (Chicago: Praxis Research Institute Press, 2003) xiii.

27 Tim Cook says he was inspired to call it this name by the allegory, which tells of the ten warriors.

28 <www.consciousharmony.org/programs_and_activities>.

29 Bernard McGinn, *The Foundations of Mysticism, Vol. 1: The Presence of God: A History of Western Christian Mysticism* (New York: Crossroad, 1991).

30 Andrew Louth, *The Origins of the Christian Mystical Tradition: From Plato to Denys* (Oxford: Clarendon Oxford University Press, 2007).

31 A few of the leading lights of the contemplative—or mystical—tradition of the early church are Clement of Alexandria (c.150–216), Origen (c. 185–253), St. Anthony the Great (c. 250–357), John Climacus, Augustine (354–430), and Dionysius the Areopagite (c.500). There are many others that could be named in a useful way, but suffice to say that a very helpful overview of the history of the mystical tradition in Christianity can be found in Andrew Louth's *The Origins of the Christian Mystical Tradition: From Plato to Denys*, 2nd ed. (Oxford: Oxford University Press, 2007) and Steven Fanning's *Mystics of the Christian Tradition* (London: Routledge, 2002). For a more accessible approach, see Richard Rohr, *The Naked Now: Learning to See as the Mystics See* (New York: Crossroad, 2009).

32 Wayne Teasdale, *A Monk in the World: Cultivating a Spiritual Life* (Novato, Calif.: New World Library, 2002). For a useful introduction to the distinction between the contemplative life "in the world" versus the "flight from the world," see Thomas Merton, *The Wisdom of the Desert* (New York: New Directions, 1970).

33 <www.consciousharmony.org/who_we_are/testimonies.htm>.

SEVEN *Leaving Christianity for Christianity*

1 Tim Cook, Sermon. The Church of Conscious Harmony, Austin, Texas, July 26, 2009.

2 For a useful case study of the emerging role of spirituality versus traditional forms of religion and the steady decrease in congregational attendance, see *The Spiritual Revolution: Why Religion Is Giving Way to Spirituality*, edited by Paul Heelas and Linda Woodhead, *et al.* (Oxford: Blackwell Publishing, 2005).

3 C. S. Lewis, *The Abolition of Man* (New York: Collier Books, 1982).

4 See Ken Wilber, *Sex, Spirituality and Evolution: The Spirit of Evolution* (Boston: Shambhala, 2000). Wilber is drawing the concept of "Flatlanders" from Edwin Abbot. Wilber is one of the most important thinkers and writers of our generation, and has profoundly outlined how our ideas of God have been developing and changing over the course of history—what Alfred Whitehead called, "the creative advance into novelty." Wilber has integrated the work of the developmental psychologists with many of the spiritual traditions, and has provided a "spiritual map" for human/spiritual development that helps locate where on the spectrum of development various spiritual traditions/ expressions are. I believe his summarizing work is the most important contribution to spiritual studies since the Reformation, and, if studied and taken seriously by spiritual leaders, will have an equally revolutionizing role for Christianity in the decades to come.

5 From Blaise Pascal's fourth letter to Mlle. Charlotte de Roannez (October 29, 1656) in

Blaise Pascal: Letters, The Harvard Classics (New York, P. F. Collier and Son, 1909–1914) Vol. XLVIII, Part 2.

6　This is one of the positive sides of the great humanistic project—it connects us with the beauty of being human.

7　Such as the classic evangelical tracks, "Four Spiritual Laws" and the "Roman Road."

8　For example, many Christians' fiercest cultural fights are over their desire to reverse the moral decay they perceive scientific, modern culture has brought about, whether it be teaching the theory of evolution or alternative views of human sexuality.

9　Although the church fathers didn't share this tension with rationality, they worshiped God with their minds. For an exceptional survey of the early church's spiritual thought see Robert Louis Wilken, *The Spirit of Early Christian Thought* (New Haven: Yale University Press, 2003).

10　John D. Zizioulas, *Being As Communion* (Crestwood, N.Y.: St. Vladimir's Seminary Press, 2002).

11　For a good overview of the new science and its relationship to personal relationality see Danah Zohar, *The Quantum Self: Human Nature and Consciousness Defined by the New Physics* (New York: Quill/William Morrow, 1990).

12　For a full account of the various levels of human development and the way in which rationality is transcended, see the brilliant syntheses of Ken Wilber. A good place to begin to understand his model of the development of human consciousness is *A Theory of Everything: An Integral Vision for Business, Politics, Science and Spirituality* (Boston: Shambhala Publications, 2000).

13　From the song "Stand Up Comedy." No Line On the Horizon, 2009. Universal-Island Records.

14　Ibid.

15　For an excellent exploration of the inner, contemplative Christian tradition see Richard Smoley, *Inner Christianity: A Guide to the Esoteric Tradition* (Boston: Shambhala, 2002).

16　G. K. Chesterton, What's Wrong with The World (Feather Trail Press, 2009).

17　For example, the soteriological writings of theologians Anselm and Aquinas.

18　For a useful critique on this kind of Christianity and the perspective of the Generation X and Millennials, see David Kinnaman, *Un-Christian: What a New Generation Really Thinks about Christianity* (Grand Rapids, Mich.: Baker Books, 2009).

19　Richard Dawkins, *The God Delusion* (New York: Houghton Mifflin Books, 2006) and Christopher Hitchens, *God Is not Great: How Religion Poisons Everything* (New York: Hachette, 2007).

20　Tim Keller, *The Reason for God: Belief in an Age of Skepticism* (New York: Dutton, 2008).

21　For example, the role of monasteries in the early formation of universities; the development of the scientific method and the basis for capitalism. See Rodney Stark, *The Victory of Reason: How Christianity Led to Freedom, Capitalism, and Western Success* (New York: Random House, 2005).

22　St. Augustine, *The Confessions,* trans. Henry Chadwick (Oxford: Oxford University Press, 1992) 3.6.10.

23 Ken Wilber, *A Theory of Everything: An Integral Vision for Business, Politics, Science and Spirituality* (Boston: Shambhala, 2000).

24 Blaise Pascal, *Pensées* (Oxford: Oxford University Press, 2008) 285.

Conclusion: In All Things God

1 Alister McGrath, *Evangelicalism and the Future of Christianity* (Downers Grove, Ill.: InterVarsity Press, 1995) 120.

2 I'm not advocating the "adoptionist" viewpoint of Marcion. I agree with the developmental insights of psychologists such as Piaget and Erickson, and the theological interpretation of their writing provided by practical theologians Donald Capps and James Loder, who simply take the "fully human" Nicene confession to its logical conclusions in light of the insights of the developmental psychologists.

3 Quoted in Maurice Friedman, Encounter on the Narrow Ridge: A Life of Martin Buber (New York: Paragon House, 1991) 293.

4 G. I. Gurdjieff as told by Maurice Nicoll, *Psychological Commentaries* (Boston: Weiser Books, 1996), Vol. 4.

5 Flannery O'Connor, *The Habit of Being: The Letters of Flannery O'Connor* (New York: Farrar, Straus & Giroux, 1988).

Appendix A: The Relationality of God: A Reflection on the Nicene Creed

1 For a full treatment on relationality, see James E. Loder and W. Jim Neidhardt, *The Knight's Move: The Relational Logic of the Spirit in Theology and Science* (Colorado Springs, Colo.: Helmers and Howard, 1992).

2 For a more detailed overview of the integrated worldview see Ken Wilber, *Integral Spirituality: A Startling New Role for Religion in the Modern and Postmodern World* (Boston: Shambhala, 2007).

3 See Cletus Wessels, *Jesus in the New Universe Story* (Maryknoll, N.Y.: Orbis, 2003) for further treatment of the developmental understanding of God's story to and with humanity through Jesus the Christ.

4 See *Documents of the Christian Church*, edited by Henry Bettenson (London: Oxford University Press, 1967); *Christology of the Later Fathers*, edited by Edward R. Hardy (Philadelphia: The Westminster Press, 1954); Theodoret of Cyrus, *Ecclesiastical History*, I.v.1–4; in *Die griechischen Christlichen Schriftsteller der ersten Jahrunderte: Theodoret Kirchengeschichte*, edited by L. Parmentier and F. Schweiweiler (Berlin: Akademie Verlag, 1954) 26.1–27.6.

5 Recent interest in Trinitarian thought suggests an optimistic outlook and potential change in practice. In particular, feminist theologians, in rethinking relationality, have rediscovered the importance of the Trinity for Christian spirituality. See, for example, Catherine Mowry LaCugna, *God for Us: The Trinity and Christian Life* (New York: HarperSanFrancisco, 1991); Jürgen Moltmann, *History and the Triune God: Contributions to Trinitarian*

Theology (New York: Crossroad, 1992); *The Trinity and the Kingdom: The Doctrine of God* (Minneapolis: Fortress, 1993); Colin E. Gunton, *On Being the Church: Essays on the Christian Community* (Edinburgh: T & T Clark, 1989) and *The One, the Three, and the Many: God, Creation, and the Culture of Modernity* (Cambridge: Cambridge University Press, 1993).

6 See Karl Barth's list on analogies in *The Göttingen Dogmatics: Instruction in the Christian Religion* (Grand Rapids, Mich.: W.B. Eerdmans, 1991).

7 There are divine trinities outside of the Christian tradition, such as the Hindu triad of Brahman, Vishnu, and Shiva.

8 For a detailed history, see Jaroslav Jan Pelikan, *The Christian Tradition: A History of the Development of Doctrine, Vol. 1* (Chicago: University of Chicago Press, 1971–1989) 172–225; Paul Tillich, *A History of Christian Thought* (New York: Simon & Schuster, 1968) 68–79.

9 For background on these movements consult, J. N. D. Kelly, *Early Christian Doctrines* (New York: Harper SanFrancisco, 1978) 22–28, 56–60.

10 For an excellent general history and overview of the councils, see Justo L. Gonzalez, *The Story of Christianity: The Early Church to the Dawn of the Reformation Vol. 1* (New York: HarperSanFrancisco, 1984).

11 See James E. Loder, *The Logic of the Spirit: Human Development in Theological Perspective* (San Francisco: Jossey-Bass Publishers, 1998) 17–45; James E. Loder and W. Jim Neidhardt, *The Knight's Move* (Colorado Springs, Colo.: Helmers and Howard, 1992) 19–124.

12 Karen Armstrong, *A History of God* (New York: Alfred A. Knopf, 1994).

13 John Calvin began the *Christian Institutes* with the presupposition that the knowledge of God and man are interrelated.

Appendix B: A Brief History of Christian Mysticism

1 *The Old Testament Pseudepigrapha*, ed. James H. Charlesworth (New York: Doubleday, 1983).

2 Bernard McGinn, *The Foundations of Mysticism, Vol. 1: The Presence of God: A History of Western Christian Mysticism* (New York: Crossroad, 1991) 14. 14.

3 Ibid., 16.

4 Ibid.

5 Ibid., 22.

6 St. Augustine, *The Confessions*, trans. Henry Chadwick (Oxford: Oxford University Press, 1992) 123–124.

7 Quoted in Tomas Spidlik, *Prayer: The Spirituality of the Christian East, Vol. 2* (Kalamazoo, Mich.: Cistercian Publications, 2005) 203.

8 Ibid., 204.

Appendix C: Contemplative Practice and the Apostolic Church

1 For a useful survey of the contemplative dimensions in the early church, see Robin Maas and Gabriel O'Donnell, OP, *Spiritual Traditions for the Contemporary Church* (Nashville: Abingdon Press, 1998).

2 Granted, the life of inquiry and critical thinking must be central to the Christian community, but we behave and believe tempered by the phrase: faith seeking further understanding. We stand facing the future, while learning from the past. We don't blindly follow fads and trends. We remain firmly fixed upon the long view of the maturing of ideas through prayer, study, and community dialogue. In a word, we are guided by the *tradition.*

3 For example, Thomas Merton, *Bread in the Wilderness* (New York: New Directions Books, 1997).

4 Ken Wilber, *Up From Eden: A Transpersonal View of Human Evolution* (Wheaton, Ill.: Quest Books, 1996) 346. See also Wilber's *A Sociable God* (Boston: Shambhala Press, 2004).

5 <www.charterforcompassion.org>. Bold in the original.

6 Bernard McGinn, *The Foundations of Mysticism, Vol. 1. The Presence of God: A History of Western Christian Mysticism* (New York: Crossroad, 1991) 71.

7 Dietrich Bonhoeffer, *Life Together: A Discussion of Christian Fellowship* (New York: Harper and Row, 1954) 134.

8 Tomas Spidlik, *Prayer: The Spirituality of the Christian East, Vol. 2* (Kalamazoo, Mich.: Cistercian Publications, 2005).

9 <www.contemplativeoutreach.org>

10 Keating, *Intimacy with God* (New York: Continuum, 1997) 32.

11 See James Torrance, *Worship, Community and the Triune God of Grace* (Downers Grove, Ill.: InterVarsity Press, 1997).

12 In addition to the quiet prayer of the heart, there are three expressions of prayer that foster the discipline of public prayer in a relational, communal way. Grounding all public prayer, of course, is the private prayer that fosters further formation of Christ within us. The first expression of public prayer is the prayer concert—a gathering of Christians in a local community for the sole purpose of praying together. Usually the concert includes individual silent prayer, corporate prayer, huddle-groups, prayers from the pulpit, scripture reading, worship in song and music, and other items such as times of confession, silence, and so on. The prayer concert is a powerful alternative for the church because it can function as both ministry outreach and intercession for the local area.

The second expression is a prayer walk. The prayer walk is ideal because it's a visible expression of the church's commitment to prayer and demonstration of our faith in the existence of a God who listens and responds. It's also a tangible communication to the community (and the spiritual forces therein) that the church is interceding on behalf of that local geographic area including its people and various idiosyncrasies. For instance, as the community prayer-walks, particular prayers are offered for the items that come into view. Thus, the community of Christ can walk around its own context communicating with God in prayer, but also to the community in silent enactment of this sacred, intercessory relationship.

13 See Sydney Ahlstrom, *A Religious History of the American People* (New Haven: Yale University Press, 1972).

14 It's not just parishioners either. A 2005 survey by Ellison Research revealed that only sixteen percent of Protestant ministers in the U.S are very satisfied with their personal prayer life. Forty-seven percent are somewhat satisfied. In addition, the survey showed that thirty percent are somewhat dissatisfied, and seven percent very dissatisfied with their prayer life.

15 For example, Diogenes Allen, *Christian Belief in a Postmodern World: The Full Wealth of Conviction* (Louisville, Ky.: John Knox Press, 1989).

16 This movement has been well documented by Claude Welch, *Protestant Thought in the Nine-teenth Century, Vols. 1–2* (New Haven: Yale University Press, 1985).

17 Centering Prayer is one form of meditative or contemplative prayer. It has been revived in the West through the writings of Thomas Merton and Thomas Keating. Interestingly, the Eastern and Russian Orthodox Church never lost their tradition of contemplative, hesychastic prayer. One reason may be that they didn't experience the same cultural tensions resulting from modernity in their more Eastern cultural environments.

18 For such a comparison, see Scott McKnight, *Praying with the Church: Following Jesus Daily, Hourly, Today* (Brewster, Mass.: Paraclete Press, 2006). And from an Eastern Orthodox perspective, Tomas Spidlik, *Prayer: The Spirituality of the Christian East, Vols. 1 and 2* (Kalamazoo, Mich.: Cistercian Publications, 2005).

19 See Thomas Keating, *The Human Condition: Contemplation and Transformation* (Mahwah, N.J.: Paulist Press, 1999).

20 Robert Kegan, *The Evolving Self: Problem and Process in Human Development* (Cambridge, Mass.: Harvard University Press, 1996); James Loder, *The Logic of the Spirit: Human Development in Theological Perspective* (San Francisco: Jossey-Bass Publications, 1998); Benedict J. Groeschel, *Spiritual Passages: The Psychology of Spiritual Development* (New York: Crossroad, 1998); and James Fowler, *Stages of Faith: The Psychology of Human Development* (New York: Harper Collins, 1998).

21 Such as Erik Erickson and Daniel Levinson.

22 See Ken Wilber's *Sex, Ecology and Spirituality: The Spirit of Evolution* (Boston: Shambhala, 2007) and *A Theory of Everything: An Integral Vision for Business, Politics, Science and Spirituality* (Boston: Shambhala, 2000).

23 Thomas Keating, *Open Mind, Open Heart* (New York: Continuum, 2007, 20th Anniversary Edition) 1–2.

24 For a useful overview of contemplative prayer see, Tomas Spidlik, *Prayer: The Spirituality of the Christian East, Vol. 2* (Kalamazoo, Mich.: Cistercian Publications, 2005).

Appendix D: Answering Important Questions

1 For a basic overview of the theological discussion and history on these terms see Donald W. Musser and Joseph L. Price, eds., *A New Handbook of Christian Theology* (Nashville: Abingdon Press, 1992) 494–499.

2 Emmanuel means, "God with us." See Matthew 1.23.

3 See Jacob Needleman, *Lost Christianity: A Journey of Rediscovery* (New York: Tarcher/Penguin, 2003) or Robin Amis, *A Different Kind of Christianity* (Chicago: Praxis Instituted Press, 2003).

4 This is a journey, on which we'll be asked to release that which blocks awareness, and receive that which heightens awareness. The dual process of releasing and receiving is the essence of Christian spirituality, and one of the primary means through which the Holy Spirit brings about our inner healing and transformation. St. Paul spoke of it as "death" and "resurrection" (Romans 5).

Ending Quotation

1 Karlfried Graf Durckheim, *The Way of Transformation: Daily Life as Spiritual Practice* (Sandpoint, Ida.: Morning Light Press) 6.

About Peter T. Haas

Peter serves as Associate Pastor for Community at Westlake Hills Presbyterian Church in Austin, Texas. Peter received his M.Div. from Princeton Seminary and is currently writing his doctoral dissertation on contemplative leadership for deaconate ministry. *The God Who Is Here* is his first book. Peter writes daily prayers, essays and poetry at the blog: www.ContemplativeChristians.com. Peter welcomes your comments and questions at PastorPeterHaas@gmail.com.